MW01147555

WRITE THROUGH IT

WRITE THROUGH IT

AN INSIDER'S GUIDE TO PUBLISHING AND THE CREATIVE LIFE

KATE McKEAN

Simon Element

New York Amsterdam/Antwerp London
Toronto Sydney/ Melbourne New Delhi

SIMON ELEMENT

An Imprint of Simon & Schuster, LLC
1230 Avenue of the Americas
New York, NY 10020

For more than 100 years, Simon & Schuster has championed authors and the stories they create. By respecting the copyright of an author's intellectual property, you enable Simon & Schuster and the author to continue publishing exceptional books for years to come. We thank you for supporting the author's copyright by purchasing an authorized edition of this book.

No amount of this book may be reproduced or stored in any format, nor may it be uploaded to any website, database, language-learning model, or other repository, retrieval, or artificial intelligence system without express permission. All rights reserved. Inquiries may be directed to Simon & Schuster, 1230 Avenue of the Americas, New York, NY 10020 or permissions@simonandschuster.com.

Publisher's Marketplace Deal Report reproduced with permission of PublishersMarketplace.com

"How to Read a Literary Agency Agreement" was first published by *Poets & Writers* magazine (July/August, 2022). Reprinted by permission of the publisher, Poets & Writers, Inc., 90 Broad Street, New York, NY 10004. www.pw.org

Copyright © 2025 by Catharine McKean Landon

All rights reserved, including the right to reproduce this book or portions thereof in any form whatsoever. For information, address Simon Element Subsidiary Rights Department, 1230 Avenue of the Americas, New York, NY 10020.

First Simon Element hardcover edition June 2025

SIMON ELEMENT is a trademark of Simon & Schuster, LLC

Simon & Schuster strongly believes in freedom of expression and stands against censorship in all its forms. For more information, visit BooksBelong.com.

For information about special discounts for bulk purchases, please contact Simon & Schuster Special Sales at 1-866-506-1949 or business@simonandschuster.com.

The Simon & Schuster Speakers Bureau can bring authors to your live event. For more information or to book an event, contact the Simon & Schuster Speakers Bureau at 1-866-248-3049 or visit our website at www.simonspeakers.com.

Interior design by Julia Jacintho

Manufactured in the United States of America

1 3 5 7 9 10 8 6 4 2

Library of Congress Cataloging-in-Publication Data has been applied for.

ISBN 978-1-6680-5554-0
ISBN 978-1-6680-5555-7 (ebook)

TO HOWARD,
WHO TAUGHT ME
EVERYTHING I KNOW.

CONTENTS

INTRODUCTION

IS THIS NORMAL?

The most common question I get from my clients as a literary agent is: "Is this normal?" Is it normal to wait this long to hear back from editors? Is this advance amount normal? Is it normal to not like my book cover? Is it normal to get so many starred reviews? Is it normal to not sell the movie rights? Writers want to know how their experience measures up to others' because, well, that's what humans do. But every author's experience will vary. Most things are normal because writing and publishing a book can go so many different ways. The scope of normal is vast. But I want all authors to know that it's normal to feel lost while trying to write a query letter. That it's normal to hate your book about a quarter of the way through, and then again probably toward the end. That writers are not alone in the complicated, uncomfortable, and scary—but also exciting, euphoric, and proud!—feelings that come with writing and publishing books. Writing is a very solitary experience, but writers are never alone in how that writing feels. With this book, you're not alone, either. So, is it normal? Yes. Whatever it is, someone's probably experienced it too.

HOW DO I KNOW?

How do I know all this? Because I have been everywhere you have been and a lot of places you want to be. I am a writer and a literary agent. I've sold hundreds of books, and written six and a half, including this one. And just like you, most likely, I dragged my feet for years.

It wasn't until my early thirties, after about ten years of working several side hustles because my job as a literary agent at the Howard Morhaim Literary Agency is commission-only (i.e., not salaried), that I really got my shit together and started to write. I would get so upset at myself for not writing more sooner. *I could have had a book published already!* I would say to myself. I wanted so badly to be published, but I wasn't doing the writing. It took a long time for me to realize the only solution to this problem was to write.

Between deciding that I wanted to be a writer (about age eight) and today, writing this book, I have done *a lot* of avoiding writing. I took all the writing classes I could in high school and college, and I wrote everything the night before it was due. (Didn't we all?) Then in undergrad, instead of writing, I started working at the University Press of Florida, at the suggestion of my very smart sister, and I learned about how books were actually made. My fantastic boss there suggested I read this new email newsletter called *Publishers Lunch*, and that's where I learned what a literary agent was. Even at nineteen years old, I knew this was the job for me. It was as close as I could get to writing books without having to do it myself! Maybe I didn't see it that way at the time, but it sure is funny how life works out.

After working at the University Press of Florida for a year after graduation, I went to the University of Southern Mississippi for my master's degree in fiction writing. *This is where I'm going to sit down and really write*, I thought. No more distractions. Just work. I got a carrel in the library, a beautiful little closet with shelves and a desk and a window, even though I had a super cheap, one-bedroom apartment to myself to write in. It was lonely in that carrel, it turns out. It was lonely in a new place, making new friends, leaving one life behind and starting another. But after a few semesters, I decided I wanted to be an adult with a job, not a student (maybe because all that writing was hard?), so I graduated early and drove to New York City.

Eventually, I got a job as the assistant to *seven* literary agents.* Guess what you don't have time to do when you're living in New York City making roughly $30,000 a year in the early aughts? Write. Everything was working out perfectly. I had infinite excuses about why I wasn't writing. Anything sound familiar?

I know you're already thinking that there's no way we're the same because I'm on the *inside* of publishing, the place you probably want to be so badly. I've been working in and around publishing for more than two decades, so obviously I know all the secrets, and my path to this here book was paved in gold. Just wait, dear reader. It will surprise you how being on the inside of publishing has helped me and how it has not. The primary thing it has given me, besides a thick skin, is the knowledge that it's different for everyone. What happens to my book will not be what happens to your book. What a friend gets in a marketing plan won't compare to what you'll get. (And notice if you assumed that your friend would get more than you. I didn't say that.) You're going to know something your friend doesn't know, and vice versa. You're going to find something in these pages that you cannot *believe* you didn't realize before. This is OK. This is expected. This is *normal*. This book will serve as a kind of baseline, a way to fill in the gaps of what you know and don't know. It is not a blueprint for How All Books Are Written and Published™.

---

* Pro tip: Never do that.

No one can give you that. You're going to do things differently than I will and differently than your friend will, and that's OK. My goal here is to make sure you understand *why* things vary, so you can understand if that variation is a red flag or a green light, a cop-out or an innovation.

I'M GLAD YOU'RE HERE

I can't tell you how to write a book, the definitive way to get it published, or if it will be successful. No one can. It might sound like a cop-out, but no one knows the future. Your book is your own, and the next one you write will be its own thing too. Your book might be a success because it got written. Your book might be a success because it sells a lot of copies. Maybe both.

Why this book, then? Because the only way out is through. You have to write the thing to see if it's going to work and even then, it feels like you can see only as far as your own headlights. But with knowledgeable advice gleaned from years of experience, you can go into the endeavor of writing and publishing a book with your brights on. You'll gain more knowledge and familiarity, so that when things happen to you that haven't happened to your friends or colleagues, you'll say *Oh, I heard about this* or *I know where to look to figure it out.*

In this book, you'll find all the nuts-and-bolts things I tell writers about traditional publishing. We'll go over how to format your manuscript, how to write a book proposal and when you don't need to, how to submit your work to agents, and how to know it's time to quit. We'll talk about the ins and outs of building a writing community.

We'll talk about what happens when an agent offers you representation and how to know if it's a good fit, how your agent submits a book to editors, and how editors buy books. We'll discuss book deals and what the money part means, as well as the editing and production process of the actual book. We'll talk about the tougher stuff, too, including making peace with self-promotion, how to weather your book not selling, and how to get back on the horse for your next one.

And we'll talk about the emotions that go with these things. How to deal with waiting, waiting, and more waiting. How not to read into an agent's form rejection. How to distract yourself through the many times you'll wait even longer for news about your book. We'll talk about silencing your inner critic and dealing with the complex feelings of cheering on your fellow writers without being overcome with jealousy or resentment. If you're wallowing in your feelings or if you feel like you're the only one, it will hold you back from doing your best work and could derail your entire career. The goal isn't zero feelings. It's realizing the feelings are pretty typical and are just feelings, not truths.

A few caveats and best practices as we move forward. This book is aimed at those primarily interested in traditional publishing in the United States, as opposed to indie or self-publishing. Hybrid authors, who do a mix of traditional and self-publishing, will benefit from reading about the traditional side of things. Traditional publishing means the big (as of this writing) five publishers like Penguin Random House, Hachette, HarperCollins, Simon & Schuster, and Macmillan, as well as the other many (what I call) mid-major publishers, often—but not exclusively—located in New York. These publishers offer advances against your future royalty earnings and distribute books in bookstores of all sizes, digitally and in print. Indie and self-publishing is a rich and wonderful world, but that's a whole 'nother book. Publishing industries vary in other countries, and I do not know the ins and outs of every one of them around the world. Feelings, though, are universal.

We'll also be talking mostly about novels and nonfiction books of all stripes for adults and kids for a trade audience. The academic publishing world is its own beast, and for that check out Laura Portwood-Stacer's excellent *The Book Proposal Book: A Guide for Scholarly Authors* (Princeton University Press, 2021). I'm sorry, but I know very little about screenplays and poetry. This might not be the best book for you if those are your main areas of interest.

A BRIEF EXPLANATION ABOUT WHY THIS BOOK DOES NOT DISCUSS SELF-PUBLISHING

I have kept up on the industry news regarding self-publishing, and I've poked around the sites and such. I've had detailed conversations with my clients who have done their own self-publishing and seen how successful, and not, they have been, but I'm not an expert in self-publishing.

I also know enough about the general process of writing, editing, publishing, distributing, and marketing a book, regardless of whether that's through a traditional publisher or not, and whew! It's a lot! Some books and authors are well suited to self-publishing and some are not, and if you are wondering if that's you, there are other books you can turn to aside from this one. Jane Friedman's *The Business of Being a Writer* (University of Chicago Press, 2018) has a great series of questions to ask if self-publishing is right for you.

The absence of self-publishing information here is not a judgment of its use or viability. If you want to self-publish, you should do it. It should be a fair, uncomplicated (notice I didn't say easy), transparent, accessible process. It should always be an option, especially as traditional publishing is not a fair, uncomplicated, transparent, or accessible process. Neither one of these things has to win, or be better than the other, or be the last publishing process standing. We can have both. I hope self-publishing never goes away.

WHERE I'M COMING FROM

My grandfather, we called him Grumpy, wrote a book about his time in the Marines as a brigadier general and weapons battalion commander at Parris Island. It came out from The Dial Press in 1958, and his military portrait is the full back cover of the book. After he passed away, I inherited a box of his notebooks and writing books. One was a meticulous ledger (c.f., Marines) about the writing and editing of his book. In a self-made table with ruler-straight lines, he wrote down each of the tasks he needed to do for each chapter, the words written or edited, and the completion date. I wasn't particularly close to my grandfather in life, but I have always felt close to him as a writer. He left me a road map of sorts. When I first held a copy of his book, I knew that writing was for me. I was going to do that too. Now I keep my own ledgers.

I spent a lot of time talking about writing but not actually writing. When I finally completed my first novel, I did it word by painstaking word. Even with my publishing experience and the example of so many writers, there wasn't a thing that made the task easy or painless or effortless. It was the opposite of those things.

I finally wrote a novel, by getting to my desk and putting the damn words on the page. I was in my early thirties. I wrote a YA novel about teens who built an app poised to change the world, until their social-climbing friend compromises all their user data and it all comes crashing down. This was 2013, and the post-*Twilight* surge of YA novels was still going strong. Twitter was about six or seven years old by then. Snapchat was two. But when I was finally done with that novel, I knew the story would be outdated before the pages hit the tray of my inkjet printer. I let a few people read it, and they gave me some notes, but I never revised it. I've never even reread it. My publishing knowledge combined with what I was learning about my own writing led me to one conclusion: this book would flop. I put it aside.

And this was fine! The project was a success because I had proven to myself I could do it. I could sit down and rack up the words. Face the blank page. I could start and finish a project and be overall happy with it, even if it would never see the light of day. I wrote a book and survived. And I survived not publishing it too.

Then I had a kid, and my whole life changed. My whole personhood changed. I didn't have time to hem and haw in front of my laptop, clicking over to social media or taking BuzzFeed quizzes. If I really wanted to be a writer, to sell a book, to at least *write* a book I had any hope of selling, I had to get over myself right quick. I went to a coffee shop at 7:00 a.m. twice a week and eventually I wrote another novel.

I wrote a middle-grade novel and two picture books. With one of those, I got an agent. Yes, I had to send out query letters too! After we tried to sell those projects with no luck, I had to face the fact that I was writing them in an attempt to get *any* book published. I was desperate, impatient for it. I'd wanted it for so long. Eventually, I realized I had to write for myself and not the market. That the point was to write and see what happened, not write any old thing just because I thought it had a better chance of being published.

So I wrote another novel. It was inspired by a short story my great-grandmother Maud had written over a hundred years ago. I worked and worked on it for about two years, and in the end, my agent liked it (so did I) and sent it out in May 2020. It was a kinda rough time then, and it didn't sell. Why? I have some ideas.* I can't blame the pandemic alone because goodness knows it's not a perfect book. But I can't really know exactly why, and it's never just one reason anyway. It didn't sell, and that was that.

---

* Quiet, literary novels about motherhood in Brooklyn aren't exactly burning up the charts.

NEWSLETTERS AND FEELINGS

While that was happening, I was in the second year writing my *Agents & Books* newsletter. My goal was to give writers easier access to writing tips and publishing knowledge, and to keep myself distracted while my solo writing career failed to launch. I covered query letters, word counts, publishing contracts, and all that jazz. I didn't write about my own writing that much, except to say that I'd done it and to talk about my process in general, but I didn't post a play-by-play of the submission process for my novel or all my rejections. As I was actually going through it, I started thinking more and more about the *feelings* side of the writing and publishing process. The part that was nowhere in Grumpy's books and ledgers and notes. I absolutely had a lot of feelings about not selling that novel. All that work, all those mornings away from my baby, all that effort, and nothing. I was crushed. I cried about it. I began to realize that I might *never* publish a book. Me! A literary agent with an MFA! With my own fancy agent! Who's edited dozens and dozens of books and sold many times more, for other people! With all my privilege and knowledge, not to mention ego, I always figured I'd get a book deal one day. (I know, I know. I am aware of how this sounds.) I was over forty by this time, and I had to look this fact dead in the eye: I might never publish a book. I had no control over this process, regardless of how much I knew about query letters and "the market." I had to make peace with it, somehow, if I was ever going to have the heart or stamina to try again.

So I started writing about that on my newsletter, instead of the specific rejections to my novel. And the response from readers was great. I got countless emails telling me *I feel this way too!* And *I really needed to hear this today!* And *Get out of my head!* Writers related to the doubt and fear and anger and confusion. I needed that boost. But also, it was comforting. As a literary agent, I know all the nuts and bolts of how books are bought and sold, but as a writer, I also felt the strain of getting all these words—any words!—on the page.

AND NOW HERE'S THIS BOOK

I got a book deal after all! And it didn't happen because of some magic confluence of clout and opportunity (but not zero of that either, because all cards on the table here). It happened because I tried and failed and had the ability and privilege to try again. Because I eventually got my act together to sit down and write. Because I have been in the publishing industry for many years, and I know how it works.

I can't give you privilege, opportunity, or experience. I can't give you status or power. But I can give you knowledge and encouragement. This is my ledger for you. Because if you're reading this, you probably want to be published as badly as I did, and I want to help you get there. Anyone can tell you how to pull the cord on your parachute if you're skydiving. But you also need someone to tell you how to have the courage to jump.

I want readers of this book—you—to come away with the knowledge that *you are not alone* in these feelings. *Everyone* feels this way. Some people even feel worse than you do! And some people have figured out how to manage it (enough) to get on with their writing. I did. When my novel didn't sell, I went through the five stages of grief. *Of course my novel is going to sell. How could they not buy my novel? Maybe this one person will actually buy it. Fuck, it's over. It's not selling.* And finally, *Yeah, it's not selling, and that's OK.* When I got through that, I ended up asking myself why I wanted to write in the first place. Because I love it, even when I don't wanna do it. I love putting words on the page in ways that make me happy. That last part eventually sunk in. I could just write things that make me happy. Maybe they won't get published, maybe they will. Maybe that's not the only thing that matters.

I want to give you permission to feel all your feelings about writing and publishing your book. Feelings are annoying, and I would prefer not to have them! And I definitely avoided them for most of my writing life. But tuning in to your feelings about writing and publishing will help you figure out if something is a big deal for you or just a bump in the road. You can't rely on what everyone else does/feels/thinks to guide your path. Tuning in to your feelings is how you develop intuition so that when issues come up, and they always do, you'll have a better understanding of what they mean for *your* career and book. I'm going to say many times over the course of this book that *it depends* and *every book is different*. There is no one way to write and publish a book. How you feel about what's happening can tell you so much about those variations. Feelings don't predict the future, but they can help you know when to pump the brakes.

When I started to feel my feelings and tune in to what *I* liked and wanted to accomplish with my writing, I actually started to enjoy it. I was *excited* to sit down and work on another novel, not to mention this book! Will I ever sell a novel or another book?* Who knows? Confronting this, though, has made it easier to rack up the pages and to feel less precious about editing and less stressed about where it's going and what's going to happen. I've felt great writing this book, and I've had all the boring, negative feelings too. If any other writer told me that's where they were in their writing process, I would tell them they'd figured out the secret to the whole thing. If I have the secret now, I want to share it with you.

---

* **Well, actually, while I was writing this book, a picture book I'd been working on for SEVEN YEARS sold, kinda out of the blue! I'll tell you more in chapter 5.**

Chapter One

ARE YOU READY TO GO?

So you want to publish a book. You want to say *When my first book came out . . .* at cocktail parties and maybe even have someone recognize you on the street (or at least on the internet) as that author who wrote that great book. Maybe you don't want all that attention, but you still want to feel the weight of those pages in your hands, to go to a bookstore, see your name on a spine, and know you did a huge thing.

Are you ready to get started? Great! Here's the process:

1. Write book.
2. Find agent.
3. Get book deal.
4. Cash checks.

Lol, no. It isn't that easy, but it's not *not* that easy either. It's just hard to know *how* to do any of those things, except cash the checks. You've written a book, but are you done editing it? You know you need an agent, but which one? And what's a good book deal? We're going to talk in detail about agents, query letters, book deals, and checks in later chapters, but here the goal will be to figure out if you have what you need to take the next steps, and how to steel yourself mentally for the road to come.

HAVE YOU WRITTEN YOUR BOOK?

You have to finish your book or your book proposal before you take the next steps. That doesn't mean you have to stop reading this book right now (don't stop reading this book right now), but it does mean that first you focus on the writing, and *then* you focus on the publishing. It's most helpful to do things in that order, though I'm sure you'll be daydreaming about how you will decide between the many agents beating down your door and how big an advance your masterpiece will get. Go ahead and daydream. But do the work too.

I'm assuming you're not starting from scratch. I can't give you a book idea to write. I can't tell you what markets are hot (and they'd be cold as soon as this book hit the shelves) or whether you should write for kids or adults, fiction or nonfiction. That's your decision. But if you have those things, I can tell you what to do next.

WHAT DO YOU MEAN I HAVE TO WRITE THE WHOLE BOOK FIRST?

If I had a nickel for every time I've heard that, I could buy the whole hardcover bestseller list. But in most cases, you have to write the whole book before you can submit it to agents, and ultimately to publishers. I know! That takes a lot of time! And you are not paid for that time, either, at least not in an hourly wage/regular paycheck sense. It is very hard to write a whole book in a vacuum, without help, when you don't even know if an agent will like it, a publisher will buy it, or anyone will read it. I don't have a fix for that, unfortunately. It is just how the industry works.

But that's mostly true for novels and other fiction formats. You don't have to write the whole book if you're writing nonfiction, and in fact, editors don't want you to! Instead, you'll write a book proposal, as well as a sample chapter or two, which we'll talk about in chapter 4. If you're doing an illustrated book like a graphic novel, art book, or craft book about sewing or knitting, etc., you'll need to include the relevant illustrations in there too. If you are writing a picture book and you do not plan to illustrate it yourself, you do not have to provide illustrations. Yes, this is all confusing. That's why you're reading this book!

Memoirs, though, are kind of in between. Some writers choose to write the whole thing first. Some find this necessary so they can map out the story or find out what they want to say and how to say it. But other writers find it sufficient to write a book proposal, and that works for many agents and editors too. I've sold memoirs from both proposals and full manuscripts, so this is really a case-by-case basis. If you don't know which applies to you, keep reading, especially the book proposal chapter (chapter 4), and see what feels right for your book, subject matter, writing style, and goals.

For novels and children's picture books, though, you have to write the whole thing. Best not to assume you are the exception to any rule.

OK, BUT WHY THE WHOLE THING OF ONE AND NOT THE OTHER?

You have to write the whole novel because agents and editors need to know if you can stick the landing. I'm sure you're thinking *But I can just tell an agent how my book will end and they can trust me that it will be good.* Sure, that could happen. Sometimes literary agents take on clients based on a partial novel manuscript and cross their fingers (me included). But most agents most of the time want to see the whole novel before they offer representation, so you better get cracking. You might find an agent who will be willing to send out a partial manuscript for your debut novel, but they're few and far between. When an editor buys a book, they share it with many of their colleagues—from marketing, publicity, sales, and more—hoping to convince them it's worth buying. Editors saying *And when the author eventually writes the ending, I'm sure it will be good!* doesn't make for a very strong argument. So, you have to write the whole novel. Sorry.

You don't have to write the whole book when you're writing nonfiction because . . . we've always done it that way? Prior to globalization, cheap and widespread mass communications, and the internet, if you wanted to know what was going on somewhere else, you had to send someone there to check it out. And that cost money. Nonfiction is often a less risky investment because it is easier to link sales to subject matter. I mean, I like historical novels about Paris, but I'm not interested in *all* historical novels about Paris. When I was a kid, though, I read every biography of the Beatles I could get my hands on. Whether this plays out in empirical data or not, it's easy to make a case for it, and well, I guess it stuck.

You can make a very strong argument that it's more critical for fiction to stick the landing than it is for nonfiction. How many novels have you read that were *great* until the very end? And did you say to your friends *Gee, that was great until the most unbelievable thing happened in the end?* Weak endings don't lead to robust sales from word-of-mouth marketing. I suppose it doesn't take too many flops in any genre for a publisher to figure out which works best for them.

HOW TO WRITE A BOOK

I can't tell you what to write about, but I can tell you how to get more words on the page. Of course, writing a book isn't just putting a lot of words on the page. There isn't any one-size-fits-all advice about plot, character, theme, subject matter, structure, thesis, etc. This book will not tell you if your novel should be in past or present tense. Instead, I have insight to share with you about what can make writing easier or more manageable and how to deal with all the messy feelings that come along with it.

To start, you need something to write with. Fountain pens and vintage typewriters might be kitschy and inspiring, but traditional publishers will require you to send your manuscript as a digital file. You can write it longhand and type it later if you want, and some find this is a good way to edit.

You don't, however, need the fanciest laptop in the world to write a novel. Heck, you could type it out on your phone, if you have the thumb strength. You can use the computers at your school or library. Most of publishing uses Microsoft Word in editing manuscripts, so eventually, you're going to have to use that. You can draft your book in Google Docs or Pages or Scrivener, but somewhere down the line, you'll need Word, and a passing familiarity with Track Changes. But I'm getting ahead of myself.

There are *many* laptop-adjacent devices that promise to boost your productivity. You can whip out a tablet with a keyboard and write anywhere. There are e-ink devices you can write on with a stylus and that will convert your handwriting into typewritten text (the Kindle Scribe is one). You can get distraction-free devices like the Freewrite Traveler or Alpha that are basically digital typewriters—a keyboard and small screen but no internet browser. They even back up to the cloud. You can dictate your work into your phone or computer. There's a device to suit any ability or productivity profile. You might even be able to borrow some of these devices from your library or buy them used. But you don't have to have the biggest, latest, fanciest thing. It's not the device that makes the writer. It's the writing. You might think you'll be more productive if you have X, Y, or Z. But really, you'll be more productive if you just write more. (And turn off the internet. That helps *all* the time.)

I know lots of people who swear by Scrivener, a program with a *lot* of different functions to help write, organize, and edit any kind of writing. There's a learning curve to it, so be prepared. Also be prepared that if you ask your writing friends about it, the true evangelists won't stop talking about it. They're like vegans (love you, vegans). They want everyone to know they use Scrivener (love you, scriveners). Personally, it has a few too many bells and whistles for my tastes, but I did seriously consider using it for this project.

A certain kind of pen bring you joy to use? Get it. You don't need any more reason than you want to. Easily distracted? Try earplugs or noise-canceling headphones. I'm an old lady with a repetitive stress injury from looking down at laptops, books, and phones, so I'm going to tell you to be mindful of your ergonomic setup while you're working, but I also know you'll just contort yourself on your bed or couch anyway, so don't forget to get up and move around once in a while.

Get all this stuff and the writing will be easy! No, of course it won't. You don't need imported, Italian leather–bound notebooks or gold-plated, noise-canceling headphones or a candle burning and one specific ASMR video on YouTube to write a book. Some of these things might make the experience more pleasant or convenient for you, but they won't make you a better writer. For that, you just need to write. You don't want that candle to become a crutch.

DO I HAVE TO WRITE EVERY DAY?

You do not have to write every day. I do not write every day. I can't. I have a full-time job and a kid and a compulsive need to watch mediocre Instagram Reels and this pesky desire to leave the house sometimes and also get at least seven hours of sleep a night. If you do not or cannot write every day, you are not any less of a writer.

But. Unfortunately, there is a *but*. The times when I have written *most* days are the times I've been the most productive. Not only because there were more cumulative minutes at the keyboard but also because more frequent writing sessions meant less time reminding myself where I left off and what I needed to do next. I could just pick up from the day before and keep going. I also found the ideas were fresher in my mind, so I thought about them more, and tricky narrative knots worked themselves out more readily. I had more brainstorms on long walks or in the shower. (Why is it always in the shower?) I was thinking about it more, so, well, I thought about it more.

I don't write for two hours every day or anything. Sometimes it's 500 words or fifteen minutes. Sometimes I sat down with a swath of free time in front of me and pecked out twenty words before I realized I was just too tired to keep going, or the phone rang, or my kid needed something. I still touched my project that day. You have to work within the constraints of your daily life and also steal time whenever you can. But you are not a failure if you do not write every day. And the answer to your productivity problems is not big chunks of uninterrupted time (what even is that?). Can your brain handle writing for seven hours straight on a Saturday after a busy week? You can run one mile five days a week more easily than you can run five miles straight without any prep.

Routines are lovely to have, but not all routines are daily ones. If you find something that works for you, guard it with your life. But if you don't or cannot commit to one, you're still a writer. Try to touch your work most days. Aim for that and do your best.

HOW TO KNOW WHICH WORDS TO PUT ON WHICH PAGE

You probably know what you want your book to be about, whether that means something abstract, like *an exploration of the intersection of motherhood and roller derby*, or something more concrete, like *what happens when four college roommates find a million dollars hidden in the wall of their dorm*. Either way, stuff has to happen in your novel, large or small, or your nonfiction has to show your discovery or answer a question or provide the reader a solution, and you have to write down those things in some kind of logical order. How you do that puts you in either the plotters club or the pantsers club.

PLOTTERS

A plot is what happens in a story. But it also means the act of writing those things down. You might call it a synopsis or an outline, but either way, it's a document that contains everything that happens in your book, in order. In nonfiction, your story or argument or investigation or plan has to proceed logically, or your reader will get lost and miss the point entirely. In fiction, your story should proceed according to the logic of your book and something, big or small, should happen. Otherwise, the reader will get bored or confused and stop reading.

I, for one, have always been a plotter. I often use spreadsheets, and here's what mine looks like at the moment of this writing.

Chap 1	Chap 2	Chap 3	Chap 4	Chap 5	Chap 6	Chap 7	Chap 8	Chap 9	Chap 10
Intro	Writing/ Prep	Literary Agents	Book Proposals	Editors/ Subs	Book Deals	Editing/ Pub	Self-Promo	Failure	Next Book
Feelings	whole book	what agents do	why you need one	agent subs	what's in a deal	production process	everyone hates it!	most people don't sell their first book (anecdotal evidence)	assess what you learned
Writing	word counts	why you need one	when you need one	waiting, etc.	advances	editing feelings	you have to do it	my first book sale, of five tries	with time, you may see what didn't work about the other book
"Is this normal?"	YOU ARE HERE plot vs. pants	how to get one	BP elements	How an editor buys a book	royalties	typos	publishers aren't magic	you are not your book	there may not be a good reason
Manging both	drafting	the pitch	when you don't	getting close	payout	when you have to stop editing	you have the best market	you have other books in you, I promise	write THIS book on its own terms
Set up for success	editing	query letters	different types	editorial notes	rights	cover fights	do what you can	get back on the horse	be willing to begin again
Practice, rigor, ritual	manuscript formatting	how do you know your genre?	illustrated books	good signs/ bad signs	delivery	worrying about your editor's feelings	no magic pill	how to assess what happened	find joy in the process
Writing every day	trust your gut	sub strategies	formatting	comparison is the thief of joy	no ticker tape parade	worrying about your own feelings	swallow your anxiety	how to find confidence again	HAVE FUN
Tools, books, crutches	self-doubt	finding an agent	nothing is perfect	channel the query process	you might not be able to tell anyone	"it's not perfect"	no one is paying as close attention as you think	how to know when it's time to quit	all writing sucks, but try to enjoy it if you can
	letting go	saying yes to rep	letting go	distract yourself	your life won't change overnight	nothing is perfect			
	getting ready for what's next	dealing with waiting	think of the reader	don't stalk people	dealing with $$ disappointment	perfect is the enemy of good			
		rejection			enjoy it too!				
		making peace with chance							

This probably doesn't mean much to you, but it's enough of a guide to keep me on track. I find that I can write and write when I know where I'm going. I don't fret over each sentence because I know I can go back and edit things later. It's the worrying about what comes next, what characters are going to do or what topics I need to cover that slows me down, and with a solid outline, I worry about that way less. Using this chart, I wrote the first draft of this book in four and a half months.

There are a lot of differences between this chart and the final book. That's how it's supposed to be! Things changed as I wrote and definitely changed in editing. But this road map kept me moving forward with my draft. You can't edit what you don't write.

Your plot or outline can take many different forms. Some people use a spreadsheet like this or a bulleted list. You might adopt the format you learned for the five-paragraph essay, regardless of whether you're writing fiction or nonfiction. (Obviously, your book will have more than five paragraphs.) You might even write something that's more like a narrative synopsis, a very long description of what happens in your book, formatted into paragraphs. That's what I'm working from for a novel I've been writing, and that document is fourteen pages long, single-spaced, and *full* of notes and cross-outs and marginalia about new ideas or changes that need to be made or questions I should answer before the end. You don't have to do it this way, of course. I'm sure programs like Scrivener have similar outlining functions, or you can find templates online. You can pin note cards to your wall or write it out on a whiteboard. You get to use whatever works for you, for your specific book. Your next book might require a different format. You never know!

I find that plotting and outlining is a good way to stress test a book too. When you start writing it down, all the holes in your story and argument reveal themselves. You might discover that your idea isn't long enough or even too long, or if you have enough evidence to support your argument. If you don't know how your story will end, writing an outline is a good way to figure out how to get to that ending.

Not sure where to start? Pick a place to begin: the beginning, the middle, or the end. It's likely you have an idea of at least one of those points in your story. Write it down, in whatever format you choose. It's even better if you know two of those points so you can start to see how one leads to the other. You might write multiple outlines to see how it all works together. I've even written long lists of different endings or middles or twists or other plot elements, just to get them out of my head. I wanted to clear away the low-hanging fruit, to get the most obvious plot ideas out of the way so I could home in on the more interesting or unexpected ones. It looks something like this.

My main character could:

- go back to school
- drop out of school
- write a book
- have to plan her friend's wedding
- have to plan her teacher's wedding
- have to plan her enemy's wedding

OK, that got dark kinda quick. But see how just riffing on an idea can reveal what's boring and what's interesting and unexpected?

As you work on your plot and outline, you can go back and change things, move things around, scrap ideas, and even start over. It's going to feel like a lot of work that's *not* writing. You're going to put in a lot of time and not come out with a higher word count, which is the metric writers often use to gauge productivity. You're also going to sit down to write and realize that some part of your outline doesn't work, you can't get some crucial research in time, you have a brainstorm that changes everything, or your characters themselves take you down a completely different road. That's OK! That's part of writing! Follow where your characters or research or arguments lead, and if you have to go back and rethink your outline, or scrap it altogether, then so be it. Everyone does that. Staying flexible will keep you moving forward.

You could spend weeks outlining, and when someone asks how far you are into your book, you'll be tempted to say *I haven't started yet.* But you have. All this work counts as writing, even if it's not in your final word count. It's real work. It's not wasted time. It's time you're spending now so that the actual writing part later goes smoother and sometimes even faster. It's the tortoise approach. You don't need to be the hare.

PANTSERS

A *pantser* is someone who just wings it, as in *from the seat of their pants.* You just sit down and write and see what happens! Chaos!

Pantsers scoff at an outline. You cannot be hemmed in. Part of the joy of writing is sitting down and following where the story leads, being surprised by what your characters say, what argument you make, finding things out about your story—and yourself—you never imagined. There is freedom in the blank page (though probably not the absence of anxiety).

As a pantser, you probably have an idea of what you want to write about. It's not like your keyboard is a Ouija board and you're just waiting for the spirit to possess you. Though that *could* be interesting! You may start with a question, character, conversation, setting, or world, and see where that takes you.

Pantsing requires very focused editing after drafting. It's unlikely your book will come out fully formed in terms of plot, argument, story, logical progression, research, character development, tension, pacing, or conclusion. Be ready to seriously scrutinize your first (and second and third) draft to produce a book that doesn't feel like it was, well, written by the seat of your pants.

If you told me I had to write a book without an outline, I would say *Never! I can't do it!* That was, until I tried.

I learned the five-paragraph-essay format in the third grade in the North Carolina public school system. When I moved to Long Island in high school, I was *stunned* that my friends were learning it for the first time in their sophomore year. Sophomore year! Of high school! I'd been using this method for *seven years* when my classmates in New York first encountered it. It definitely explains my dedication to outlining everything, on top of being a type-A, Taurus sun, Capricorn rising, classic overachiever. I've been known to outline particularly long emails!

And I've outlined all the books I've finished writing so far.* Over and over. For one novel, I even wrote an alternate outline to see if my idea worked as a thriller—a genre I don't really read at all. Surprise! It didn't work. But I gave it a shot. My enthusiasm for that idea petered out, and I was at a loss for what to write for a while.

Until one day, I just started writing. I had a scene in my head and I just decided to write it. Why not? I could just write for fun without it being *for* anything. I could follow wherever my heart and keyboard led me. It could just be for me. I knew what I wanted to write *about*, but I didn't know what was going to happen to those characters, and I didn't know what kind of ending, or middle for that matter, I was working toward.

I was always sure pantsing would end with me staring anxiously at a blinking cursor. But it was working this time! I got more than 25,000 words in without plotting anything! And it was fun! Was it good? I have no idea! But it was a joy to write, and it was interesting to watch my characters find their way on their own. Do I think I could write a whole novel this way? Probably not, but even just getting a third of the way into something without an outline was such a revelation that I no longer

---

* *Finished* is the operative word there.

evangelize for Plotting Only, Pantsing Never. Now I think I'm more Plotting Mostly, Pantsing Sometimes. But that's just me. You, writer, are allowed to do it any way you want. You may find that your mind actively rejects anything as rigid as an outline or that kind of executive functioning is just not your forte. Knowing this about yourself is key, and I give you explicit permission to do it any way that works for you.

After you write your outline or decide to pants it, the next step is to write the book. Ready, set, go!

What comes next in this is not what story beats your plot must hit or whether you should use present or past tense. The writing part is on you. But I will help you handle all the feelings that go along with that writing, and what comes after, and I promise that will help.

HOW MANY WORDS IS DONE, THEN?

A question for you. Is your book done when you reach the end of your story or research, or when you hit a specific number of words? If you answered *both*, you are correct. Your book should be as long as it needs to be, *and* that tends to be within a general word count range depending on your genre and audience. This is a topic of much discussion.

I totally get it. I myself have typed THE END and then looked at the word count and thought *Oh, that's not long enough at all.* What we all really want to know is *Have I typed enough???* Or *Have I typed too much???* ¯_(ツ)_/¯

Notice I am not saying *page count* here. Agents and editors do not care how many pages your book is (except picture books) because I can make the text very big, and suddenly my book is twice as many pages. Every word-processing program will tell you how many words you've typed. Measure your work in words, not pages.

So how many words does your book need to be? Here's a guide:

For Kids

- **Picture Books:** They're typically thirty-two or so published pages, including the copyright page and stuff, and you can put few or many words on a page. They are often 500 to 1,000-ish words total, but it's more important to think about what words go on what page, and how turning pages affects the story, as well as what it sounds like when you read it out loud.

- **Chapter Books:** 5,000 to 12,000-ish words. These are very short, often lightly illustrated books for kids, almost always written to be a series. (These are super hard to publish, so don't think you have it made in the shade writing one of these a week for the rest of your life.)

- **Middle Grade Fiction and Nonfiction:** 30,000 to 50,000-ish. These are stories aimed at kids aged roughly eight to twelve and usually feature main characters in those same age ranges. Science fiction and fantasy for this audience can be longer, but even those are rarely more than 90,000 words.

- **YA Fiction and Nonfiction:** 50,000 to 100,000-ish, again on the longer end for science fiction and fantasy. These are books aimed at readers thirteen to roughly eighteen.*

---

* There is also a burgeoning audience known as New Adult, which targets readers eighteen to twenty-one-ish. College-aged. The word counts here are the same for adult novels.

For Adults

- **Adult Fiction of Basically All Stripes:** 50,000 to 125,000, again on the longer end for science fiction and fantasy. You'll find some shorter novels for adults as well as much, much longer ones, but on average, most fall in this range.
- **Adult Novellas:** 30,000 to 50,000. At the time of this writing, this format is most robust in science fiction, fantasy, and horror, but you'll occasionally find them in other genres as well.
- **Prescriptive Nonfiction (How-To, Self-Help, etc.):** 25,000 to 75,000. Word count varies widely here, depending on the format and content of the book. Nonfiction with a lot of instructions, pictures, tables, or fill-in-the-blank-type pages will have a lower word count, but I have found most still cross the 25,000-word mark.
- **General Nonfiction:** 50,000 to 100,000. Depending on topic, format, and what the general audience wants, there's a lot of variation here too. A too-short book may signal to me that the topic cannot sustain a book-length treatment and is more likely a magazine article. A too-long book may signal that the author's subject is too broad or the book needs a hefty edit.
- **Memoir:** These function much the same as adult novels in terms of word count.

For Graphic Novels

These are measured by final, finished, fully illustrated page count, not by word count. If you're not sure, go to the bookstore or library and look at the page counts of books similar to yours. Books have certain common page counts because of specifications of printing, so if you think your book will be eighty-nine pages but most of the ones you see are ninety-six pages, this is OK. You'll notice a lot of graphic novels include pages of character designs, sketches, alternate covers, and the like. This is probably because they had extra pages to fill! Or the content was particularly good, so they made room for it. It's OK if your estimate is 10 percent off in either direction. It is important for agents to know, though, if you are envisioning a 400-page graphic novel or a 100-page one, and what audience you are targeting.

In very, very general terms, these are the following common page counts for graphic novels per audience/genre:

- **Younger Readers:** Think Meggie Ramm's *Batcat*, or Ben Clanton's *Narwhal and Jelly*, 80 to 128 pages.
- **Middle Grade:** Think Dav Pilkey's *Captain Underpants* and *Dog Man*, 208 to 224 pages.
- **YA:** Think *Heartstopper* by Alice Oseman, and Mariko Tamaki and Rosemary Valero-O'Connell's *Laura Dean Keeps Breaking Up with Me*, 200+ pages.
- **Adult:** Varies! There can be short, slight, graphic novels for the adult audience or huge bricks. It's my experience that very, very short ones and very, very long ones are hard to sell, so you might want to aim for the middle, 200+ pages.

There is also a lot of crossover reading in graphic novels, between adults and kids. I personally read all genres of graphic novels, from *The Baby-Sitters Club* graphic novelizations to graphic memoirs about Vietnamese diaspora like Thi Bui's (spectacular!) *The Best We Could Do*. Kids read whatever they can get their hands on, and your book might be interesting to a wide swath of age groups. You might think that saying your book is crossover or will appeal to readers nine to ninety-nine makes it more enticing to agents and publishers. But that's not quite true. Each book targets a primary market, and that's where you should focus your efforts. You will probably know who you're talking to—kids or adults—because you probably set out to do one or the other. The other age groups who come to your book are icing on the cake, but when you query, have your target audience in mind.

But, Kate, you're thinking, *if I'm writing nonfiction, and I am not going to write the whole book right now, how do I know if it's going to be long enough? And how do I know what to put for my estimated word count, which I've seen people put in query letters?*

If you haven't started writing it yet, you aren't going to know if your idea is long enough for a book. We'll talk about that more in chapter 4 about book proposals. When you write your proposal, though, you'll write both a chapter outline and up to two sample chapters. After that you do some simple math. Take the average word count of your two chapters and multiply that by the number of chapters you have. That will give you a *very rough* idea of your word count, and you can go from there. You will probably think *My intro is short, so I'm going to pad this final number with about 3,000 words*, and you probably won't be wrong.

WHY SHORT BOOKS AREN'T ALWAYS EASIER TO PUBLISH

Why is it hard to publish a very short adult book, but not a very short children's book? Capitalism, baby. Shorter books are not necessarily cheaper to produce, at least not enough to overcome the consumer's perceptions about how much a shorter book should cost. Your 20,000-word adult novel would be slimmer than *Vogue*'s September issue, heck, probably slimmer than their January one. The publisher still needs to charge more than about fifteen dollars for it in hardcover (even less for paperback) to cover the costs of production. Would you be willing to spend $15.00 on something that is approximately the same length as a long story in *The New Yorker*, which currently has a newsstand price of $8.99? Even if you were, it probably wouldn't be very often.

This holds true for long books, too, which can cost more in paper, printing, binding, and shipping when they're significantly longer than average. According to the preface of the 1990 "Complete and Uncut" edition of Stephen King's *The Stand*, it wasn't his editor who asked him to cut 400 pages from the original manuscript—it was the accounting department! Otherwise, the retail cost necessary to recoup costs would have been more than they thought readers would have been willing to pay. Once he was a big star, they knew readers would be willing to pay the increased cost for the longer book!

You may have noticed that the price of your favorite doorstop-sized fantasy novel is more than $30.00 in hardcover. But how many readers are willing to spend $32.00 or $38.00 for a 700-page epic from a debut author? Few. President Barack Obama's 2020 book *A Promised Land* was 768 pages and retailed for $45, but that book had the trifecta of being very long, by a very important and well-known person, and highly anticipated. And Barbra Streisand's 2023 memoir came in at 992 pages and sold for $47! Babs's book is a steal compared to Obama's, price-per-page-wise.

But books aren't priced by the page like bananas are by the pound. It's possible that the average word count of any genre or for any audience is what works best for storytelling. Too long and you may bore the reader. Too short and it might feel underdeveloped. It's also that consumers have a general idea of how much they're willing to spend on a book and how much book they want to get for their money. If a publisher has to charge a lot more to cover the costs of a long book, they need to be sure there's a public waiting to buy it. Prices don't break down small enough to make it significantly cheaper to publish short books.

You'll notice that I put "*-ish*" after the specific word counts here. That's because if your book is a 50,001-word-long middle-grade novel, you won't be automatically rejected. Even if it's only 29,999 words. Literary agents and editors are not that strict. Only worry if your book is at least 30 percent longer or shorter than these guidelines. A 75,000-word (non-fantasy) middle-grade novel might signal to me that it needs a good edit. A 15,000-word middle-grade novel says to me that the plot or characters may not be developed enough. Word counts are not a litmus test. They're a guide.

Of course, everyone can think of a superlong or supershort book that sold millions of copies. You might be thinking you can do that, too, and you might be right. But it's unlikely those books worked *because* of their word counts. Were the authors already famous? Was their research groundbreaking? Was it truly one of a kind? When a book falls outside the norms, you've got to work even harder to make a case for it. Publishing is not an Olympic sport with strict regulations and guidelines. It is where business meets art.

COMIC SANS IS NOT YOUR FRIEND, AND OTHER FORMATTING NECESSITIES

One thing that will save you time in the writing and editing process is to use general manuscript formatting guidelines from the jump, so you don't have to go back and fix it all later. When your book finds a publisher, they will give you a document that outlines their house style, but in the meantime, these generally accepted guidelines will put you on the right path.

- Use a 12-point font throughout, even for headers and chapter titles.
- Use 1-inch margins all around.
- Pick a common font like Times New Roman or Arial. (Don't get fancy. Courier is for screenplays and Comic Sans is for memes.)
- Include page numbers (bottom right is most common).
- Make sure your whole book is one file. (Do not send anyone each chapter in its own file unless requested to do so.)
- Save your file as a .docx, .rtf, or .pdf file. Do not send links to files saved in the cloud, even Google Docs (unless your file is extra-large, including many illustrations; we'll talk about that below).
- Indent each paragraph using the global formatting templates in your word-processing program. Don't hit the Tab key every time.
- Do not separate paragraphs with a line break. (This is often the default in Google Docs. It's a HUGE PAIN to take this formatting out down the line, so save your future self some time and do it now.)
- Do not put two spaces after a period. Search your manuscript for this and change it.
- Double-space everything using the Double Space function, not the Enter key!
- Do not repeatedly hit Enter to put things on a new page. Learn how to use the Insert > Page Break function.

- Remember, hyperlinks don't work in a print book, so take those out of your manuscript.

- When using footnotes and citations, use *The Chicago Manual of Style* as your general formatting guide.

- If you're going to use a ~~**~~ (called a dinkus or an ornament) to denote a space break, use the same one throughout. Keep it simple.

- Keep the styling to a minimum. Bold or italicize things if you really need to. (You do not need to indicate something should be italicized by underlining it.) It all gets redesigned by an actual book designer in the end, so save everyone the trouble and keep it simple and clear. It won't go from your computer to the printer as is.

- Most of us have been reading text messages for at least a decade, so you don't have to get fancy about how you transcribe those in your book. We get it.

- Make sure you don't leave Track Changes on when you're ready to send your book to agents or editors.

- If you want to make a text box or some other kind of fancy formatting, just put it in angle brackets: <text box here>. Don't try to format it yourself. Editors and agents will understand.

- If you are a designer (or not!), I know you will want to lay everything out like a finished book. You can do this for fun, for yourself, but don't do this for your submissions. The program you use to make your manuscript look like a book is not the same program a publisher uses to typeset a book. Your goal is not to make a printer-ready manuscript. It's to make an *easily readable* manuscript. Plus, you don't know your publisher's interior design conventions. You'll just have to take all your own formatting out later, and it's a big pain. Keep. It. Simple.

- If you're writing a graphic novel or other illustrated book, these formatting suggestions still apply to you. When you're showing text, like chapter openers or recipes, use the text formatting guidelines above. If you're writing a graphic novel, your script will look like a screenplay (about which I am not an expert, so feel free to google that). We'll talk more about how to show your pictures, illustrations, or comic panels in chapter 4 about book proposals.
- Remember, you won't get automatically rejected if you send an agent a book in 11-point type, but you could be making it harder to read your work. (Have mercy on the agent's poor tired eyes.) Taking care of things like this means your readers can focus on your actual words and not your purple font and dancing GIFs.

THE LAST STEP IN WRITING A BOOK

There's one last thing I want to talk about before we get into the nuts and bolts of editing your manuscript and finding an agent and seeing your book out in the world. You need to ask yourself how you feel about your writing, your art, your heart and soul, and how that intersects with commerce. If you're reading this, publishing your book so that someone can buy it in a store is likely high on your priority list. Publishing is a retail industry where money changes hands. It's not that different than selling shoes or widgets or knitting patterns on Ravelry. Everything that comes next in this book is affected by the place where art and commerce meet, and it's best to understand how you feel about it, so you know how to account for that down the line. If you don't, it can be a bumpy ride.

Some writers want to ignore it altogether, preferring to never think about money or the market. Some writers don't have that luxury, and others think about it almost exclusively. Or it could change book to book. Regardless of where you fall on that spectrum, if you are aiming for publication by a traditional publisher, then you're going to have to think about commerce at some point. If you want to be paid for your writing, you'll need to think about who will read it, and whether they want to exchange money for the ability to read it. (Even if your readers go to the library, the library has to figure out how many of their patrons will want your book before they invest their scant resources in it.) I'm sorry if it makes you itchy to think about money and consumerism.

Agents who read your queries and editors who pass on your book are not a royal court capriciously proclaiming or denouncing your name as an artist. They are people who exchange their labor for money to pay their rent and buy food. Their jobs are to find books that other people will buy in stores. Is this a crude description of a many-layered and nuanced job? Yes. But agents and editors and everyone else on the traditional side of publishing *do care* about your work as an artist and your book as art. There are so many kinds of art! But everyone's goal—including yours, likely—is to make money, so you have to think about money.

Not only is money hard to think about when it comes to art, it has this pesky tendency to correspond with *value*. The reader, a consumer, has to decide if a particular book is *worth* exchanging their hard-earned money (and/or time) for, in a never-ending sea of more books. Whenever you get flustered or panicked or heartsick about the money side of publishing, of art versus commerce, put yourself back in the reader's shoes. Think about how *you* decide to spend money or time, or not, on different books. Personally, as a reader, I buy a lot of books, because I have the luxury of being able to do so, and I love them, and it makes me feel good. I also get books from the library, especially graphic novels and audiobooks. These are worth very much to me as art, as entertainment, but they are also expensive, considering how fast I go through them. I frequently request that my library buy new graphic novels and audiobooks, and guess what—they often do! This not only means the author gets a sale but also I get to read it and so do other people. Then the library might even buy more titles by the same author or in these genres. Everybody wins, even if I personally didn't spend any money.

Yes, the reader will assess whether your book is *worth* buying. They will take note of which of their friends are reading it or if it's on the front table at a store or if a celebrity recommended it. They might think *That sounds good* or *That's not for me.* If they're on the fence or strapped for cash, they might put it on hold at the library. People get books many different ways, for money or for free. Readers want to exchange time and/or money for books because they think they will get something out of it. They aren't buying or reading a book because you worked really hard on it or because you deserve the royalties or because they *should.* They're doing it because they want to. You read books because you want to. So, what's in your book that readers will want? What's in it for them? What do you want to share with the reader?

Readers might decline to buy your book because, *wow*, that first chapter had a lot of detail only you thought was interesting. They might have bought your book because the subject matter sounded great, but—*oof*—the first chapter was so harrowing they couldn't get through the rest. That may also mean that they don't tell their friends to buy and read your book, because they never finished it. These are all considerations to make when you're thinking about what you want your book to do and how readers will respond to your book—with their dollars or attention or lack of both.

I find that following this path takes some of the squicky feelings out of the art-versus-commerce debate, at least for some writers. It doesn't negate or erase or obscure the fact that readers exchange money for books under this capitalist system, and that it is subject to the problems that plague all systems under capitalism. You don't have to write or publish under this system. If you want your book sold in stores, though, you do. Try to frame your thinking about what value your book can provide to the reader (Fun! Knowledge! Guidance! Sexytimes! Recipes!) instead of its worth. It's already worth something, most importantly, to you.

ARE YOU DONE?

At some point, you're going to type the words *The End* for the first time in your manuscript. WOOO HOOO! That's amazing! You finished the first draft! That means you can start writing your query letter, right? Wrong.

First: celebrate. You did it! You wrote your first draft of a book! Whether it's your first or your twenty-first book, this is a reason to congratulate yourself on a job well done. You're not *done* done, but you certainly did something!

It's normal to cycle through a lot of emotions when you finish a draft. You might (should!) feel pride about your accomplishments. You might feel anxious about its value or prospects. You might be daunted by the next stage(s) of editing. This may have been one of your lifelong goals. And you did it! All of these are common, normal, understandable things to feel after finishing the first draft of a big project. Feel your way through whatever is coming up and try to remember that this is just one step on the long road of writing and publishing. And pat yourself on the back for completing this part.

Second: put your book aside for a period of time and let it rest, let it cool, like a cake out of the oven before you frost it. Why? So you can forget what you wrote.

When you read something too soon after you're done, you aren't really seeing the words on the page. You're remembering them in the idealized voice in which you wrote them. That's how you easily read over typos and words you left out, and how you don't realize the middle bit doesn't make any sense. You're not reading what's there; you're reading what you hope is there. Letting your work rest for a bit sets you up for your first round of editing and helps you prepare for your second, third, fourth, and more drafts.

While your book is resting, read some other books. See some movies. Put down the computer and see the sun. Catch up on all the stuff you neglected when you were feverishly finishing the first draft of your book. After that, it'll be time to sharpen your red pencils and move on to editing.

Chapter Two

HOW TO EDIT YOUR MANUSCRIPT

ARE YOU READY TO EDIT?

Editing your manuscript can feel like staring up a steep staircase. You know you want to go to the top, but you also know it will be hard work getting there. Isn't it nice just to stand at the bottom for a while, not doing anything? Yeah, I like that too. The problem is then you never get to the top. You have to take editing one step at a time.

The first step in editing your book is figuring out if you're ready to edit. There are the practical considerations: Have you incorporated all the necessary research? Have you written all the parts you know you want to write? Have you said all you want to say? And then there are the emotional considerations. To many, editing feels like correcting what is wrong in a book. And, yes, part of editing is correcting typos and putting the commas all in the right places. But just because you move a chapter around or cut a subplot doesn't mean you did it wrong in the first place. It just means you thought it went there and now you know it doesn't. Editing takes a lot of time, as does writing, and I know I've thought, *Ugh, if I had just done it right the first time, I wouldn't be in this mess.* No one does that, though. No one writes it right the first time. That is my brain being mean to me with unrealistic expectations. There is always editing after writing.

It can also be hard to admit or accept that something you love has to go. Guess how many ¯_(ツ)_/¯s I had to cut from this book in editing. (A LOT.) And it was fine, because even though I love my shruggie guy, less is more when it comes to him. You're going to have to make some hard cuts in every book you write and edit. You'll have to kill your darlings. This is OK! You can copy and paste them into a new document and use them later. I have done this for years and never used things from that file, but it feels good to know they're there. Trimming, changing, cutting things with impunity is the sign of a good writer and good editor. It's all in service of the larger goal. You are strong enough to do this. I know it.

The second step is remembering that there are no completely done and 100 percent perfect manuscripts. Ask any published writer, and they will tell you the things they want to change about their book, no matter how long ago it came out. Books are done mostly when we have to stop working on them, either because of a deadline or for our own good, not because they are perfect. If you are waiting for a definitive sign that you're absolutely done with the writing part and you are unequivocally ready to edit, you won't get it. There are few definitives in publishing. Does this contradict step one? Only a little. You're ready to move on to editing when you've done all the writing you can do *at this point in the process.* There will be more editing and writing to come, and that's OK. You can't work on a first draft forever.

WHAT GENRE IS YOUR BOOK?

Before you get started chopping your manuscript into bits, it's important to know what genre your book is first. Why? Because genre guides so much of your publishing path to come. It can guide you in edits, as you keep the conventions of your genre in mind. If you're writing a picture book and your manuscript is suddenly 47,550 words, you'll know why you'll need to cut it *way* down. Not all genres have hard-and-fast rules like this, but some do, and you need to know what you're dealing with. It will also guide you in choosing what agents to query, but we'll talk more about that in chapter 5.

It seems like an easy question, right? Of course, you know if you're writing a literary novel or high fantasy or a gardening how-to book or an essay collection. But when I ask first-time writers what genre their book is, I often get an answer that's more about theme. You might rightfully describe your book as a coming-of-age story, but that is not a genre category that will help you in the publishing process. Authors also frequently give me seventy-five adjectives to describe their genre, and that's not going to help you either. It's worth it to nail down the best genre to describe your book from the jump.

I know you're worried you'll be wrong. You might be! But it's unlikely you'll be so wrong that you'll miss your target altogether. You probably already have a good idea of your genre because you read widely in it either before or as you were writing your book. You probably read and write in this genre because you enjoy it. If you haven't read other books in your genre, I would do so now. While you don't have to read every Regency romance ever to write one, you should be very familiar with the conventions of the genre. You probably aren't going to have your love interests texting each other while their chaperones are occupied with the quadrille. Or if you do, you'll know when bucking the trend is fun and when it's annoying.

To figure out your genre, imagine you are putting your book on the shelf at the bookstore. Where would it go? That sounds pretty easy, right? But—you only get *one* shelf. Your book can't be on both the Memoir and the Fiction shelves. You can't be on the Cookbook shelf and with the diet books.

Some genres are easy. You probably know if you wrote a cookbook or a novel. But your novel with a few recipes in it (which I see surprisingly often) can't go on both shelves. It would go on the Fiction shelf because if you were looking for a cookbook and you picked up that one, you'd think *Hey, what's this novel doing here?* The presence of one recipe doesn't make it a cookbook. Meeting the broad expectations of the general reader of that genre does.

It is helpful, too, to have some specificity in describing your genre, without going overboard. Few writers would just call their work fiction, even though that's a big section in the store. On top of your higher-level genre (cookbook, graphic novel, mystery), it's helpful include one or two adjectives to describe it: *Baseball history. Romantasy. YA thriller. Illustrated nonfiction.* You might even have *literary historical fiction* or *queer narrative nonfiction.* But don't get carried away. The more adjectives you add doesn't make your book's potential market bigger or make agents think more readers will like your book. It actually narrows everything. Readers of your Steampunk Grimdark Autobiographical YA Romance have to like *all* those parts together, not just each of them separately.

You can also describe your book in more than one way. You can have a romantasy and a contemporary fantasy. Which one is it? Both! And they would both go on the same shelf at the store too. You might send it to some agents as a romantasy and to others as a contemporary fantasy. This is allowed! The query police will not come looking for you.

Remember, there is no rubric that will spit out your one true genre. You have the best insight into how to describe your book's genre because you wrote it and you're reading other books in the genre too. Books can be described in multiple ways. But don't let the amorphous nature of genre confuse or paralyze you. Make the best determination you can and go forth.

THERE'S NO ONE-EDIT-FITS-ALL

The third step in the editing process is up to you.

Every manuscript needs something different. You might have done a stellar job with the time line and setting of your book, but another writer may find that their whole book happens in a week of Thursdays and not on purpose. You might find that, whoops, you basically wrote the same thing in chapters 3 and 4 and now need to combine them or cut one. I personally never remember what season it is when I'm writing fiction, so I have to do an editing pass where I take out or put in appropriate clothing or weather markers. Sometimes it doesn't matter if a character has a coat on, but sometimes it does! That's just something I know I need to watch for. You'll find you have something you need to watch for too.

When you first set out to edit, it will feel overwhelming. It will feel like an impossible tangle of yarn, like if you pull one thread, the knots will get worse. That's how I felt when I started editing this book!

But these feelings are normal. It's hard work to edit a big project, and it was already hard work to get the first draft down. In many cases, editing is more important than writing, and you can do this too! Remember that you won't do it all in a day, and it's OK if it takes a while. It's *supposed* to take a while. Skimping on editing will only come back to haunt you later, trust me. I know you will be worried that you won't fix the *right* things or that you barely know what to fix in the first place. You will worry that a change you make will not be the same as what an editor or an agent thinks you should make, and you'll have to go back and do it over again. (I mean, that might happen anyway, but you won't know until you get there.) You'll be worried about doing it right, because doing it wrong takes more time and you want to be done and on to the next step already. Editing will always be time-consuming; there's no way around that. Or you'll worry it could mean you don't get this book published. I know this because I have also felt all these things. Even about this very book. The only solution is to take a deep breath and begin.

Katie Adams, a freelance book editor, says that she sees common mistakes in authors' manuscripts, especially first novels. There, she says, "I often see a trauma dump, where the writer seems to feel they have to put all of their hard-earned insights about pain, all of their life's worth of ideas, into this one book because it's their big chance." In nonfiction, she sees the writer's "devotion to research that was fascinating to discover or hard to come by but doesn't actually need to be in the book." Both of these things prioritize the writer's aims and desires over the reader's experience. A trauma dump, especially in the early pages of the book, can overwhelm a reader and make them stop reading. Too much unnecessary detail can bore a reader. You might be doing both or neither of these things, but regardless, it's important to consider the reader's experience in your book.

I have different editing strategies for fiction and memoir versus nonfiction, but you can take any tack that works for you. Here's how I do it, just to get you thinking about the editing process overall. (Your memoir might function better under my nonfiction suggestions, so keep that in mind as you read.)

HOW TO EDIT FICTION AND MEMOIR

To make such a big job more manageable, I break it down into different editing goals. I ask myself, and my book, different questions and make sure I've answered them on the page. It often requires a full reread of the book for each, so it can be time-consuming, but it's easier for me to read for one or two issues at a time, instead of just a FIX EVERYTHING approach. Only some of these questions may apply to your work, but if you're lost for where to begin, this should help. Some of the individual things I focus on in these instances are:

Plot

- What happens in the book? Write a sample summary, like you'd see on the back of a published book. How would you describe it if you could say anything you wanted?
- Can the plot be described succinctly and enticingly? Does anything happen? If not, is there anything at stake emotionally for the characters?
- What's the climax of the story, and how does it resolve? Will the reader be satisfied by the ending? Have you read other books with a similar ending? How did that make you feel as a reader?

Setting

- Is the setting clear? Does the reader know what they need to know about how this world works (especially if it is different than our own)? Does that information come early enough in the story so that the reader isn't frustrated and confused?

- Does time move in a linear fashion and consistently? What does the reader need to know about time? If the time line shifts, are those changes clearly marked, either in the prose or in a heading?
- If time does not move linearly, is the reader confused, or do you signpost time changes to them in some way? Are you playing with time because the story needs it or just to be clever?

Character

- Does each main character want something? Is the reader aware of that? How and when are they made aware of it?
- Which characters get what they want and which do not? Why or why not? How does that form and inform the story? How will the reader react to that?
- Does the main character do things, have agency? Or do things just happen to them and they react?
- Do the characters interact? Do they talk in groups or just in dyads?

Details

- Are the characters' names, ages, and descriptions consistent? If you mention every character's eye color, does the reader really need to know that? Do you mention the race or ethnicity of all the characters except the white ones, leaving the reader to assume the default race is white? Do you avoid stereotypes and ableist language?

- Are the setting names consistent?
- Do you leave room for the reader to imagine non-crucial details? For example, does it matter if the kitchen table is oak or teak? (Probably not!) Don't over-stage-direct your scenes.
- Do you mention when every character takes off their shoes or puts their jacket in the closet, and do you need to?

HOW TO EDIT NONFICTION

Remember that spreadsheet I made for this book? When I was done writing according to this outline, changing, deviating, eliminating things as necessary, and after the manuscript rested, I went back and outlined it again. I read the book and wrote down what I had *actually* written on the page. I didn't compare it to my original outline, because my goal wasn't to make sure I stuck to that. It was to see what I actually put on the page and to make sure that made sense. I wrote it as a list of topics, not a spreadsheet, mostly using the section titles to guide me. In fact, I did this every time I significantly edited a chapter. I needed a bird's-eye view of what I'd done.

After I did that the first time, I saw that the chapter 2 about literary agents had forty sections and the original chapter 4 on self-promotion only had eight. That became chapter 3 about agents and 5 about query letters, and chapter 4 became chapter 9 about self-promotion.

I could also see that this very chapter wasn't working *at all* in its original form, and the numbered list helped me organize what went where. The first three sections of the first draft of this chapter didn't make it into the final book! (I saved them, and they eventually became posts on my newsletter.)

On top of this, or in place of it, you might want to ask yourself these questions:

- What is your book's thesis? What is the promise your book makes to the reader? Does it fulfill the promise?
- How does it fulfill that promise? Does it progress logically? Are there transitions between logical steps?
- Does each section serve to support the book's promise (instead of just being there to look/sound cool)?
- Is the structure easy to navigate? Does the organization make sense?
- Have you correctly and accurately cited any sources? Most publishers use *The Chicago Manual of Style*, and so should you.
- Have you made sure you haven't (inadvertently or not) plagiarized anything? Do you give appropriate credit when you cite others' ideas? Do you use a variety of sources and voices?
- Do you need any charts/graphs/illustrations, and do you have a plan for how to professionally produce them?
- Do any of your chapters start with "Webster's dictionary describes [your topic] as . . ."? I *strongly* encourage you not to start anything this way. It's become very clichéd.
- Do you explain any jargon the reader might not know?

HOW TO EDIT PICTURE BOOKS

I want to talk specifically about editing picture books here, even though I can't discuss the ins and out of editing every other genre or type of book. Picture books are their own special case. The shorter the book, the harder it is to sell. I say this all the time, but nowhere is it truer than in picture books. Everyone thinks they can write one, and lots of editors put them on their wish lists. But picture books are incredibly hard to make stand out in a crowd and take a lot of fine-tuning. You won't spend more total time editing a picture book, but that doesn't mean it's quick and easy.

Before you even start, I highly recommend reading an enormous number of picture books, most of them published in the last ten years. I mean like more than one hundred books. Really! You have to be familiar with recently published picture books and not just the classics of your childhood or your children's childhood. You'll see how some rhyme and others don't, and the difference it makes when each rhyme lands perfectly and when it doesn't. You'll see what's conveyed in the illustrations and what's not. You'll see how fun the *teach you a lesson* ones are to read (or not) and how charming the *purely for fun* ones are (or not).

With this knowledge base, you'll discover more about your own book than you thought possible. And when you're ready to start editing it, here's what I recommend:

- Ask a friend to read it out loud. Note where they stumble over the words, even on the first read through. You won't stumble because you've read it so many times. It should roll off the tongue without too much fumbling.

- If your book rhymes, are the rhymes natural or forced? If your book has a specific meter (think: iambic pentameter, etc.), does everything conform with your pattern, without being forced?

For a great example of this, read Julia Donaldson's *The Gruffalo* out loud. It has a perfect rhyme scheme and flawless meter.

- Have you considered what words will fall on what pages and how the story is affected when the reader turns the page? Think of how you wait with anticipation every time you turn the page in *The Monster at the End of This Book* by Jon Stone and Michael Smollin. If you move a reveal in your story to its own page, does that create more suspense? If you make an emotional moment its own two-page spread, does that give it more emotional weight? If you put a lot of very active bits all on one page, does that make it feel more frenetic? These may or may not apply to your story; in fact, they could have the opposite effect. But where in the story a reader turns the page has a big impact on their experience of the story.
- Have you considered what elements of the story will be told in the illustrations (even if you are not drawing them) and thus don't need to be written out in the text? Have you included necessary art notes? Do you need to say "Edgar had a bad day" in the text if you envision an illustration of a wet cat with a broken umbrella?

UNIVERSAL QUESTIONS

Here are some editing tips that apply to all genres and formats:

- Is any referenced material used correctly (quotes, epigrams, song lyrics, etc.) and do you have permission to use it? You don't have to get this permission when sending a book to an agent or editor, but you will need it before the book is published, which includes paying for it yourself. It can be difficult and/or expensive to use song lyrics or lines of some poetry, so use them sparingly if at all.

- Have you spell-checked everything and read it over for missed words, homophones, and typos? Did you use the right *breath/breathe*, *their/there/they're*, *its/it's*, etc.?
- Is the word count consistent with your genre? Does it conform to the standards of the genre in the way readers want (and/or subvert them in an interesting way)?

The answers to all these questions will point to where you need to spend the most time editing. Can't answer what your characters want? You probably need to work on character development. Can't describe what happens in your book in an enticing way? You might need to work on your pitch, or you may need to beef up your plot. (Something happens in every book, whether it is a big, active thing or a small, interior thing. If nothing happens in your book, then you have written a book of description, and while beautiful, it may be hard to convince readers they want to read it.) Does your argument make logical sense? Is it supported? There is no single, correct answer to any of these questions, but what you have trouble answering will point you to where you need to bolster your book.

WILL YOU READ MY BOOK?

It's natural to get to the end of a book project and think *Who can tell me what's wrong with this thing?* There are lots of people who can tell you what's wrong—and right—with your manuscript. Some cost money and some don't. The first thing to tap when you're at this point is your writing community.

Your writing community can be many things: the people you complain about publishing to, your critique group that meets once a week, your former classmates from a workshop or online course, your internet friends, a group at the library. It can also be where you develop relationships with other writers who may become your beta readers. A beta reader is someone who reads your book and offers their honest reactions in a supportive and productive way. A beta reader's job isn't just to heap praise on your genius but to help make your book better. You are not required to have beta readers. But it is a tool you can use if it is available to you. And it's a role you're expected to reciprocate.

Who's a good beta reader? Someone you trust. Someone who is widely read in your genre. Someone who might be a writer, too, but not necessarily. Someone who can give you constructive criticism and someone from whom you can receive constructive criticism.

Who is not a good beta reader? Someone you're related to or partnered with. (Maybe, but tread lightly there.) Someone who has never read a book in your genre. Someone who thinks little of your genre. Your cousin who's a tenth-grade English teacher. (Just because they're an English teacher doesn't mean they know anything about your genre or writing books.) (Love you, English teachers.)

Sympathetic readers like family and close friends may not be the best beta readers, but they can be valuable in other ways. They can be your cheerleaders. They can be the ones you write for when you would rather hurl your laptop into a lake. They can be the emotional support you need, even if they can't be practical help.

BETA READERS DON'T GROW ON TREES

How do you get one of those communities and some beta readers? Slowly. You aren't going to type *The End* one day and send it off to newly found beta readers the next. It takes time to find the right group, to get comfortable, to meet willing readers, and to make time to read and be read. Luckily, there are many ways to find your people, and you can tailor your search depending on where you live, how you like to communicate, what genre you're writing, and your overall lifestyle. You can find groups online through your social media connections, even just posting "Anyone want to start a writers' group?" is a good first step. You can search Facebook or groups in your genre or area or find like-minded people in the places you already are online, like message boards and fandoms. There are hundreds of in-person and online writing classes, workshops, conferences, and groups in your backyard or across the world. Writers' associations like Science Fiction Writers of America, Horror Writers Association, and the Society of Children's Book Writers and Illustrators, among many others, are great places to start. Look in the back of any issue of *Poets & Writers* magazine and you'll see countless ads and listings for classes, conferences, and workshops that might be just right for you. Start looking. If you want to meet IRL, check out your local indie bookstore, library, community college, or university to see if they have groups, classes, or workshops. Yes, it's scary to be the one who reaches out first. Yes, there's no guarantee what you find will be what works. But the number one way people fail at finding a writing community is never looking at all.

The most important thing to remember is it's going to take time. It might take years. It might take six months to realize you don't like any of those people in your monthly Zoom and it's time to find something else. This sucks, I know, but it's part of the process. It's true for everyone. But you won't have tomorrow what you don't start building today.

And if you can't find a group you like, start one! I know that suggestion makes a lot of you cringe, but sometimes that's what it takes to get what you want and need. Every group needs a person to do the admin and emailing, and if that's your strong suit, lean into it. If it is not your strong suit, find a well-established organization, like a regional writers or genre-based group, and follow the rules to find your right spot.

Finding beta readers isn't the only benefit of seeking out community. You'll learn things and share things and find support when you need it most. You might find your agent through a friend, or you might share your own with another. It takes a lot of work and time, both of which we all feel we do not have, but the benefits greatly outweigh the costs. I've been in a book club for more than twenty years (!!!!), and a fellow member sent me a friend's manuscript that I read and loved and signed right up. Not only did that writer's community benefit him, but mine benefited me. I've also been in a writers' group since 2015, and it's been invaluable. Sometimes we meet and don't have pages to talk about, so instead we share highs and lows—good things happening with our writing and the bad—and it's always just what I need. I've been in other writing groups before, and you know it when you land in the right one.

If you don't have your writing community yet, don't worry. Beta readers aren't a requirement when editing your book. Start today and maybe you'll have a great one lined up for your next book. Try not to be discouraged by the effort it will take. It's worth it.

HOW TO TRUST YOUR GUT

You might be thinking *I don't have any beta readers! My book is horrible! It'll never be published!* Rest assured, everyone feels this way, many times throughout the course of writing. When I edit my own work, I alternate between thinking I'm a genius and a fraud, so there you go. The thing is, you don't know if any of that is true, especially at this point. You don't know if anyone will want to publish it unless you finish and send it to agents and editors. Very few books are pure shit. Your book is going to be amazing to some and *eh* to others, and this is true whether it sells five copies or five million, whether you hit the *New York Times* bestseller list or win a Nobel Prize. Passing judgment on your work before it's even finished is just anxiety, not objectivity. Keep going. You're not alone. Just focus on the task at hand to the best of your ability and learn to listen to your gut.

The voice that says *This book is horrible* is not your gut. It is fear and doubt, and that is not the same as your gut or intuition. What's your gut when it comes to writing? It's that small voice inside you that says, *I'm not sure that part makes sense.* It's not the part that screams *This is worthless!!!!* It's much quieter than that, and it rarely passes judgment. It just calls your attention to the work you need to do, to the questions you need to ask or answer. Remember, kindly deployed criticism is not judgment. Something can need fixing in your book and that doesn't mean it's bad. You especially know this voice is your gut when it tells you to do something and your reaction is *Ughhhhhhhhh I don't want to.* That's how you know it's a really important thing you have to do to your book. How do you develop this? Just by writing and reading, listening and trying, and not panicking.

When I'm reading a book, published or not, my gut is asking questions all the time. *What day is it now? Did that character come back from the place yet? Hold on, who said that part? Why the heck did that character do that?* Most times, I can go back a page and find the answer, but sometimes I've discovered a thing the writer missed. Not a mistake, but an assumption they made that I didn't. They guessed I would understand why the heck that character did that thing, but I didn't. And my gut found it. (This doesn't lead to an automatic rejection of the work, but too many instances is a sign it's not ready for the next step.) See the chart below for some common things your gut will say versus what's just fear talking.

GUT	FEAR
Are the stakes high enough in my story?	No one will ever want to read this shit.
Are there too many footnotes?	Gah, my book is boring.
Did I *fade to black* in chapter 3 because I like it or because I don't know how to write that scene?	La la la la la I can't hear you nothing's wrong with chapter 3 la la la la la la.
Do I have a vision for who my reader is?	Is anyone going to care?

You can develop this skill, I promise. It's harder to tell the difference between what's on the page and what lives in your head, but that's another skill you develop as a writer. And you can start with whatever you're working on right now. Practice by reading your book and writing down all the things your gut/fear tells you, even the things like *This is crap*. Write them in the margins or in a notebook and then look back on them. You'll start to see the difference between fear and actionable things you can address in your text. You might notice sections where you feel the most fear and doubt are sections that need extra attention. Go back to those and tell yourself, *I'm OK. I can do this. What do I need to address on the page here?* You might need to psych yourself up for this the first few times, but this is how you develop your instincts as a writer.

When you've gone through your editing evaluations, you can go forward with the actual editing in whatever way suits you best. You can save all your notes and do one big, massive edit, or you can do each pass—character, setting, logical progression, typos—separately. Yes, you are probably going to spend an hour working on a paragraph that you later decide to delete entirely and that is OK. Do not despair that this is wasted time or that you should have known that in the first place. It is all part of the process. Editing takes a good chunk of time however you approach it. You are not a bad writer if your first drafts need a lot of editing. You're just a writer like the rest of us.

HOW I EDITED THIS BOOK

Coming into this book with my fantastic outline and my wealth of knowledge, I figured it would fall out of my fingers and onto the screen near perfect. See? Agents are just like writers. I knew I would do some editing, of course. But then I started it in earnest.

I finished the first full draft at a residency at the Spruceton Inn in the Catskill Mountains of New York. It was *perfect*. A tiny little room all to myself, and nothing to do but write. I finished writing the last bits on day two of a five-day visit, and I actually wished I'd had more drafting to do. I wanted to take my own advice and let the manuscript sit, marinate, settle before I dove into edits, and a couple of days was not going to cut it. So I typed *The End* and then I . . . took a break. Went on a hike. Read some books as research. Napped. I went back and looked at the introduction again, since I'd written it long, long before, but I didn't do any major overhauls. This was the perfect plan for me and the book, even if it wasn't the most productive. I knew I'd just have to go back and do it over if I tried to edit too soon.

After several weeks of marinating, I dove back in and started reading. The first two chapters weren't half bad! They were, of course, the ones I'd edited with my agent, his assistant, my writers' group, and my editor, who gave me early notes before the whole draft was complete. And then I hit a point in the middle of this very chapter where my gut was saying *This isn't working*. Something was wrong with the structure. I could just feel it. I didn't know how to fix it yet, so I just kept going.

Then I remembered one of my own editing tips: the reverse outline! An outline of what I'd already written! I could then compare it to my original outline! When I saw the sections all laid out, it made so much more sense. And because I numbered the sections in both my list and on a printed copy of the manuscript, it made it much easier to find the sections I wanted and move them to where they needed to go.

Of course I wrote about this on my newsletter. I was certain I wasn't the first person to come up with this idea, and I don't claim to be. Other writers chimed in to say where they'd seen it discussed, including in Tiffany Yates Martin's *Intuitive Editing*, Jeff VanderMeer's *Wonderbook*, and Matt Bell's *Refuse to Be Done*. I'm glad to be in such great company.

Once I got through the whole manuscript, even more things became clear. Remember that chapter with forty numbered sections and the one with eight? Oops! This chapter was originally part of a very long chapter 1. I was able to get a bird's-eye view of the book and decide what could be split in two and what could be combined. It really gave me a better handle on organizing the first draft. If I'd been writing fiction, I feel like this would be even more helpful, showing the narrative distance between conflicts and resolutions, secrets hinted at and revealed. Action versus exposition. I can't wait to do it again to another book.

I also line edited as I read and organized, fixing typos and cutting repetitive bits. It wasn't going to be perfect after this first edit, but I flagged everything that caught my eye.

When I got to the end of the book (and also my deadline to turn it in), I stopped. My editor was not expecting a perfect book, I knew, but I also didn't want her to waste time telling me things I already knew. I wanted to respect her time that way.

After a month or two (tbh, I was happy not to see the book for a while), Stephanie sent me an edit letter, a document outlining what I needed to address and questions I needed to answer, and it suddenly got very real. She'd read it and now I had to edit it and it was on its way to becoming a real book!

It was also a long letter. Six pages. (I've seen longer, but it hits different when it's your six pages.) This was not too long, mind you, and I wasn't surprised by anything she said. But, whew, the work ahead started to sink in.

Stephanie's edit letter made me realize that I, as an agent, needed to be nicer in my own edit letters to clients. Stephanie said some wonderful things about the first draft, and that was very encouraging to read. Then she outlined, in brief, what she thought each chapter needed and then listed some general suggestions and questions. She said what I knew she would, that the front chapters were too long and I needed to do more interviews with industry professionals to add perspectives that were not just my own. She also pointed out what I couldn't see, that the internal logic of some chapters didn't make sense, and the topics just proceeded on the page as they had exited my brain. She made suggestions on what could go where, but also, once I saw it, I could apply that advice universally, though her telling me exactly where to move some things was very nice. She suggested one part go in chapter 1, much earlier than it appeared in the first draft, but as I was working, I realized it fit better in chapter 2. She wasn't mad I didn't do what she said. Quite the opposite. She agreed it fit better in chapter 2, and she was happy I addressed the concern in the best way possible. When you get an edit letter, from an agent or an editor, it's not a prescription for how to fix your book. It's a reflection on what you've already written and how to get it where it needs to go. No two editors will say the same thing, and there is no one "correct" version of a book.

What did I do next? I sat on my edit letter and looked at my manuscript in terror for about two weeks. The clock was ticking—I knew I had to get it back to Stephanie in about six weeks if we wanted to edit it a few more times before it had to go through the production part of the publishing process. (That's design and copyediting and the steps that make a manuscript into a book.) I printed out the edited manuscript she'd given me, with notes and suggestions made in Track Changes, and I used colored sticky notes to flag the things I needed to do. Purple for questions to answer, yellow for structural changes to make, blue for suggestions. What did I do with that printed manuscript after? Nothing. But I needed to leaf through it on paper instead of scroll on a screen to get a sense of what was to come, and that was valuable in and of itself. In the end, I took off all the sticky notes and recycled everything. I made my actual changes and additions in the digital manuscript, leaving the Track Changes function on so Stephanie could see what I did.

When I was done with everything I knew I could do, including half a dozen hours of interviews, I sent it back to Stephanie. We went through the manuscript two more times, including with her fabulous colleague Karina, editing, polishing, and refining. I somehow added 15,000 words to the second draft, and then took a bunch of them out in the third. Eventually it went to copyediting, and the time of making big changes to the manuscript was over. I've been able to refine things here or there, and certainly fix things the copyeditor caught, but once it's in copyediting, you don't make big changes without creating a huge headache for everyone else. Is this book perfect? No. Does it need to be? No.

The overall lesson on editing is not that you have to do it this specific way, or any specific way, or else your book will suck. It's that everyone hates editing, and it feels murky and big and scary, but the only way out is through. There are no shortcuts. And there are no perfect books.

HOW TO KNOW WHEN YOU'RE DONE

You'll know you're done when you've taken out a comma in the morning, and put it back in the afternoon, to paraphrase Oscar Wilde. That means you stop when you're making small changes just to be doing something instead of substantive edits that will improve (or not!) the book. You may not have answered all the questions you set out to answer. You may not be sure what you've done is right, good, or sufficient. But there's a point at which you have to move on. This is where your gut comes in again. When you hear it whispering *Go back to chapter three again*, you're not really done. The voice saying *Everything is wrong, and you are the worst!!!* is not your gut, remember. That's your fear. When your gut says, *OK, I think you did all you can do*, that's when you know. Or when you don't hear it at all, when it stops pointing you to things to check. It takes practice to hear your gut, so if you're just starting out, don't worry if you're still not sure. No one's 100 percent sure. Just do your best.

You can also be done when you just can't do it anymore. Editing is taxing, and sometimes we've done all we can do. You still might not be sure about chapter 3's ending, but well, you're tapped out. We all get to this point sooner or later.

What you can't do, though, is use fatigue as an excuse to shirk your duties. Your beta readers and agent and editor are there to help you, but it's a waste of everyone's time if you know chapter 3's wonky and you don't address it. Your editor is just going to say "Chapter three is wonky," which you already knew! So don't use this as a shortcut. Ask for help if you need it. That's what your team is there for.

Done does not equal perfect. Done is going to mean something different for every draft. And there's only one draft where your *done* manuscript will be going to the printer—and you'll know exactly which one that is!

HOW TO EDIT YOUR EXPECTATIONS

Now that you've done all the editing and writing you can do, it's time to get ready to send your work out into the world. This is terrifying! It's normal to be scared of this part. But it's also normal to be excited and anxious and hopeful and convinced you wrote a bestseller. (I hope you did!) It's all of these things, sometimes all at once, sometimes one at a time. Hold on tight.

Before we get into the nitty-gritty of sending your book out to an agent or editor, take some time to think about what you want to happen and what is most likely to happen. What we all *want* to happen is an agent offers representation mere hours after submission and there's a six-figure book deal by the end of the week. I can say with confidence that is not going to happen. If I sold a book the same week I took on a new client (who didn't already have a relationship with an editor) in my whole publishing career, I don't remember it. It would be nice if it happened that way, but I wouldn't write it down as a goal.

What you can expect going forward is for everything to take a very long time. I know, it sucks. It takes a long time to read a book, for an agent or an editor. (How many books have you read this week, month, year?) And your book is just one of many in their inbox. Agents and editors want to read submissions quickly, but the slush pile (i.e., queries that come directly from authors) is not any agent's or editor's first priority. I know that sucks to hear too.

An agent's top priority is their current clients. And when you are one, you'll want that to be true too. An agent may get a few hours to read queries and requested manuscripts some weeks and only a few minutes in others. Yes, agents want to find new clients, and an agent just starting out, who has a lot of room on their client list, may spend more time in the slush pile. An agent with a full client list may be less frequently in the slush pile or closed to new queries altogether. This isn't because your work isn't worthy of time and attention. It's because agents have many other tasks to complete in their days. We'll talk about this more in chapter 3 about agents and in chapter 6 about submissions, but this is just to prepare you for why everything takes so long.

As time passes while your book is out to agents, you will think *Surely an agent could have read my book by now!* And they probably could have—if it was the only thing they had to do. If I had no other obligations, I could read three or four books a week and hundreds of queries! But I have many other obligations, not just work, and reading time usually comes after hours. Your novel is in the queue with all the other reading an agent has to do, for their current clients, prospective clients, market research, and even books they just want to read for fun. I read upwards of eighty books a year, and it can still take me weeks and weeks to read a submission. There is just a lot of reading to do all the time.

Agents, too, do not get paid to read queries or submissions. I know what you're thinking: *Of course they do. That's their job!* But most agents are paid on commission, not on salary, so they do not get paid until they sell your book. Thus, they are not getting paid when they read queries, edit unsold manuscripts, or send out submissions, but those are the steps that must happen to eventually get paid. (This is also why agents can't give you feedback on your manuscript if you are not already a client.) Many agents are in the business because they love books. But it's also what provides them with money to shelter and feed themselves and their families. When it feels like your book has been out there forever, just picture it in the middle of a tall stack of others, all of you in this together.

You should also prepare yourself for more editing. You may do editing with your agent, and you will most certainly do several rounds of edits with an editor. That doesn't mean that your book sucks right now, or that you don't have to do your own editing because someone will just tell you how to change it later, but it does mean that the professionals you work with will help you make your book even better. Again, don't think of editing as fixing things that are wrong. Think of it as bringing out the best in your work. Michelangelo didn't carve marble because the rock was the wrong shape. He did it to find the sculpture inside.

At the end of all this, you will have a manuscript ready to go out into the world. You will have a good idea of your genre. You will know you've taken the editing as far as you can go. You will still feel unsure and maybe insecure. You will not know what to do next (hi, that's why you're reading this!), and you will feel your desire for success even more keenly. There's still a long way to go from here, but you can't do anything without the work you've already done. Just keep going.

You Have My Permission to Write

I've read many craft books, and after my almost twenty years of publishing experience, I've found writing advice comes down to one thing: giving yourself permission to write. Craft books are still useful because sometimes we need to hear the same advice over again in a different way to really absorb it, but to me, it all boils down to permission. You are allowed to write. You are allowed to try. You are allowed to take the time from other things to write. You are allowed to take the time for yourself, no matter how brief or long, to write whatever you want. You are allowed to write even if it's bad at first, even if you never get published. If you can't give it to yourself, I'm giving it to you here.

Maybe you will never even show your writing to anyone. Maybe your heart aches with longing to be published and lauded or at the very least seen. (You're allowed to want any and all of those things too.) It doesn't matter. You cannot control what happens to your writing, most of the time. But you can control *if* you write, and this is your explicit permission to do it. Today, tomorrow. Instead of the dishes or reading your book club book or watching that show you aren't particularly interested in anyway. Instead of the thing you *should* do. Instead of mowing the lawn or vacuuming or getting the cobwebs down from the corner of the ceiling that no one but you notices anyway. How dare you write instead of doing something else, something someone else thinks you should do? Because I said you could. Because you want to and because you can.

Chapter Three

ALL ABOUT LITERARY AGENTS

WHAT'S A LITERARY AGENT?

It will come as no surprise that I think you should have a literary agent. I admit all my own biases. But before I give you the hard sell, I want you to know what literary agents actually do, and do not do, so you can decide for yourself. You might not need one, or you might not want one. I will not be offended if that's your decision. Bottom line: agents want what's best for authors, even if it means not working with them.

Writers often ask me if editors will be mad if they get an agent, especially if they've been talking about a project for a while. I can say with confidence that editors on the whole do *not* feel this way. Most editors love it when an author gets an agent because it means they can talk to them about the book and save all the money/deal/negotiating stuff for their agent. It means the editor doesn't have to explain what an option clause is and instead can spend their time working on the actual book they want to buy. Editors have told me that if they have to play hardball with an agentless writer about the book deal, it might sow distrust in their relationship. The writer might ask for something an editor just can't give (and that an agent would tell them not to worry about). Editors aren't out to screw over writers, but they are also not paid to advocate for them over their publishing house, i.e., the entity that signs their paychecks. Editors aren't worried that agents are going to drive up the cost of a book when they get involved. Any increase in the advance an agent asks for, that the publisher can grant, is money well spent, from what I hear from editors.

So, what does a literary agent do? A literary agent represents authors to publishers. That basically covers it. This means they speak with specific publishers about specific works on behalf of their clients' best interests. Literary agents are paid primarily when they sell a client's work, not up front. Agents, like authors, do not work for publishers; they work *with them.* (My family continues to ask what publisher I work for, and I answer, *None of them.*) A cynical view is that agents are middlemen, gatekeepers. A generous view is that agents are advocates. It's likely your experience with any one agent will dictate which way your opinion leans. Agents are not, however, a monolith.

There is no degree, licensure, or certificate* required to be an agent. Most learn through an apprenticeship with a more experienced agent, and to me, this is *vital.* There isn't a way to study how to be an agent except by doing the job, because an agent's primary job is assessing a situation and figuring out what to do about it. Every book, every publisher, every author is different. Even the agents I know who are also trained lawyers say that their contract law classes barely prepared them to be an agent, because publishing contracts are their own narrow area of contracts.

* There are publishing certificate programs at universities like New York University, Columbia University, Pace University, and the Denver Publishing Institute, but these programs give you an overview of publishing, not intense, specific training.

I know agents who have, of course, English degrees, or who moved over from other areas of publishing, like editorial or marketing. I know agents who worked in politics, who worked in Hollywood, who were any number of things before they became agents. I think the only requirements to be an agent are a love of reading (or at least stamina!), the ability to juggle lots of things all at the same time, and a keen attention to detail. The rest you learn along the way.

WHAT DO AGENTS DO?

Agents review and evaluate manuscripts and proposals to see what they think they can sell. (Notice I didn't say *to see what they think is good.*) Agents study the marketplace, as much as they can, and make judgments about what may or may not be successful in the retail book market. Sometimes those decisions are financially driven, sometimes they are artistically driven, sometimes both. Sometimes it's just a feeling. Sometimes they're right. And sometimes they're wrong. No agent has a crystal ball.* It takes a long time and a lot of work to sell a book, so agents don't take things on just for the heck of it.

Agents get clients by reaching out directly to authors, through network referrals, and through queries (which we'll talk about a lot, don't worry). They read websites, magazines, journals, newspapers, and social media to find talent. It could be anywhere. Honestly, sometimes I think *too much* about what could be a book. All these things work together to help an agent build a robust client list.

* Elisabeth Marbury, one of the early female (and openly queer!) theatrical and literary agents in America, wrote a book called *My Crystal Ball* in 1924, but it's more *looking back through the mists of time* than *predicting literary futures*.

Agents hope these clients will all be successful writers. They hope to vary their list so that if the market swings one way or another, their business (and the business of their clients, don't forget) doesn't tank. That's why you see agents who represent romances and memoirs and picture books and self-help. It's not smart to put all your eggs in one basket. There is no perfect number of clients to reach this goal. Some agents have large client lists and are supported by assistants, contracts managers, bookkeepers, and many other staff. Some agents have highly curated lists of just a few writers and work either by themselves or with a lean or outsourced staff. One way is not better than the other. It's what suits the agent and their business.

Once they join forces, the agent does what needs to be done to get the author's book ready for market. That could mean editing a proposal or manuscript, or not. It might mean doing research on comparable titles, appropriate publishing houses, or the right editor to send the book to. Sometimes agents know the second they read something which editor is going to love it. Once an agent is established, they have strong connections with editors in at least a few genres. But editors move jobs, get promoted, or leave the industry all the time. Imprints spring up, merge, reemerge, or close. Publishers are acquired by bigger ones. And sometimes whole new publishing houses emerge. The industry is in a constant state of flux. That means agents have to keep up with who went where and when and what editors are able to acquire what. They do this by reading industry publications like *Publishers Lunch* and *Publishers Weekly*, going out to lunch, coffee, or drinks with editors (really!), or having calls or Zoom meetings. Some publishers send out rosters of their editorial staff (and we agents thank them mightily for it!). An agent doesn't have to know an editor personally to send them a manuscript. I send things to editors before we've chatted or gone to lunch all the time. I've done my research about what they can and want to acquire by seeing things they've previously purchased on websites like PublishersMarketplace.com or by asking friends or colleagues for recommendations. Sometimes the best way to get to know an editor is to sell them something.

Agents compile a list of editors to send a proposal or manuscript to, called a submission list. There's no perfect number of entries on these lists. Some are big, in genres like commercial fiction or picture books, because there are a lot of editors who acquire them and lots of publishers who publish them. Some lists are small because of a limited number of houses or editors or because an exclusive list is better for the submission. Agents also use their prior experience with a publisher to decide on future submissions. I'll admit there are a few traditional publishers I just don't do business with anymore, usually because I think their contracts or business practices are harmful to authors. But I could probably count them all on one hand. Most agents, as far as I know, don't just send a book out willy-nilly. A bad contract or the wrong house for a book is *worse* than no deal at all. It's not *any port in a storm* when it comes to publishing.

When something doesn't sell, which does happen, the agent then works with their client to figure out what's next. A revision? Another round of submissions? A new project? They work together on what's best, and the agent guides the author according to their experience, instincts, and the author's wishes. I have definitely told clients we've hit the end of the road with a submission, even if there wasn't a sale. It sucks, trust me. Each book and each client is different and requires a different strategy.

Then there are the times when a book *does* sell! This is the goal, obviously, for many reasons. One: it's an agent's job! There are no guarantees, but it is the point of the whole endeavor. Two: it's what the client wants! And three: that's when everyone gets paid.

THE MONEY PART

Most agents work on commission, which means they are paid a percentage of all the money a book brings in until it stops bringing it in. We call this "the life of the book." The standard commission rate agents earn in the US is 15 percent of domestic deals, and 20 percent to 21 percent for foreign and subsidiary rights, depending on a few different factors, which we'll get into later when we talk about book deals. Some agents earn a salary from their agencies and might get a bonus depending on their total commission earnings. Some get a "draw," which is like an advance against their future commission earnings (just like a book deal, which we'll talk about soon, too), and if they don't earn it back after a certain number of years, their contracts might not be renewed. According to a 2023 survey by the American Association of Literary Agents (AALA), 63.9 percent of those member agents surveyed are paid, in full or in part, on commission, which means they don't get paid until you get paid. They may split that commission with their parent agency in a number of different ways and may or may not get benefits like 401(k)s or health insurance.[1] It varies widely in the industry. There are large corporate agencies and small "boutique" agencies and everything in between. There are big-name talent agencies that represent actors, screenwriters, celebrities, and, yes, authors. There are agencies that do only books. The size and structure of any agency you sign up with likely doesn't matter too much. You may have preferences one way or another, but most often, authors pick the *agent* they want to work with, with a side of the ambient prestige of their agency. Some agents are known by where they work, and some are known more by their own reputation. I think connecting with an agent's personal reputation is the best approach to finding an agent, rather than being attached to saying *Oh, I'm represented by Big Name Agency.*

If you're already notable in your area of expertise or have a big platform that includes audio or video work, it's possible a talent agency is right for you. They often have the resources and connections to coordinate between the many professionals this type of author or public figure works with—like a manager, a talent agent, PR professionals, and assistants—but it's not a rule that you have to join such an agency.

A book that has very, very strong chances to cross over into other formats, like a TV show, movie, or high-profile podcast, might also benefit from working with a large talent agency. But working with one doesn't guarantee your book will be a movie, and not working with one doesn't guarantee it won't, either. We all think our books would make great movies, podcasts, breakfast cereals, stationery lines, and calendars, but few will be offered as anything other than a print book, e-book, and audiobook. That's OK! That's normal! Focus on getting the book published in the first place and then worry about all that other stuff.

A BOOK DEAL AND AFTER

Let's say your agent has just sold your book and is negotiating your deal. Woo hoo! You'll talk about what it all means, what likely can or can't happen, and your agent will give their recommendations. They'll tell you why *just ask for one million dollars* is or isn't the way to go. They'll keep you posted on how everything progresses, and you always get the final yes or no. It's your deal, after all. We'll cover all the ins and outs of book deals in chapter 7.

I like to tell clients that my job from that point on is to do what needs to be done. I take care of the business stuff so the author can have a purely editorial relationship with their editor. I bug people if the checks are late. I send follow-ups about when the marketing meeting should be scheduled. I ask when we'll see a cover sketch. Not that authors can't ask these questions, but I'm usually aware of what's late and what's not, and authors are . . . not, especially first-time authors. Agents can't *force* a publisher to do anything, but we sure can be annoying when we have to be! The squeaky wheel gets the grease.

I also tell my clients that it's my job to be the bad guy and say the things the author doesn't want to or doesn't know how to say. If an author is uncomfortable nudging their editor *again* for edits (love you, editors), I am more than happy to send those *Just following up!* emails. If bad news needs to be delivered or received, it usually goes through me. That's OK. That's what I'm here for.

This all goes the same for your first book or your fifteenth, until we both ride off into the literary sunset. Some agents may contract with an author on a book-by-book basis, and some work with an author for decades. You'll know going into your relationship which it is, and one might suit you better than the other. Between books, I brainstorm ideas with my clients or seek out or suggest them for new opportunities I hear about from editors. When it's time to sell another book, we do it all over again, together.

WHAT AGENTS CAN'T AND WON'T DO

Agents do so many other things besides deal with the money parts, like help with marketing and publicity, decode royalty statements, advise on next projects, help authors network with other authors/clients, and so much more. But there are also things an agent *can't* and *won't* do.

Agents cannot guarantee they will sell your book, at all or for a specific advance. Would that it t'were true. Agents can't force a publisher to give them a certain amount of money for a book, regardless of whatever rumors you've heard about whatever big-name agents do or don't do. Agents can't get marketing plan promises—like a billboard in Times Square—written out in the contract. Publishers just won't do that. Sometimes an agent will have such a hot book or author that they can say *We need $X for this project.* And the publisher can either say yes or no or give the number they are willing to spend. If an agent says *We must have $X or we walk*, they—and you—must be prepared to walk. Playing hardball doesn't always work. Any agent who says they guarantee sales or dollar amounts is a schmagent, or someone to be avoided.

Agents cannot tell you what to write. I mean, sometimes we go out into the world and say *I really want a book about debutant hedgehogs or how to dismantle the American health care industry*, but that doesn't mean we have a full outline waiting for you or a publisher on the hook. Agents are not necessarily looking for a stable of authors to hand book projects to, though I know authors out there who would jump at that chance. *Just tell me what to write!!!* is a common refrain I hear, especially from those who've been querying for a while. Agents usually prefer to work with an author who has an idea of their own.*

Agents are not therapists. Do agents support authors? Yes. Help in times of need? Yes. Do agents and clients sometimes become close friends? Yes. Can you be yourself with your agent? Yes. But most often, agents are not trained therapists, and while we always want to help, we're not a replacement for professional care.

Agents are also not banks. Most of the time you are paid by your agent, not your publisher, as in the publisher sends the agent the advance payments, and the agent takes their commission and remits the rest to you. That doesn't mean they are a bank with unlimited reserves that can give you

---

* Tbh, authors' ideas are usually better than mine. It's easier to find the passion needed to write a whole book from within rather than to ask someone to give it to you.

an advance on your advance. Agents have a fiduciary responsibility to pay their clients within a certain period of time, so they aren't just swimming in cash. The client account needs to zero out as often as possible, meaning all the clients have received all their money. What's left over is the agent's operating costs and paychecks. If you are in dire financial straits, talk to your agent. Chances are they are just as anxious to get paid as you are.

Agents do not have crystal balls, like I said. If we did, I wouldn't be writing this book—I'd be on a tropical island sipping mai tais or at least reading leisurely in my library (one with a library ladder, of course). If we could predict the future, what will or won't sell, what will or won't be a hit, what trends will pop up next, then we'd be right all the time, and all authors would be millionaires. But that is not the case, obviously. My least favorite question as an agent is *What trends do you see right now?* Because if it's a trend anyone can see, that means books are already selling, either in the retail market or between editors and agents, and if that's true, then those books were written two to three years prior, if not longer, and if you started now, you'd be two to three years behind. It's better to make the trend yourself than follow someone else's.

This isn't an exhaustive list, but it's a good start. If you need or want something from your agent, just ask. We can't always deliver, but we'll do what we can.

WHY YOU NEED AN AGENT

Now that you know what agents mostly do and don't do, you might ask yourself why you need one. You don't need one to say you're a writer. You might not need one right now, or ever. You probably need one if you want to be published by most traditional publishing houses, because editors there are not allowed to accept unagented manuscripts or ones sent to them directly by authors. There are some publishers (Chronicle Books,

Harlequin, and others) that do accept unsolicited manuscripts, and you can send your book straight to them according to the guidelines they post on their websites.

When you do this, it will likely go into the slush pile or the inbox where all unsolicited manuscripts go, and someone will look at it . . . whenever they look at it. Some have "slush parties" where everyone gets into a conference room and binge reads queries, looking for good stuff. Some assign this task to specific team members (not always but not never interns), and some get to it whenever they can.

And things do get picked up out of the slush pile at publishers! I've seen it with my own eyes. (An editor might also reach out to you directly, but we'll talk about that later.) It's possible! So if that happens, you don't need an agent, right?

People ask me all the time if they really need an agent, with varying levels of sincerity. I reply with a little *gotcha* question too. *What is the standard export royalty for hardcovers shipped to the UK by your publisher?* I ask. Of course they don't know that! Who would but agents? The point of having an agent, imho, is to work with an expert in a field you don't know. And you need that person from the jump. Once you sign the book contract, you can't say *Oops, I have an agent now; can we start over?*

In the beginning, there's a power imbalance in the author-agent relationship. The agent has all the knowledge and the power that goes with it, and the author needs all that knowledge to get where they want to go. What I'm doing with that cheeky question about export royalty rates is fluffing my feathers and saying *Don't forget you need me!* Agents have to act responsibly with that power and not let it go to their heads. In reality, agents can't do anything without the books authors write, and once the author gains a little more knowledge, the power dynamics stabilize. If you are scared of your agent, nervous to ask them questions, or fearful of their response, examine the power balance between the two of you, how you perceive it, and what it actually is. I've heard of so many people terrified of agents, of their agent, and it makes me sad. Writers need agents, and agents need writers, and we all need to work to remember that.

An agent is there to help get you money and favorable deal and contract terms, but they are also there to figure out what *your* book needs and if publishing can give it to you. Think of an agent as the publishing interpreter for your book and career. You might be able to figure it out yourself. But you don't have to.

HOW TO GET AN AGENT

I know you're thinking *OK, Kate. I want an agent, but how the heck do I get one?* I won't lie and say it's easy. It's complicated, confusing, and opaque. Fun, right? I'm sorry it's not easier. There is no single *find all the agents here* website or *submit all your stuff here* portal. (No, not even QueryTracker, which we'll discuss.) There are many tools you can use to gather what you need. I'll try to make it as clear as possible.

You might have done some casual looking or note-taking as you were writing, but I suggest waiting until you're actually done with what you need to write before you start your search in earnest. Why? Because sometimes what you set out to write isn't what you end up writing, and that can change who you send it to.

WHAT GENRE IS YOUR BOOK, REDUX

Agents specialize in specific genres of books, because frankly we can't be an expert in all things. Individual genres have different rules and conventions (like a Happily Ever After in romance or a strong read-aloud quality in picture books) as well as whole slates of editors the agent must know to sell those books to. We can't know everyone! We specialize in different areas according to our tastes, strengths, business acumen, or dumb luck. Early in my career I found myself the go-to agent for craft books (sewing, knitting, etc.), not because I thought *Wow, this will make me money!* but because I have always been a crafter, and I understood what readers might want in those kinds of books and how that could match up with what publishers might want. When I barely had any clients, I reached out to crafters whose blogs I read or whose projects I saw in magazines like *Make:* or *Bust*. And it worked! I've sold more than forty craft books in my career. I didn't plan it that way, but I'm glad it happened.

You want to target agents who represent writers in your genre* because they know the market, the conventions of the form, and the editors who buy those books. You start by making what I call a Big Messy List. Just a bunch of names in a format that works for you, spreadsheets, paper and pen, Notes app, whatever. If you see an agent that reps your genre, write down their name.

WHERE DO YOU FIND THESE NAMES, THOUGH?

Here are the best places to start:

Publishers Marketplace, PublishersMarketplace.com

This is a subscription-based website that costs $25 a month as of this writing, and is worth every penny, if even for a few months while you're in an intense research period. You can even get a twenty-four-hour Quick

* Agents will provide lists of the genres they represent on their websites and various other online resources. This info can change, so I think it is best practice to use the agent's own website as the final word in what they are looking for and not necessarily an interview, submission manager website, or blog post from a decade ago.

Pass to check it out for $10. Don't let the spare graphic design fool you—it's an industry go-to when it comes to publishing news, contacts, and deals. Subscribe to their (free) newsletter, *Publishers Lunch*, or the paid version, *Publishers Lunch Deluxe*, and it will provide a wealth of publishing news and insight.

But for agent-finding purposes, navigate to the Deals section. Agents, authors, and editors announce new books this way, using the website's specific format. The deal announcement for this book looked like this:

Publishers Marketplace **Deal Report**

Category: Non-fiction: How-To *July 27, 2023*

WRITE ON **By Kate McKean**

Imprint: Atria

Vice president of Howard Morhaim Literary Kate McKean's WRITE ON: PUBLISHING, BOOKS, AND NAVIGATING THE CREATIVE LIFE, a guide to publishing and managing the ups and downs of a creative life, based on the author's newsletter, Agents and Books, to Stephanie Hitchcock at Atria, in a pre-empt, for publication in summer 2025, by Michael Bourret at Dystel, Goderich & Bourret (world).

You'll notice there, too, is a genre designation, next to Category. You can search the whole deal database, going back to 2000, by category and/or keyword. You might look at all the books sold in How-To in the last few years (going back too far might not yield the most relevant results) and put those agents' names down on your Big Messy List. You might look at other genre/topic designations to see if something else might be relevant. The agent or editor posting the deal chooses the category and results vary. Your How to Survive Climate Disaster book could be How-To, but it could also be Current Events. It's OK to cast a wide net at this point because it's a big, messy list.

Within a genre, especially larger ones like General Fiction or Mystery, you can search for keywords. Maybe your book is historical, and you want to target agents who do historical mysteries. Maybe you want an agent who knows a lot about vampire books. Search broadly and write it all down.

QueryTracker, querytracker.com

QueryTracker is a query management and research tool online. In its free version, you can research agents, make lists, track your submissions, and read comments others leave about that agent. (*Gulp*. And guys—I read these. I'm sorry it takes me so long to respond!) For $25 a year, you can get premium features such as an agent's average rejection time or manuscript request rate as well as many other features.* QueryTracker's own user guide suggests you also double-check the information on their site, like agents' chosen genres. All databases are only as good as the data.

Literary Marketplace, literarymarketplace.com

The *LMP* is a physical book you can find in most libraries and great for people who want a tactile research experience. It's almost like the phone book for agents and publishers, if you remember phone books. There is an online component, but a subscription is required, and it's very possible your library has that subscription too. Ask your trusty librarian for help accessing it. Published yearly (the 2023–24 edition is its eighty-fourth!), the print edition is only as accurate as the information

---

* No, I don't get a commission if you sign up for any of these services.

they had at printing time. I would definitely suggest cross-referencing any information you find there with more current resources, but if you want to just leaf through and look at lists of names, this is how to do it. You can buy your own, but they cost around $500 each.

Manuscript Wish List (#mswl), manuscriptwishlist.com

This site, which started as a Tumblr hashtag back in 2013, and then turned into a website by a group of writers, editors, and agents, specifically focuses on what agents and editors want and do not want, as well as whatever fun facts agents and editors want to include about themselves. I actually use this website when making submission lists, either for specific information about editors or even just as a vibe check. If I have a dark fantasy novel, and that editor's MSWL page is all unicorns and rainbows, they might not be the best fit for my project. It's one of many resources I use, and you can use it that way too. Agents and editors can log in and edit this information at will, but there's no telling how often they do that. (I have updated my profile a few times over the years, but not more than that.)

Association of American Literary Agents, aalitagents.org

This is the website of the governing body for literary agents. Not all agents are part of the AALA—they report almost five hundred members in their survey—but all member agents "must meet AALA's professional qualifications and agree to adhere to its widely respected Canon of Ethics"[2] and be approved by the Board of Directors.[3] They might not be the right agent for you, but they aren't going to be an outright scammer. This site has a searchable database, and agents submit this information. It is another resource to use to add to your big, messy list of agents.

Social Media

Who knows what social media will look like when this book is published? If it's still around, agents will be on it. As you make your list, search for those agents on whatever platform you prefer. It's likely agents will be on the text-based ones more often than the video-based ones, but I do know some agents who participate in BookTok. Regardless of the platform, you can get a sense of their personality (at least the public-facing one), what they talk about, maybe even what they are looking for. Not all agents are on social media, but a lot are.

Actual Books

Authors often thank their agents (and many others) on the acknowledgments page in the back of their book.* You can sit down in front of your genre's section at the library (or bookstore, but please don't treat it like the library) and see who authors are thanking, add those names to your big, messy list, and research those agents further later. If you're doing this later in your research, you'll be familiar enough with a lot of agents to recognize them when the author just lists a name and doesn't say "thanks to my agent."

In-Person Events

Many authors want to go right to the source and talk to an agent face-to-face. Many have called an agent's office requesting a meeting, but unfortunately, that's not a thing anyone's schedule will allow. The next best thing is a writers' conference or other literary event. Many conferences offer pitch events (*Writer's Digest* sponsors many) where you can meet and/or pitch agents directly and in person. I've met hundreds of authors

---

* You can use the Search Inside function, when available, on books at Amazon.com or Google Books and search for "agent," "thanks to," and/or "acknowledgments." That's my secret hack to find out who edited a book!

this way. But I've offered representation to three clients at a conference, and two accepted. That's not a great hit rate for any of us.

It's OK to seek out an agent at a conference, whether that's at the closing reception or a pitch event. It's great to meet agents and learn they are just people who love books and not all-powerful beings that will bestow upon you the power of Publishing. It's also very good practice to pitch an agent because it forces you to home in on what's great about your book and practice talking about it confidently. But that ten minutes you get to sit down with an agent is not going to make too much of a difference as to whether they represent you or not.

Why? Because the point of books is reading them. Meeting authors is great, and their enthusiasm can be contagious. But in the end, it comes down to the book and if I can sell it or not. I can't tell that in one ten-minute meeting. It's a *start*, but I still need to read the materials.

What writers don't realize is that meeting agents is only one tiny benefit of going to conferences. Besides that, conferences offer tremendous opportunities to learn about writing and publishing (often directly from agents), to meet and network with other writers, and to build or expand your professional (and/or social) community. Very few people walk out of a conference with an offer of representation in hand. But most, if not all, walk out with knowledge, contacts, or resources that get them closer to that goal.

If conferences are too expensive or not accessible to you, keep an eye out for virtual ones that may better line up with your schedule or needs, as well as ones that offer scholarships or reduced fees. You might also look for literary events in your community (free or ticketed) where local or visiting agents might be. I do not suggest pitching an agent your book while they're trying to listen to a reading or enjoy an event, but it's OK to network and meet people at these things, whether they're agents or not. This is part of community building, and you never know where it's going to lead. (Just don't be creepy.)

If you can't make it in person, don't feel like you're at an acute disadvantage. Most people find their agents using the above online resources and not conferences.

Please, though, be considerate when approaching an agent at a conference or event, especially if you want to pitch them. Please don't pitch an agent in the bathroom or slide your manuscript under the stall door. (Yes, this has happened.) Please don't pitch an agent while they are hurriedly scarfing down lunch between panels or clearly conducting business on the phone or with colleagues. And please reconsider your plan to pitch your book after a few drinks at the bar. Wait until morning! An agent is a human being you'd like to talk to, not your one shot at fame and fortune.

HOW TO NARROW DOWN THE BIG MESSY LIST

You'll eventually start to see the same agents pop up again and again in your searches, and adding new names to your big, messy list will slow to a trickle. That's when you know you can move on to the next phase of your research, where you narrow this down to a solid list of agents to send your work to. The goal is not to include *all* agents who could possibly be interested in your book, but enough to give you a fighting chance. Your friend who writes thrillers might send to twenty agents, and you might query fifty for your YA novel. That's OK. You're both right. There's no perfect number of agents to query.

How do you make your big, messy list more targeted and best suited to your book? Start by answering some basic questions:

- Is this agent still in the business?
- Is this agent still at the agency I thought they were?
- Is this agent currently accepting queries? Do I know if they will close to queries soon?

- Am I interested in more than one agent at the same agency?*
- Does this agent say they want my genre?

When you've made that first pass at your list, you can further winnow it down with these more specific questions:

- Has this agent sold a book in my genre in the last few years?
- Has this agent recently said on social media they do or do not want a book like mine?
- Has this agent recently sold a book very, very, very much like mine?†

It's easy to read too much into the answers to these questions. Is a book that also has a character named Mary in it "very, very much like" your book? (No.) If an agent sold a mystery three years and eight months ago, is that "recently"? (Yes.) If an agent *hasn't* said they want unicorn military fantasy, does that mean they don't? (No.) Try not to spiral and overthink things. If in doubt, include them on your submission list. The worst they can do is say no, and that's true about everyone.

SHOULD I GO WITH A BIG-NAME AGENT OR A NEWBIE?

There's logic to the advice that if you want a better chance at getting an agent, you should send your queries to new agents who are looking to build their lists. This is a great thing to do. Agents just starting out in their careers, but who are still part of a larger agency they can lean on for

* If so, check that agency's website to see if you can query more than one agent there. These rules vary from agency to agency.

† If so, you might try someone else. They may not want a new client that competes directly with a current one.

support, are hungry for clients and may have more time to focus on edits or book development. Writers worry, though, that the newbies won't have the sway necessary to land a big deal. Some are insistent on the fact that you need a big-name agent to get a big deal. Literary agent and founding partner of Neon Literary Anna Sproul-Latimer says she encounters writers who think: "Surely there are some agents out there who can sell things on name recognition alone? Is there no person left who can just make a phone call and get a half million for a debut author on the strength of their endorsement?" She and I agree that no, there isn't! This was true maybe fifty years ago, but that's not the publishing world we have anymore. This line of thinking focuses too much on what will make things *easier*. Easier to get an agent, easier to get a book deal. That's the wrong focus. You want the agent that *gets* your work and that you feel comfortable working with.

Simon & Schuster senior editor Yahdon Israel said he believes a lot more writers have agents than book deals. When writers make a clear goal to get an agent and they achieve it, they can stall out there. He says writers don't "understand that an agent is but a means to getting a book deal and getting a book deal is a means to getting published" and everything else that comes after. If your sights are only on the agent, that might be all you get. Think bigger. Think about your next book and the next and the next. Find the person who is right for you, not right for right now.

WHAT ARE SUBMISSION GUIDELINES?

Every agent or agency decides what they want authors to send them so they can best evaluate a project. These are their submission guidelines, and sometimes they even vary agent to agent within an agency. They usually all request a query letter, but they can ask for a number of sample chapters or pages, a synopsis, an outline, or none of these things.

Each agent sets these according to what they know they need to make a decision about the work they want to represent.

Agents commonly ask for these things in their submission guidelines:

Query Letter. This is a letter of introduction or cover letter that tells us about your book. Hold tight: we're going talk all about them shortly.

Sample Pages. An agent might ask for the first five or fifty pages or the first three chapters. Pages are defined according to the manuscript formatting guidelines I talked about in chapter 1. Always send your first chapters. Absolutely under NO circumstances should you send chapters from the middle of your book or nonsequential chapters. Do you read books out of order? Neither do we! If chapter 8 is your best chapter, then why is it all the way back in chapter 8, and what can you do to improve chapter 1? If things don't really get going until twenty-five pages in, see what you can do to those first five pages to draw the reader in more. If you have a prologue, that counts in your chapter/page count, and you should include it (unless you discover, like most writers I know, that they don't really need that prologue anyway). If it says, "Send your first fifty pages," and chapter 3 ends on page 52, *send the fifty-two pages*. But be reasonable. If the agent asks for five and you send fifty, it just looks like you can't follow directions. You won't get automatically rejected for not following the guidelines—at least that's not what we do at my agency—but you want to avoid deviating from them as much as possible. Agents ask for these things because they want this info, not to make your life needlessly difficult.

If it says you can attach a file, attach a file. I suggest using a .docx or .rtf file, as those are usually easier to view on e-readers, which isn't always the case for .pdfs. If your proposal or materials are illustrated or particularly large, a .pdf is fine. Unless specifically permitted, try not to send agents a Google Docs, Dropbox, OneFile, or other cloud storage link for text files. They're hard to get on our e-readers. Again, you can send very large files via these methods, or you can host your materials on your own website and provide a link there. But first and foremost, follow the submission guidelines.

PUT ALL YOUR CHAPTERS IN ONE FILE. Please, please, please do not save your manuscript chapters as individual files. All one file!!!! And label your file something other than MYBOOKFINAL_FINAL_FINAL_REALFINAL_THISONE.docx. Your last name and the book title is a good way to go. You can personally make several versions of your submission materials to have on hand, like the first three chapters in one file and name the file thusly. Just make it easier on us when we're looking at the contents of our Kindles to remember which FINAL FINAL FINAL draft is yours.

Sample Art. If your work is illustrated, like a graphic novel or illustrated how-to book, agents will want to see some visuals. Prepare a low-resolution PDF of your materials to include so that the file is small enough to upload or email. Don't worry—those files will not be going to the printer. How much should you include? Opinions vary, but I think ten fully inked and colored graphic novel pages, one whole project for a how-to book, or a chapter's worth of illustrations, however that works for your book. The point here is not only to give the agent an idea of your style and skill but also to represent what design specs your book requires and whether that is possible, reasonable, or logical.

Synopsis/Outline. Some agents request a synopsis or outline of your work. The goal of either of these documents is to give them an overview of your work, the scope, or the plot. You aren't being graded on this (though I know it feels that way). You aren't being judged on the artfulness of these documents (though they should be clear, clean, and enjoyable to read). The point is to show the reader what happens in your book, the logical progression, the scope of your argument. Some agents ask for this document to be one to two pages, and I think that's fine. These aren't the blueprints to your book; they're a more detailed look at the highlights. A three- or four-page synopsis wouldn't bother me at all.

No One Is Going to Steal Your Work

Some writers are nervous that if they email their work to an agent, that agent is going to steal their work or their idea, strip their name from it, and pass it off as the agent's own or give it to one of their current clients. That is a good plot for a novel, but this fear is unfounded. You have *so much* data on your side—the email query you sent, the files you've created on your computer—that if an agent wanted to steal your work, it would be so easy to catch them. Also, you own the copyright to your work from the moment you create it, whether or not you register it with the Library of Congress. (You don't have to do that.) The rumor that agents are going to steal your work is right up there with hidden razor blades in Halloween candy. Don't fall prey to conspiracy theories.

BUT WHAT IF AN EDITOR REACHES OUT TO ME?

While you can't send an unsolicited query to an editor at most traditional publishers, editors can reach out to you, and many do. They might read your work in a newspaper, blog, literary journal, or see your illustrations at a convention. They may email you and say *Have you ever thought about writing a book?* And you can answer them freely! You don't need an agent to talk to them! They aren't looking for a hapless author to scam, so you can proceed with the normal amount of caution you use when talking to any stranger on the internet.

They may ask to see your work, and you can send it to them, even if you don't have an agent. It's also possible that they can make an offer on your book, even if you do not have an agent. But they also should be patient if you want to go out and get one, and even recommend a few (always more than one!) agents to reach out to.

This isn't scammy. This isn't an agent and editor colluding to take advantage of you. It's one of the normal ways the business of publishing works.

I get emails all the time from authors who say *I have an offer in hand. Can you take a look at my stuff and maybe help me out?* Sometimes I can, and sometimes I can't. You still want to approach agents who work in your genre(s), so they'll be the most help to you. Above all, you should take the time necessary to do this the way that works best for you. If an editor is putting undue pressure on you to accept their offer or not to get an agent, my antennae would go up. Your offer should not disappear just because you want to take a few weeks to find an agent.

And editors won't get mad at you if you want to find an agent yourself! They won't think *Gee, does this person think I'm going to scam them?* They won't be offended. They won't assume you're just trying to drum up your advance. (Editors expect you to ask for more money.) This isn't the most common procedure to get an agent, offer, or book deal, but it happens plenty. The primary difference is the order of operations, and not your opportunity to find representation and get a fair deal.

Chapter Four

BOOK PROPOSALS AND WHO SHOULD WRITE THEM

Oh, you lucky ducks who only have to write a book proposal and not the whole book. I've done both, and it's much faster to write a book proposal. But it's not necessarily easier.

A book proposal is a document that gives an agent or editor everything they need to know to evaluate a book. It tells them what the book is about and what it will do for the reader, who the author is and how they might promote the book, what other books are like it, and sample chapters of the actual work.

A book proposal is a semi-formal document that has semi-standardized parts. They can vary a little, depending on the subject matter, the author, and the advice of different editors, agents, or writers. You won't get automatically rejected if your Marketing section comes before the Comparable Titles section. Agents and editors get it. We want the overall information, not adherence to an arbitrary checklist.

You need a book proposal when you're writing nonfiction or a graphic novel (which can also refer to a work of nonfiction told in sequential art). You may also write a book proposal for a memoir, but there are some downsides to consider with that. You will rarely write a book proposal for a novel, *especially* your first one. Maybe when you're sending the option proposal in for your third novel, you won't write the whole thing, and the document you create is close but not exactly like this kind of book proposal. So, if you're writing prose fiction only, you might think this chapter won't apply to you, unless you have plans to write nonfiction down the line. But we're going to talk a lot about platforms and comparable titles, so keep reading.

BOOK PROPOSALS FOR NONFICTION

Nonfiction traffics in book proposals because sometimes the thing the author wants to write about hasn't happened yet. They are *proposing* a book idea. Sometimes the author is going to report on an event on top of putting it in a larger historical context (so it's not just a newspaper or magazine article). Proposals are also used to sell books that would take a lot of materials or production costs to produce, like a sewing or knitting book, a photography-based art or design book, or an illustrated book like a graphic novel. You aren't going to knit all thirty-five sweaters you propose in your knitting book before you sell it, and the publisher does not expect you to. But you do have to know which thirty-five sweaters you intend to knit and show some kind of visual of most, if not all, of them in your book proposal.

There is a lot of conflicting advice about book proposals, mostly because there is no single way to do them. You're allowed to riff a little. I maintain that you have to know the rules before you break them, so here we're going to talk about each element of a book proposal: Overview, Platform, Marketing, Annotated Table of Contents, Comparable Titles, Sample Chapters, and About the Author. We'll discuss the how and why of each of them, so you can figure out what works best for your idea. I wrote a book proposal for this book, and you can see most of it in appendix 2.

OVERVIEW

The overview is like an introduction to the proposal and very often overlaps with the actual introduction to the book. Yes, you can use the same text in both. It's fine. An overview is shorter than a book's introduction—I'd say they usually run about 1,000 to 1,500 words, but there's no absolute rule here, and it will vary according to the subject matter. The overview should outline what your book will do and why that is something the reader wants. I often refer to this last part as the "reason to buy" (see below). But first, the overview needs to tell me what you're going to write about and how you're going to get to your conclusion. If you're writing a self-help book, your overview should tell me all about the steps I will need to take to become self-actualized or whatever your book claims. If it's something reported, tell me what you hope to find out and how you're going to do it. If it's how-to, tell me what you're going to teach me and the things I'm going to learn along the way. If it's a graphic novel, tell me what's going to happen in the end.

About that "reason to buy." I see a lot of nonfiction that boils down to *look at this cool thing I found!* And I like cool things. But I don't need a book about all the cool things in the world. Sometimes I only want an article or (let's be real) an Instagram post about it. Maybe I just want individual sewing patterns or recipes I can get one at a time. It should be clear in your book proposal why readers need your idea *in book form.* Is it a perfect gift for Mother's Day or graduation? Is it a manual they'll come back to again and again, compiled nowhere else? Is it the longform exploration of what you do on YouTube or TikTok or your newsletter? (Cough cough.) The *people will just think it's cool* reason to buy is elusive, if it exists at all. Do people think your idea is cool enough to hand over their ten or twenty or thirty dollars for it? And thinking people *should* read about your subject because it'll be good for them is even more shaky ground to rest your book on. No one wants to be told to eat their vegetables, literally or figuratively. Which leads me to the next part.

PLATFORM

Sometimes, an overview can bleed right into the platform section in a narratively seamless way. You've just told the reader all about your revolutionary new way to make friends, and you transition right into something like: *And who am I to write about this? I am the author of the award-winning blog makingfriendsiseasyyourejustbadatit.com*, etc. An author's platform is how readers already know your name, and the marketing you do is how you *already* can reach them. I see a lot of proposals that say "And when the book comes out, it'll build my author platform!" No. That's not how it works. The book does not build the platform. The platform comes first.

Sometimes folks think that their platform is just or mostly social media. It can be, but not exclusively. It depends on your readers. Are *they* on social media? Broadly speaking, if you're writing about parenting, you're probably reaching the bulk of your readers on TikTok or Instagram. And with how much social media is always changing, it's smart to diversify where you reach readers. There are many other things that can be valuable aspects of your platform. The important thing to evaluate in each one is how you, personally, can directly reach readers and who those readers might be.

Other things besides social media that make up a platform can be: personal blogs or newsletters; organically grown (not purchased) mailing lists; recent publications online or in print; professional organizations wherein you can reach out to the membership through social media, emails, newsletters, etc.; public appearances/speaking gigs you have ready access to; classes you teach; online webinars or other similar events; TV/radio appearances; conference attendance; panels; keynote addresses; and more. The most important aspect here is that these things are already in full swing when you're writing your proposal, that they're things you already have your hands in. The publisher will help market your book, but they specialize in the book-facing areas they already know. They aren't likely to get you the keynote address for next year's National Conference on Miniature Bookbinding, or whatever you're doing. You have a better shot at that because you're already involved in your subject's community, right? Right.

I am often asked how many of [x] you need before you can get a book deal: newsletter subscribers, social media followers, unique views on your blog, etc. There are no official numbers you have to reach that equals a book deal. Ten thousand followers on Instagram does not mean a publisher will say *OK, this is worth looking at.* Too few followers may signal to the agent or editor that not many people have eyes on this person or thing. A lot of followers may mean a lot of people do have eyes on it, but that doesn't mean they will all (or even a small percentage of them) buy a book on your specific topic. These things are measured together: idea + platform. What I look for in a successful author platform is visibility in relevant venues (e.g., a reporter published in recognizable periodicals, or a self-help influencer with a sizable and engaged following online) plus an idea that their followers might be eager to buy *in book form*.

What's an engaged following, you ask? There are no specific metrics for this one either, but agents and publishers want to see that your audience is interacting with you and your posts, not just scrolling by without hitting Like or anything else. An engaged reader is more likely to be a loyal fan who will buy, share, talk about your book. We've all heard content creators say *Like and subscribe!* Because those actions are what creators use to show others (advertisers, sponsors, agents, editors) that there are real people behind those follower counts. The changes in social media algorithms make this engagement both more crucial for creators and harder to attain. I don't have a fix for that, unfortunately. It's just another reason to stay curious and flexible when it comes to social media and do what's right for you and your work.

I know it feels like I just asked you to climb a mountain. And it might take you a while to get to the top. That's OK. That's normal. That's true for everyone. You won't ever get there, however, unless you start. Senior editor at Simon & Schuster Yahdon Israel said, "The bedrock of a platform is the sincerity of what it is you're sharing, and not necessarily who you're talking at but who you see yourself in conversation with." It takes time to have a conversation.

Most people start with social media, since that's the lowest-hanging fruit. Begin by deciding which social media platform to focus on first. You can't do them all at the same time. Choose the one where you find the most content about your subject, or most active people doing your same thing (like knitters on Instagram or novelists on X [formerly known as Twitter]) *and* the one you like to use the most. If you absolutely hate using a site, you don't have to use it. After you decide which one(s) you want to use, go out and use it. Post things you're authentically curious about or interested in and find other people talking about those same things. Comment on their stuff, link back to it, share great things you've found—without any expectation that someone will do the same to your work. If people feel like you're fishing for a Share or Like, it will turn them off. When others see you have something to say or share, they may follow you back and interact with your posts. This is not a linear or quick process, but authenticity will yield the best results. With platform building, it's not *if you build it, they will come.* You have to give readers a reason to follow you. How do you do that? By examining why you follow other people and finding ways to apply that to what you want to do online.

You can also find places your community is already gathering—Facebook Groups, Discord servers, message boards—and join in the conversation. No one likes the person who only comments to link back to their newsletter or website, so spamming these places will have the opposite of your desired effect. Your attitude when approaching these groups should be *it would be great to learn something new and talk to some nice people* and not *I'm going to post eight times a day and hope to gain fifteen followers for each post I make.* There's no formula to posting that yields specific results, and any "social media expert" that says so is trying to sell you something.

If you want to grow your platform in other ways that don't revolve around social media, find venues in which to write about your subject and pitch articles. Participate in events (book readings, discussion groups, volunteer opportunities) to network with people IRL. Become active in an organization and see what you can find. Growing your platform, on or offline, is a long, time-consuming process, and I don't have any secrets to make it easier, faster, or more effective. But the number one way to fail at it is to not start. Remember that these are people you want to be in community with, not just get something from.

MARKETING

If a platform is where you can reach readers directly, marketing is what you say and do on your platform to let readers know about your book. This could be anything from hosting an AMA (ask me anything) on Instagram Live to putting a link to your book's preorder page at the end of all of your newsletters. Everyone who reads your proposal will know that any marketing ideas you put in there are speculative, that you're not guaranteeing anything will happen. No one is going to hold you to every single promise you make in the proposal. But don't say you're BFFs with the guest booker at the *Today* show if you're not.

Publishers, too, aren't looking for you to take out full-page ads in the *New York Times*. Advertising can work! But in a proposal, agents and editors are more interested in what you can do for your direct market, the one only you can get to with your platform and network. Can you propose panels or talks at conferences with high attendance? Can you offer webinars or classes (and maybe include the book as course material)? Do you know editors at websites or magazines who might do an interview? Can you run special, not-in-the-book content on your newsletter? Can you reach out to the membership of the organizations you are a part of with an email blast? That's the kind of thing that should go in your book proposal's Marketing section, not skywriting and bumper stickers and prime-time television ads.

It is tempting to aim big in your marketing section. Oprah! Twenty-city book tours! A pilot for a spin-off TV show! It's great if that's within reach for you. But agents and editors are more impressed with a marketing section that shows the many smaller ways you can reach readers, especially after the *I wrote a new book!* messaging gets old, than to be wowed by one high-impact but short-lived idea.

What Is the Difference Between Marketing, Platform, and Credentials?

It's easy to use words like *platform* and *credentials* interchangeably. But there comes a point when you need to differentiate between them and understand what they mean in publishing circles.

- *Marketing* is what spreads the word about the book. You (and the publisher) can market your book and/or yourself as an author.
- *Platform* is the way people learn more about you, right from the source. This can be online (newsletters, social media) or IRL (teaching, speaking engagements).
- *Credentials* represent your authority on a subject and could include advanced degrees, many years' experience, previous publications (articles, books), or even TV appearances.

A platform can create or support credentials. Credentials can sometimes create a platform. But credentials alone are not a platform if no one knows who you are.

ANNOTATED TABLE OF CONTENTS

This is the part of the proposal where you tell readers what will be in your book. I've always called it the "annotated table of contents" because that's how I learned it, but it could also be Summary or Book Outline or similar. You can write it as a list, with a paragraph or two about each chapter. You can write it in a more narrative way, like the story of the book or a synopsis. It can be illustrated with pictures, if relevant, like in the case of photography books or project-based craft books. It's OK to let your content dictate the form here. What's important, though, is that the reader sees the full arc of your book. Your arguments and solutions. The path the reader will take to fulfill the promise you make. All the projects you're proposing. If you're speculating, as in a reported book where you haven't done all the work or research yet, explain where you hope you'll end up and how you'll get there. Agents and editors are looking to make sure you've got a book's worth of info and something that a reader wants in book form, not just something they can google or read in an article. There are many good ideas that are more article than book. That's OK. It's much better to find this out when you're writing a proposal or sending it out to agents than after you've written the whole book. It happens to the best of us.

COMPARABLE TITLES

I attended a very interesting panel discussion at the 2023 U.S. Book Show in New York about comparable titles, run by a person way high up in the finance department at a big five publisher (i.e., someone who decides how much money editors can spend on books). She explained what publishers do with comparable titles in a way that completely unlocked them for me. This may vary slightly among publishers, but the general takeaway is useful.

Editors have to create a P&L (profit and loss) statement if they want to buy a book. This form/magical number generator compares the costs of producing the book (literally paper, printing, binding, shipping, and overhead, etc.) to the projected sales to calculate the hopeful profit. That includes guessing how many copies the book will sell, using previous *comparable* books' sales as estimates. This speaker said her publisher wants three comparable titles published in the last five years, and if the author has previously published a book in that genre, it's always one of the comps. The sales of those books as well as the subsidiary rights (subrights) such as foreign sales and audiobooks can dictate how much the publisher can spend on the advance to the author. This is an inexact science. Publishers do not have access to all sales figures except for what they publish, and they can't predict what's going to sell in subrights for certain. An editor might include aspirational sales comps for a book they really want, along with more reasonable ones so that the powers that be don't laugh at their calculations. There are many ways to make a P&L work, editors tell me, and comps are just one part of it.

For the writer drafting a book proposal, the difficulty results from the fact that, from your seat in the general population, you will never know how many copies a book has sold. There's a subscription-based service called Circana BookScan,* where one can look up book sales as reported by certain point-of-sale vendors. But a subscription costs many thousands of dollars, and I'm pretty sure you're not going to pay for that. Also, it doesn't include e-book sales for all titles. It underreports sales at nontraditional retail outlets like Anthropologie, independently owned gift stores, comic book shops, and many libraries because those places don't report into BookScan. Some books, like highly illustrated ones, can be underreported by upwards of 50 percent. Your agent might have this service, and there are discounted (but still hefty) subscriptions available to Publishers Marketplace members. It's out of reach for the overwhelming majority of writers.

So you are not going to be able to tell exactly how well your comp titles sold. Fun, right? It's OK. We know you don't have the same access to these numbers as some of us do. When you get an agent, they'll help you choose the most useful ones. But at the proposal stage, you do the best you can. How? First, pick books published in the last five or so years that

* Commonly referred to just as BookScan.

have lots of customer reviews on major retail sites or Goodreads. I might also look for very well reviewed books (i.e., lots of blurbs or quotes from reviews on their Amazon page) or look for books on display on tables at large bookstores. This isn't a foolproof plan, but it's as good an indicator as we have at our fingertips.

Where do you start looking? Try to answer the question, What books (in the same genre) have readers of my book recently bought? They may be about the same subject matter or something closely related. You should specifically avoid, though, the biggest-selling books of all time. Just because your book talks about wizards doesn't mean *Harry Potter* is a comp. Or *Atomic Habits* or *The Body Keeps the Score* or *Who Moved My Cheese?* or *The 7 Habits of Highly Effective People* or whatever makes sense for your genre. Those high-selling books are outliers (including Malcolm Gladwell's *Outliers*). And they were likely published more than three to five years ago anyway, because it takes a while to rack up all those sales. Leave those aside and focus on more realistic comps.

But don't go too far the other way. The very obscure book about your topic only available by mail order, hand-bound by the author, is not a good comp either. If you're aiming for a big trade publisher, you might not want to focus on all university press–published books (love you, UPs) or very academically focused books. You don't want to include self-published books, unless you know for a fact they have sold many tens of thousands of copies.

Comp titles are tricky. The ones in your query-stage proposal are probably not going to make it into your submission-stage proposal, and that's OK. At the query stage, agents are looking to see that you're aware of the competition for your book and to learn about related titles they might not know about. (We can't know all books ever.) They'll help you hone the ones you have when they've signed you on.

Lastly, don't claim there are *no* comp titles for your book. This usually isn't true. And if it *is* true, it's not a good thing. Sometimes when there's a hole on the bookshelf, it looks to you like a perfect spot to fill with a new book. But to readers, editors, and agents, it's because no one is clamoring for that book.

Your comp titles are not just a list of books. You'll want to include some context for your choices, like what that book doesn't do and what yours does. This might also require you to—GASP—read these books. Your main focus should be *People who bought this book will buy my book because . . .* Not *This book sucks and mine is better.*

SAMPLE CHAPTERS

To me, sample chapters are the easiest part of a book proposal. All you have to do is write the first few chapters of your book! Simple, right? Well, it is compared to coming up with comp titles, imho.

Ninety-nine percent of the time, your sample chapters will be your first few chapters, depending on how your book is structured. If it's a straightforward narrative on your subject, include your introduction and chapter 1, at least. If you're doing something that's not narrative, like an essay collection or a how-to book with projects, it's OK to include something from farther back in the book *as long as* the reader doesn't need to know specific stuff to understand it, stuff that comes from the front of the book. (You don't have to include the *how to knit* chapters in this case. It's OK to just show the projects.) The point of the sample chapters is not *I will wow them with the very best parts of my book!* But instead: *I will give them what they need to understand how the whole of this book will look and feel and/or set up my argument so they're convinced I know what I'm talking about.*

It's OK if you repeat text in your Overview and your sample chapters, especially if you include the introduction. When we read the sample chapter, we put our minds in book mode, not proposal mode, to try to get a feel for the book as a book.

ABOUT THE AUTHOR

I like to include a short section at the end of the proposal I call About the Author. It looks and feels just like it would if it were in the published book itself. Turn to the back of this book and look at what I did for mine. That's exactly what I'm talking about. You can include your picture or not. (It's not a beauty contest; don't worry.) Why do I like this section, when all of this information is in other places in the proposal? I just do. It's the cherry on the sundae. It's a palate cleanser. It feels like the right note to end on. If it doesn't feel right for your book, you can leave it out as long as that info is elsewhere in the proposal.

FORMATTING/DESIGN

When I was an assistant in my first agency job, I helped clean up the formatting on many a proposal. It was usually making things double-spaced, changing the font from Papyrus to Times New Roman, that sort of thing. One day while working on a sports-themed proposal, I got some sports-themed clip art off the internet and put it on the title page of the proposal, and my boss thought I was a genius. He'd never thought of that. I figured it was one way to give the reader a feel for the book and maybe point them in a general direction in terms of cover art. (Yes, it was only clip art, but it worked for this. It was also the early aughts, and we didn't have Canva yet.)

Another time when I was an assistant, a different agent I worked for designed an elaborate presentation for a proposal. The book was about beautiful collections and was highly illustrated with photos, and the agent went out and got twenty or so records, focusing more on the album art and not the quality of the disc or music. We chucked the vinyl, put each proposal inside a record sleeve, wrapped them in brown paper, and messengered them all over town. The book sold. But we never did that kind of production for a submission again, at least under my watch. It took a *lot* of time (which neither of us had), and it wasn't what sold the book. Did it make an impression on the editors? I'm sure it did. Did it make or break the book selling? I don't think so.

This is all to say that presentation is important for your book proposal, but you don't need to make it an elaborate production. Do not send food or treats or swag with your proposal, especially to agents.* Your expensive packaging will go in the trash *especially* since you should not be snail-mailing your queries to agents anymore.

If your book is a straightforward narrative or a predominately prose book, follow the manuscript formatting guidelines I talked about in chapter 2 and make it clean and easy to read. You don't have to design it to look like a book. It's not a book; it's a proposal. Less is more here.

If your book is illustrated, then you should present the illustrations, as best you can, in the proposal as they might appear in the book. If you are not a professional photographer, that's OK, but if your book requires step-by-step photography for your sewing projects, present that in your sample chapter and do the best you can. If your business book needs charts and graphs, create them using the tools you have (Google Sheets makes pretty great charts, btw) and include them as appropriate in your sample chapters. It should be clear in your proposal how many and what kind of illustrations you want to include. Do you need 160 full-color photographs? Ten black-and-white charts and graphs? A pen-and-ink drawing at the start of each chapter? Make sure your proposal conveys that.

Editors and agents need to know this because those elements cost money, either to print or produce or both, and that can change the

---

* Your homemade cookies are probably great, but I hope you'll forgive me if I don't try them.

viability of a project. If you want twenty pages of full-color comics to illustrate the funny HR scenarios in your business book, but you can't draw, then there needs to be an illustrator budget worked into your advance calculations, as well as the costs of four-color printing. Who is going to pay that illustrator? You or the publisher? There are a thousand considerations to make when thinking about an illustrated book, too many to go into here, but if your proposal indicates what your book needs, an agent can help you determine what could work and what may make your book too expensive to produce. Yes, it *would* be cool if Mo Willems could provide pigeon cartoons to lighten up your management book. But who's going to pay Mr. Willems? And will it increase your sales proportionally?

If you, like Kramer on *Seinfeld*, have a great idea for a coffee-table book but don't have the means to produce the images for said coffee-table book, I invite you to find another outlet for your creative urges and/or to learn the skill you need to produce it. If you have an idea that would require you to travel around the world to take pictures of garden gnomes or whatever, and you want a publisher to foot that bill, I invite you to save your airline miles. Those scenarios don't really happen anymore. They're too expensive to produce. Coffee-table books still happen, but they're much fewer and farther between these days.

OTHER KINDS OF BOOK PROPOSALS

MEMOIR

As I've said before, if you're writing a memoir, you can either write a proposal or the whole book. I know what you're thinking: *Kate, why would I write the whole book when I can just write 10 percent of it!?* And honestly,

I hear you. But memoirs and their authors vary. Some need to write the whole thing to see what they have to say. Some are writing a memoir about an event that's still happening. Some agents may advise debut authors to write the whole thing to have a better shot at scoring a deal. (This is not to say you *always* have a better shot if you write the whole thing, but some authors might.) Before you have the advice of an agent in hand, you're going to have to go with your gut. If you want to write the proposal and try your luck, go for it. There is no hard-and-fast rule for when you need to do one or the other. I know you *want* an absolute here, but there just isn't one. Do your best.

The proposal format for a memoir is the same as for a standard nonfiction book, though your book summary/annotated table of contents might be more narrative than in outline form. You can do that in whatever way best suits your book. But everything else stands.

GRAPHIC NOVELS

I promised we'd talk about this and here we go. The 2010s and '20s have seen an explosion of interest in graphic novels and graphic nonfiction for all ages. With this increased interest has come an increase in graphic novel proposals on my desk.*

In a graphic work proposal, I'm looking for a story synopsis or overview (i.e., what happens in your book, all the way through to the end), author marketing and promotion (just as with other proposals), comp titles, sample script pages, and sample lettered, inked, and colored

* Many people use "graphic novel" to refer to any longform story told through sequential art, even if that story is nonfiction. Sometimes it feels weird to say "graphic nonfiction," but it's fine. Sometimes I say graphic memoir or graphic history, but these terms are in flux, and as long as the person you're talking to gets what you're talking about, you can call it what you want.

finished pages. I used to say five finished pages was a good number, but editors are frequently asking me for more than that. Now I say ten, but I push back when an editor asks for even more finished pages. Sometimes it's just not feasible.

Just like with other proposals and query materials, it's best if your sample pages are the first pages in your book. Few people start reading a graphic novel in the middle, so don't ask an agent or editor to do so either.

Some creators include character design images, sample images of locations in the book, or other ephemera. You don't have to include these things, but if you have them, it's a nice added bonus. Include all other parts of a standard book proposal in your graphic work proposal too.

ANTHOLOGIES AND ESSAY COLLECTIONS

If you want to put together an essay collection, by a single author (yourself!) or including many other authors, you follow the same format as a nonfiction book proposal, but you need to be clear about one specific thing in the overview: Why should anyone care about these essays? Sorry to be so blunt, but lots of people want to put together collections, and few have real marketability. If you are the sole author, it should be more than your greatest hits, unless you are very famous already. This goes the same for collections of newspaper articles or blog posts. Why are they in this book besides the fact that you wrote them, especially if they're available to read elsewhere for free? Your collection should have a theme, and that theme needs to be something readers specifically look for in book form. Your collection of TV reviews from 2018 is probably not that marketable. Your greatest-hits collection can't come before your debut album.

If you want to put together a collection of essays by other people (with one from you, too, usually), you'll need to come to the table with a good number of authors signed on already. Which means you need to ask them first and figure out what you are going to pay them and what rights they are going to give you for that payment. These are hard things to figure out before you sell a book! Anthologies are hard! And it's beguiling to think *Well, when someone buys it, they can just ask Samantha Irby and David Sedaris and Oprah*[*] *if they want to contribute to my book!* But no. It doesn't work that way. An editor or agent might be able to connect you with someone famous once you sell the book, if the topic is just right and you can afford to pay them, and they have the actual time to write something. Your agent may also be able to help you network with some of their own friends and clients. But you can't bank on it. You have to do the bulk of the asking yourself.

That's the nuts and bolts of creating a book proposal. Now let's talk about the feelings side of it.

THE FEELINGS SIDE OF BOOK PROPOSALS

THEY SUCK! It sucks to distill your whole book into these little sections. It sucks to reduce your life's work into marketing and promotion sections, to have to sell yourself, to reduce your hard work to a pitch. There are so many moving parts that it feels like if you get *one single thing wrong*, you're done for. When a story is personal, like a memoir, it feels like *you* are being judged, not just your book.

And you know what? Everyone feels this way. It sucks for everyone. Second-guessing abounds. No one's exactly sure what to put in and leave out. Even me! My proposal for this book went through many rounds of edits with my agent and his intrepid assistant. (Thank you,

---

* Always with Oprah!

Mike!) There was stuff we took out and moved around and clarified and repositioned. Even I, someone who has read thousands of book proposals, did not get it right on the first try.* That doesn't mean as a first timer you're a lost cause. It just means it's hard for everyone, and you're not alone.

When writing the proposal for this book, my publishing experience helped me avoid presenting something I thought editors wanted to see in place of what I wanted to write. I didn't sweat the smallest details because I know that editors are skilled at seeing through those. There were probably better or different comp titles I could have used. But I wrote what I wanted the book to be, and that lined up with what my amazing editor Stephanie thought people would want to read, and now you are reading this book. This isn't permission to half-ass your work. But it is permission to stop sweating over the tiny details and to look at the big picture. Your proposal won't be perfect because nothing is. Perfection is not required. A strong idea told by an authoritative voice that readers want to read is the only requirement. Easy, right? Lol.

But did you catch that last part? *That readers want to read*? My biggest piece of advice to you when writing a book proposal (or any book) is to never forget the reader. What would the reader be interested in? Why is the reader coming to *you* for more about this topic? What aspects of your idea do readers want to learn about in book form, and what would they just google? Do readers want a whole book about your idea, or just a magazine article? Your book is a conversation with the reader. Is there room for them in it, or are you just bloviating at them for 300 pages? I've always thought of memoir specifically like a mirror. The reader comes to it hoping to see themselves, the solutions to their

---

* There is no right either. It's best possible with current resources.

problems or support for their struggles, reflected in what you write. Is your book a mirror for the reader or yourself?

Like all things writing, there is a point at which you have to let it go. You've done the best you can do with what you have. You've tried your hardest. Tinkering more would be a waste of time and possibly mess things up. On to the next step! It's time to tackle the query letter.

Chapter Five

LIFE BEFORE AND AFTER QUERY LETTERS

A query letter is a cover letter. That's it. I know it's not that simple, but I really want to take away some of its power. Yes, sometimes that's all an agent will see of your work. Yes, that means it has to do a lot in a little space. But trust that agents recognize how hard this part is, and we know how to spot something interesting through all your nervousness and posturing and meaningless typos.

I like to break down queries into several smaller parts so you can tackle them one by one, and then make it your own.

SALUTATION

First, we start with a salutation. This is a letter, after all. You should address it to someone.

Dear Kate is an acceptable salutation. Yes! Even my first name! I don't care. If you are not comfortable with that, you can write *Dear Ms. McKean.*

If you are not sure of an agent's gender, honorific, or marital status, you can write *Dear Kate McKean.* All fine options! Just avoid assuming a gender binary or anyone's marital status. Please do not write *To Whom It May Concern* or *Dear Agent.* That just makes me feel like another number on your list. If you spell an agent's name wrong or use the wrong honorific, just take a deep breath. It's OK! Typos happen! Lots of people think my name is Kate McLean for some reason. We understand. Do not fall on your sword in follow-up emails. You may send an apology email if you must, but queries are hard and we are all human. Try better next time.

BODY PARAGRAPHS

I think it is helpful to put the most salient info about your book right up front: title, genre, word count. Your first sentence of your query might read something like *I'm thrilled to send you my historical novel called* Mrs. Vanderbilt Goes to the Market, *complete at 80,000 words.* Look at that! Title! Genre! Word count! All there up front. Right away I can tell if this is a genre I represent or am hot for, and if the word count is in a reasonable range for the genre. Sometimes a title can draw an agent in, but at the very least, it gives us a little flavor of a book. If you are writing nonfiction, tell me your estimated word count. That's fine. I just need to know that you have thought about how long the book will be. If you're wrong and I still like that idea, we'll talk about it!

Are you required to start a query this way, whether it's for me or another agent? No! But I do think it gets very important info out there neatly and right away, and I think many agents will appreciate that. And no, it won't make your query sound generic and like everyone else's. Informative is good! Being different or unique for the sake of attention getting is tiresome when an agent is reading dozens of queries at a time.

The next part is where you tell me about your book. This can be in one or several paragraphs, depending on your book and your style. There is no correct number of paragraphs or word count here. You just want me to be able to answer a few questions about your book by the end of it.

Those questions include but are not limited to: What's your book about? Who are the main characters and what do they most want? What is at stake in your book? In nonfiction, what is the promise of your book and how do you fulfill it? What happens in the end?

YES, YOU CAN TELL AGENTS WHAT HAPPENS AT THE END OF YOUR BOOK! Cliffhangers in queries do not entice the agent to read the whole book to find out what happened. Frankly, by the time we've read your whole manuscript, most agents have forgotten what your query said anyway. And by that point, whatever you did worked.

There's going to be *so* much you do not put in these summary paragraphs in your query. Whole plot lines. Most origin stories. Every character's middle name. Many of the steps that advance your argument in nonfiction. It is impossible to put everything in your query, because then it would just be your whole book. Focus on the high points and the stakes, or the book's promise to the reader. You can format this like you would the back cover copy (i.e., the summary on the back of a book) if that helps you get started. It's much easier to write long and cut back. Back cover (or flap) copy for a book is about 350 words. That's a good ballpark to aim for, but it's not a hard-and-fast rule. If you're tripling or quadrupling that number, it's a sign to cut back.

If you're really stuck, take this advice from Julia Cameron's *Write for Life*. What would you say if you could say anything at all? How would you describe your book to a friend? Or if you knew for a fact that any agent you contacted would request the full manuscript? This might take the pressure off enough to cure any fear paralysis. Run with that and see what you have! You might be able to use a lot of it for your final query letter.

Next, you'll include your author bio. This is a *much* more critical element for nonfiction than fiction, so I'll cover fiction first.

AUTHOR BIOGRAPHY: FICTION

A completely acceptable bio for a debut novel or other fiction project is "This is my first novel. By day I am an accountant for a software firm." Period, end of bio. Seriously that is OK! I promise you will not be automatically rejected if you do not have an MFA or previous publication credits or any other supposed pedigree in your fiction author bio. If you do have other relevant credentials, include them. Those could be other publication credits (usually related broadly to the genre of your book, but it's OK to put professional/other credits in there; please don't include your high school newspaper, etc.), relevant education, awards/contests won, previous book publications (including self-published works). The point of this paragraph is to give us a sense of who you are outside of this book, not to judge whether you are qualified or whatever to be a writer. You already are. You wrote the book; therefore, you are qualified to do it.

AUTHOR BIOGRAPHY: NONFICTION

Now here is where it gets tricky. Agents and editors pay much closer attention to an author's bio and platform when it comes to nonfiction. Why? Not because you have to prove you know what you're doing, not because you have to earn the privilege to write a book, but because the reader cares about your authority.

Think about how you choose a nonfiction book to read yourself. Maybe you're choosing a cookbook. Who's the author? Do they have a restaurant? TV show? A well-known Instagram or YouTube channel? Yeah, they probably do, and that means something to you. When you see an author with one million followers on TikTok, those numbers carry the weight of a personal recommendation. You might think *If a million other people like this, it must be good.*

On the other hand, you might be looking for a cookbook about a specific cuisine or technique. You'll see where that author studied or worked or where they're from and make your judgment from there. Would you spend upwards of forty dollars of your hard-earned money on a book that was just by some home cook who said *Trust me, I promise these are good*? Probably not. You may not have actually heard of the author when you choose to buy a book, but there's something about their bio that says *You can trust me, I know what I'm talking about.* What is relevant about your bio that would make a reader think this? That's what you put in your query letter.

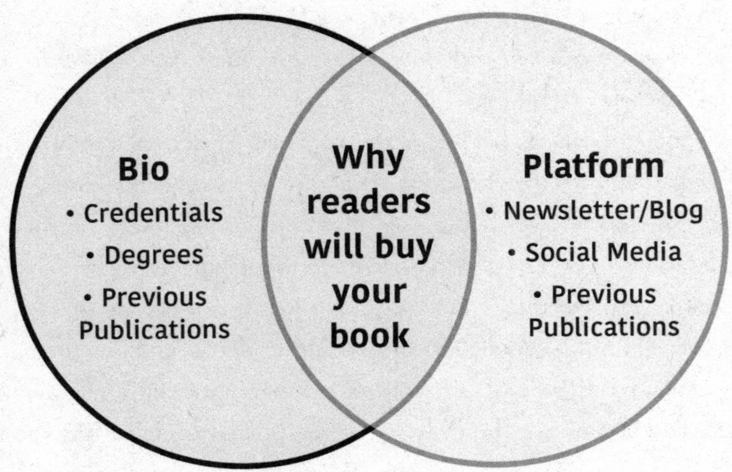

Your bio dovetails with the concept of a *platform*, and sometimes it's hard to differentiate between them. Maybe this chart will help.

As I've said before, the book you're querying cannot build your platform. It has to be there already. I've seen many queries that say *When the book comes out, I'm happy to do whatever it takes to build my platform.* That is true but not helpful. If you don't have a platform yet, focus on that instead of querying for the moment.

WHAT ABOUT AUTHOR BIOS FOR MEMOIRS?

Memoir is in a tricky space between fiction and nonfiction. Sometimes that is literal, as in the dialog in a memoir is almost never a verbatim transcript of actual conversations. In terms of how writers present their books to agents and editors as well as how readers buy those books, it's all about the *story* of how real events happened. At the same time, memoirs are judged along the same lines as nonfiction when it comes to author platform. Readers ask: *Who is this person and why should I care about their story? Have I heard of them before? Is their perspective one I trust?*

A memoir query has elements of both fiction and nonfiction queries. It likely tells the story of the memoir—what happens, what changes—like a novel but presents an author bio like a nonfiction book. Sometimes it's enough for a memoir author bio to be *I'm qualified to write about this because it happened to me.* Of course that's true. But it might not be enough to sway readers to trust and buy the book. Go look at the bios of other (non-celebrity) memoirs that you've liked. Did you notice their bio when you picked it up, or did you already know about them, and from where? If you hadn't heard of them before, what drew you in? The title? The cover? The subject matter? When you decided to buy or borrow it, what made you trust their voice and story? Can you think of memoirs where you didn't trust the voice or story? What made you think that way? How can you apply this to positioning your own bio?

CLOSING

A query is a letter, so you need a closing too. And you can use any standard closing remark you want. *Thank you for your time. I look forward to hearing from you. Sincerely, [Author].* I don't care about this part at all, but I've found it necessary to mention it when I talk about query letters because it's another part of the process that authors worry about. There was a time when it was customary to include in that closing that you were sending your query widely, that it is a "simultaneous submission." People still do that and it's fine, but I assume I am not the only agent getting your query. Don't overthink the closing. Whatever you put that isn't rude or there for shock value or attention getting is fine.

OTHER THINGS YOU MIGHT ADD

AGENT PERSONALIZATION

Some of you may have noticed that I don't put space for agent personalization in my query outline. And you're right. Many other agents suggest personalizing your query for each specific agent so that they know you are purposefully choosing them and they're not just another warm body. A reader of my newsletter *Agents & Books* wrote in to say that they were spending hours and hours researching the personalization for each query, and I was aghast. Hours for each? I would like to go on record as saying I don't care about personalization in query letters.*

* Except the salutation. Do say *Dear Kate McKean.*

Most writers say something like *I see you represent historical fiction, so I hope you like my novel set in 1940s Paris.* This is fine! But I already know I represent historical fiction, so the only part of this sentence I care about is the "1940s Paris" part, because it tells me about the book. If your query is getting long, you should cut out the *I see you represent . . .* part even if that is your only point of personalization. I wouldn't even notice it was gone.

If you have something specific about an agent to say, like you met them at a conference, read their newsletter, or loved one of their clients' books (bonus points if it's somewhat related to the book you're querying), mention that! That's true and relevant and useful. It's not necessarily useful to dig something up about the agent (in a non-creepy way) just to have something to say in whatever space you allot for personalization in your query. I went to graduate school in Mississippi, and people love to put in queries that since I'm from Mississippi (false) I will like their book set in Mississippi (maybe). I spent eighteen months in that state. I am not from there. This doesn't make me reject queries; it's just ineffective.

I give you permission to exclude personalization in your query unless you have something natural and relevant to say.

COMPARABLE TITLES

For a query letter, comps answer the question *What other book is like your book?* or *What book is already on the shelf of your ideal reader?* These are two different things, and you don't have to do both in your query. The comps you reference can be something like *My book is like* Back to the Future *meets* Ulysses. (Yes, you can use books and movies! Or TV shows! Or other pop culture references, as long as they are not too obscure.) Or you might say *Fans of* The Artist's Way *will enjoy my book* Shut Up and Write the Book

Already. The most important things to remember when picking comps is to make sure they are relatively recent (usually the last five to seven years) and aren't the very biggest books in the whole wide world. Your book is not like *Harry Potter* just because it has a magic school in it. Do not worry that agents are going to think *OMG, this person thinks their book is as good as that???* just because you use a beloved work as a comp title. You aren't bragging. It isn't a value judgment. It's more like a recommendation.

Like we talked about earlier, comp titles are used by agents and editors to help predict sales. You most likely do not have access to any books' sales information, so focus your comp titles for your query on vibes and readership, not numbers.

GENRE OR AUDIENCE-SPECIFIC ADVICE

Children's Book Queries

Queries for YA, middle grade, or picture books are not significantly different than adult novels or nonfiction books, but here are a few pointers.

It's helpful to tell the reader the age of your characters. Saying something like *high-school freshman Kiara* or *eight-year-old Miles* when you first talk about your main character is helpful. You don't have to go into great detail, such as *Kelly is twelve at the start of the book but turns thirteen in the end.* If that's important to the story, it'll probably come out naturally, because maybe her birthday is a major part of the plot. This is just to give the reader (remember, the agent or editor) an idea of how old your characters are, because that matters with kids' books. If all your characters are roughly the same age, you don't have to detail everyone's age. If it's important that one is nine and one is fourteen, well, it'll be clear why you're telling me that.

If you're querying a picture book manuscript, it is 100 percent OK not to have an illustrator attached at the time of querying. Unless you're illustrating it yourself, and you're a professional-level illustrator, it's usually better if you don't have an illustrator attached. Your publisher will hire an illustrator for you, and yes, you get a say in who it is. Your picture book manuscript likely has art notes in it, and it's OK to mention what kind of style you envision. You don't have to, though! If you want to hear what the professionals think, that's fine too. Just lead with your text and the illustration part will sort itself out.

If you're querying a chapter book series—think *The Baby-Sitters Club*, *Ivy + Bean*, *The Princess in Black*—be sure to indicate what machine keeps your series going, so to speak. For example, the Baby-Sitters had a club, and the whole series was centered around their babysitting adventures. Most publishers in this area are looking for a series that can sustain at least four stories.

Notes for Nonfiction Queries

It will be very tempting to start your nonfiction query with a statistic. Ditto with things like *Webster's dictionary defines exercise as* . . . These are common—but ineffective—ways to start your work. Statistics can be particularly useless because it's not clear where those numbers came from. And often, they're meaningless things like *A Google search of* jogging *yielded eleventy billion results.* Annnnnnd? What does that prove? Yes, eighty-seven million people have gone for a run at least one time this year, but they are not all in the market for your book about running. These things are not causal; they're barely correlative.

Notes for Graphic Novel and Other Illustrated Book Queries

Even though we've seen an increase in the market for graphic novels, there isn't more information out there about how to query this very specific genre. Graphic novelists also often start in the comics industry, where artists are less likely to have a literary agent, and they often connect with editors online, at cons, or through friends. This is OK!* A lot of projects come about with no query letter at all.

As with other genres, the guidelines for graphic novels are the same. You won't include a word count, though, and instead estimate your final book page count. You might be querying just a graphic novel script (i.e., the words), and this is OK too. Include everything else you would for querying any other book and include the script page count.

I think it's a good idea to include some information on what kind of graphic style you see the final book using, especially if you are not illustrating the book yourself. Will it look more like Raina Telgemeier or Junji Ito? You don't have to describe it in terms of others' work but instead use general adjectives like *manga-style* or whatever suits your needs. If you have had conversations with an artist who might be able to draw your work, include their information and links to their portfolio, even if it's a preliminary conversation. (And not just *I sent them a DM, but they never got back to me.*) It's OK not to have an artist attached when you query.

If you're the artist or have one on board, include finished, fully colored pages with your query. These can be a low-resolution PDF, as long as it is clear and easy to read on a computer screen. It's easiest if the files are small enough to attach to emails, but if they are not, it's OK to host

---

* But *oooooof*, those contracts from comics publishers are not great. Get an agent!

them on a service like Dropbox, Google Drive, or even your own website. Just make sure you set the permissions so that anyone with the link can see your work or include a password in your query.

How many pages do you need to send with your query? More than you think. Ideally, agents and editors would love ten or more fully colored pages as a sample of your work. This same sample would be used on submission to editors after you get your agent, so don't worry that you have to draw the whole thing before you sell it. And agents will not request the full manuscript if they like your query materials; we know that would take ages to complete. Graphic novels are sold on spec (i.e., some work done before any money changes hands), and we on the publishing side are well aware that fully colored pages take a lot of time and effort to create. This is one way the comics industry is much different than the book publishing industry. In comics, artists who draw a sample to be considered for a project are often paid for that work. Not so much on the book side of things. The good news is, book publishers often pay more than comics publishers do for a book deal, but that money doesn't come up front, before the book is sold.

If you are the script writer and you want to hire an artist to draw your graphic novel, starting with the submission materials, you may have to pay them up front. That's up to each individual artist. And that money comes out of your pocket, not the agent's. I have not been in a situation where I told a script writer, *Hey, go spend several grand on hiring an artist and then we'll talk.* I know that would be a financial hardship for most authors. If I thought a script would sell much better with an artist attached, I'd talk to the client about that, and we'd see what the best option was together.

If you are drawing your own work, I think it really is worth the time investment to include fully colored pages with your submission. Sometimes the illustration style sells the book as much as the words and concepts.

Regardless of whether or not you draw the book yourself, if you know you would like the publisher to provide certain services for the work—a letterer, flatter, colorist, etc.—mention that in your query. You might not get everything, but it's useful to know what you want. Include, too, how long you think it will take you to draw the whole book. You might say *With the help of a colorist, the fully inked and colored book could be done in twelve months.* But always add at least two months to what you think you can do, because everything takes longer than you think, and you need to build in rest for yourself and/or time for the schedules of anyone you hire to help you. If you burn out your back or neck or wrists and can't draw anymore, you'll be screwed for years to come. Don't forget to rest!

General List of Dos and Don'ts for Query Letters

- **NO MAILING LISTS.** Do not use a newsletter or email marketing service like Constant Contact or Mailchimp to send your query. It would be so easy, though, right? Not for agents! It's near impossible to follow an agent's submission guidelines that way, though it is convenient for me to unsubscribe from your list and never hear from you again. Don't do this.
- **Don't attach your query letter as a file.** Just put the text in the email. It's OK. We know how to read emails.
- **Don't show off.** A straightforward letter is always more effective than one where you're trying to be cute or clever.
- **Don't write your query in the voice of your character.** Thousands before you have tried, and it doesn't work.
- **Don't reject your own query for me.** Don't say *You probably won't like this* or similar things. You don't know what I'll like!

And if you think I won't like it, why wouldn't I trust you, the author?

- **Don't insult the agent you're querying.** You'd think this would be obvious! But it's not!
- **Don't write a non-query that's one sentence** and say *The work speaks for itself.* We need context for your work.
- **Don't respond to a query rejection.** Not with an insult (yep, it happens!) or a thank-you. (It's kind but not necessary.) Just move on.
- **Don't try to double-space your email**, even if you're pasting the sample pages in an email. We get it. We understand formatting gets funky in email. It's OK. We'll deal.
- **Do follow guidelines.** They're there for a reason!
- **Do relax and try your best.** You won't get automatically rejected because of a typo. Double-check your work and put your best foot forward.
- **Do be patient.** It takes a long time. We know, and we're sorry.
- **Do trust your gut.** You know your book best! Share that with agents.
- **Do distract yourself.** Once you've sent all your queries, write another book. Read twenty romance novels. Volunteer. Anything to keep you from obsessively checking your email.

Now, let's look at an actual query letter that worked.

MY QUERY LETTER

Hi, Michael,

So, this is a funny email to write. I'm looking for an agent. Turns out it's as nerve-wracking as all those queriers tell us it is.

I've written a picture book called BRIGHT LIGHTS, BIG KITTY about a little girl who wants to make her cat famous, like all the other cats she sees on the internet. When her fantasies don't turn into reality, she decides it's OK if Edgar is just famous to her, and not the whole world. I've attached the full text, with some art notes for direction.

I'm also working on a YA novel that's a loose retelling of the movie ***The Apartment***, but the main character turns her renovated garage into a kind of high school Airbnb. Plus a board book series called Baby Monsters where each one corresponds with milestones: baby's first tooth = Baby Vampire; baby learns to walk = Baby Godzilla; baby needs a haircut = Baby Werewolf; baby goes swimming = Baby Swamp Thing. This is already too much, so I'll stop there. I'm looking for an agent that will tell me not to do too many things at once, and I promise to listen.

As you know, I'm an agent at the Howard Morhaim Literary Agency. My work has been published in ***Racked***, ***The Toast***, ***The Billfold***, (forthcoming in) ***Catapult***, and in the anthology ***SCRATCH: Writers, Money, and the Art of Making a Living*** (S&S, 2017). I earned my MFA in fiction writing at the University of Southern Mississippi. I have a robust following on Twitter of 24k.

Looking forward to hearing from you.

Kate McKean

Isn't it perfect?

Of course it isn't. But shouldn't it be? Don't I know everything there is to know about queries? In theory, I do, but in practice, when I am writer-Kate and not agent-Kate, I'm susceptible to the same pitfalls as anyone else.

If I could go back and rewrite this, I would take out most of the stuff about the other books, except maybe mentioning I was working on a YA novel, keeping in that reference to *The Apartment*. I knew Michael would get that reference. But that board book series? What was I thinking? I was thinking I wanted to convey that I had more in me than a picture book. I was nervous agents wouldn't want to invest in me if that was all I had on deck, and I also knew I didn't want to write only picture books in my career. (It leads one to ask why I was querying that first and foremost, and that's a good question!) I knew I had the advantage of personally knowing all the agents I queried (only four!!! OMG Kate!!! What????), and of course that meant they knew me. I don't discount this head start I had. I guess that made me feel like I could take more liberties than I should have. I certainly didn't anticipate I'd be sharing my query with you guys, out in public, for all to see! The lesson here isn't *if you're an insider you can get away with anything* or *it doesn't really matter so do whatever you want*. The lesson here is that relatively small "mistakes" won't necessarily sink your chances. You don't have to be perfect. You just have to be good enough.

Want to know what happened next? Michael offered me representation, and I accepted. We tried to sell that picture book, and it didn't sell. We put it on the shelf and tried other things, and about six months after we sold this book, I went to lunch with a children's book editor who'd just taken a new post at another publisher. My writing came up and I mentioned *Bright Lights, Big Kitty*, and she said *You should have Michael send it to me*. Of course I did! She read it and offered me some notes, including changing the narrator from the little girl to the cat (genius!), and after a round of edits, she made an offer on it! Michael negotiated everything for me and somehow I went from no book deals for seven years to two book deals in one twelve-month period. The title changed to *Pay Attention to Me!* and it will be published by Sourcebooks.

You could say *Sure is easy to sell your stuff when you go to lunch with editors all the time*, and you wouldn't be totally wrong. It's not easy, but I definitely have more opportunities. And as an agent myself, I don't go around pitching long-dead projects by my clients to every editor I sit down with—though if something came up organically, like my conversation with Jenne Abramowitz, my editor, I would. To be honest, the thing I love the most about that project is the title, and we didn't even end up using it! (Don't worry, I'm going to write another book that matches it perfectly.) The real lesson here is that a good idea got my foot in the door, and patience and willingness to edit and reframe my work eventually (*eventually*) led to success. I haven't sold every book I've written, and I'm not guaranteed to do that from here on out. I don't even know if I'll sell another book after these two, but I'm going to keep trying, and that will make all the difference.

AN INEFFECTIVE QUERY IS WORSE THAN A BAD ONE

I have seen every kind of query imaginable. Fantastic ones for lackluster books. Forgettable ones about amazing books. Confounding, puzzling, and shocking ones. What these queries have in common is not that they didn't follow the rules (though a lot of them don't) or that they were not artfully written (most queries are fine in that regard) or they highlighted unsellable book ideas (lots of good ideas are not sellable). They were just ineffective.

Most ineffective queries talk more about publishing than the actual book. They outline why agents are wrong or editors are dense or why readers wouldn't know a good book if it bit them on the nose. Some writers sit down in front of their blank documents, look at all the tips and tricks, and say *Fuck that, I'm going to do this my way*. That is a choice! Maybe there are some query "rules" you can break that make sense for your book and that will turn the heads of some agents. But. BUT! The point of most rule breaking is to get attention, not to better explain a book. Breaking norms often says *Pick me! Choose me! Love me!* instead of *Let me show you my awesome book, which will make you want to represent me.*

As you craft your query, and as anxiety mounts that you will just be another file in the big slush pile in the sky, don't reach for flashy tricks to set yourself apart. It won't work. Agents have seen it all. You cannot manipulate anyone into being your agent, just like agents cannot manipulate you into being their client. Haven't I warned you against agents who say *I'll get you a million-dollar advance! Instant bestseller!* It is not effective to try the same things on agents in your query. Your query letter is the start of a professional relationship, one that can even become like a friendship. I often say if you wouldn't write it in a cover letter for a job application, don't write it in a query letter. Approach the query letter with the same respect you would want the reader to approach your work.

For more examples of query letters, both good and bad, check out appendix 1.

YOU WROTE A QUERY LETTER, NOW WHAT? SUBMISSION STRATEGIES FOR QUERYING

You've got your list of agent names and your finely honed query letter and all your sample materials ready to go! Now it's time to query.

What's the best strategy? Do you send them all out at the same time? Just to your top ten (or five? or one?) and see what they say? A test round?

From my point of view, as someone who has both read a million query letters and sent out my own (and what are my submissions on behalf of my clients but query letters to editors?), the best way to query your book is the one that gives you the most chances at success. There isn't a single perfect query you can write and send to a single perfect agent. I don't even recommend just sending out your query to your top ten or whatever number and seeing what happens. What if number eleven would have been the one?

At some point you will have to decide on a number to send. Personally, I feel ten is too few. One hundred may be more than enough. The final list of agents you want to query will be yours and yours alone, depending on your genre and your preferences. Your friend might send out forty-six queries on their first go, and you might send out twenty-six, and both of those numbers are right.

Once you have your list, send them out as close together as you can, as in the same day or week. You want agents to have roughly the same amount of time with your work, to have a roughly even playing field.* If you send them out one a day and it takes you a month to get through them all, then number one on your list will have had your work thirty days and number thirty will have had it five minutes when number one

* Do not stress over the exactness of this. I said *roughly*.

says *Hi, I love this, can we talk?* And wouldn't it be great if *two* agents read it in that first thirty days and wanted to talk? It might not happen that way, but give yourself the chance for it to. Agents are not going to read your work the second it hits their inbox. Most read in the order they are received, roughly. It's best to start from roughly the same starting point. Roughly.

I personally love a spreadsheet, so I suggest keeping track of this on one, or a paper list, if you prefer. If you use a site like QueryTracker, it can keep track of that for you, even the ones you don't send through the service. In the end, you'll want to know who got it and what they said. I think it's also helpful to note when you sent it and when they responded. But again, I like spreadsheets. Either way, it will be important for you to keep track of where you sent it, so you can comply with different agencies' submission guidelines.

And when should you send them out? Mondays at 8:00 a.m.? Wednesdays at 3:00 p.m.? Send them as soon as you're ready.* There's no ideal time to query. If we had data that told us this, everyone would query only then, and it would cease to be true. You might want to avoid the week between Christmas and New Year's and the week before Labor Day, as most agencies are closed then, but it just means your work will go on the pile, and the agent will get to it when they are back from vacation. You won't get automatically rejected because you sent your query on December 26. I'm just not going to even pretend to look at it until after January 1. Fall is not better than summer, even though publishing is supposed to be "slower" in the summer.† Just send when you're ready.

---

* If your query time is at 5:00 a.m., send then. Smart agents use Do Not Disturb, and if they don't, that's not your fault.

† It's not slower in summer. This is a myth.

AND THEN YOU WAIT

After you send it, you wait. That's it. This is the hardest part. There's so much buildup to this point. The writing! The research! The picking and choosing! The hopes and dreams! You want to see the fruits of your labor as soon as possible. But you won't. I'm sorry.

It will take at the very least a few weeks to get a response from an agent, and most likely many months. It takes a long time to read query letters, and remember that this is work that agents are not directly paid for. All agents know there are hundreds of anxious writers on the other end of those query letters. It weighs on us. But so does rent and groceries and all the stuff of being a human. Agents aren't *purposefully* reading queries slowly just to make you bonkers. There are only so many hours in the day.

There will be a point where it is appropriate to nudge the agent, to check in, to see if they are still reading your query.* Some agencies will give you an idea of when you can expect to hear back from them, but a longer wait does not mean it's a rejection. Generally, it's OK to follow up with an agent after that time period has passed. If there is no stated time period, I would wait at least three months before following up. Doing so might not bring about the answer you want, but it's an OK thing to do. You can simply reply to your own query or message through whatever system the agent uses and say *I'm following up on my query [Title], which I sent along on [date]. Have you had a chance to take a look?* A courteous salutation and closing and that's it. It's not more complicated or fraught than that.

* Some agents have a *no response means no* policy (which I dislike too!), and that will be explicitly stated alongside their submission guidelines, for example, *If you don't hear back from us in three months, that means we are not interested in your work.* Agents do this in response to the sheer volume of queries they receive. It's not great, but needs must.

If the agent has requested your proposal or full manuscript, you can follow up on that, too, after an appropriate amount of time. Three months is totally an appropriate amount of time to send a nudge here too. You can write *I'm following up on my full manuscript request sent on [date]. Have you had a chance to take a look?* This is literally what I write to editors when I'm following up on my submissions to them. We're in the same boat! You can vary this language as you see fit, but also remember, don't overthink it. Make your ask and sign off.

You aren't bothering the agent when you do this. It's a normal part of my job. Try to remember that your work is among the many things agents have to read and do in any given week, and we're not avoiding your work on purpose. We're not doing this *to* you. We're just busy!

You don't want to know this, but I'm going to tell you how many queries I have in my inbox today, right now, as of this writing: 4,717, all received in the last ten months.* I said you didn't want to know! I've only just started to have my assistant read queries with me in an effort to shorten wait times. I try to do about one hundred a week, if I'm lucky. I probably request one or two full manuscripts or proposals a month. Are you doing the math? I bet you are. Here's why you don't want to do that.

WHAT ARE THE CHANCES?

Depending on the agent, the agency, and the genre, agents receive several hundred queries a month. Depending on what the agent asks for with an initial query, they might request several full manuscripts or proposals a month. And depending on their client list or workload, an agent might offer representation to a few of those requested projects over a year. Some

---

* And yes, some have been in my inbox that long. I'm sorry! It's just so many!

agents are building their lists and asking and offering much more often. Some have full lists and can't take on many more clients. It varies greatly, which is why any data collected by one agent, or the whole body of agents, wouldn't actually predict if you are going to get an agent or not.

QueryTracker offers stats on agents, and you can look at those if you want. Users report their sent queries and the outcome, and/or their submissions made through the site are counted, so it's only going to be as accurate as those factors allow it to be. At the time of this writing, QueryTracker reports I've been sent 8,109 queries, over the full time it's been collecting data. Obviously this isn't *all* the queries I've ever received (there would be several more digits at the end of that number), but this is what people have reported. It says I've requested 49 full manuscripts. That means those who reported in had a .006 percent chance of me requesting their full manuscript. In the real world, I bet that number is higher, but it's not much higher than 1 percent.

I have not done, nor has any agent I know done, a more robust and accurate study of how many queries they receive, request, represent, and then sell or not. This would be a wonderful study to do, but we're all too busy reading queries.

Either way, you should ignore these numbers. This isn't *Moneyball*. You cannot math your way into getting an agent. If these numbers are demoralizing, I give you permission to never think of them again and/or put them into perspective. What are the chances that you met your partner or best friend, out of all the people in the world? What are the chances you found that five-dollar bill on the ground that time? What are the chances you got the last box of your favorite crackers before the store ran out? What are the chances of anything? It's just our brains going ACK, I HATE IT! THIS IS BAD! SOMEBODY FIX IT! And the fix being *Let's use numbers to bring order to chaos.* It's a coping mechanism. It won't predict your actual chances of getting an agent or a book deal. There are too many variables. Step away from the numbers.

WHAT TO DO WHILE YOU WAIT

Tom Petty was right; the waiting is the hardest part. It's hard because you can't *do* anything about it. It's hard because in that inaction, you have the chance to second-guess yourself. *Did I make a typo? Did I send it at the wrong time of day? Did someone beat me to the punch with my story idea? Does the agent hate me because I used Calibri instead of Times New Roman? Did I get automatically rejected because my query was too long?** There's just so much space and time to worry about things! All this worrying creates basically every question I've been asked as an agent.

Everyone feels this way. The first thing to do to counteract it is realize that you are worrying because everything is out of your control, and that worrying is not going to solve anything.[†] Take a deep breath and laugh at your brain a little. *Oh brain, look at you trying to make sense of this mess.* The next thing you can do is—anything else. Literally anything else. Write a lot of fanfic. Pick up Duolingo again. Volunteer. Clean out your basement. Stare at the wall.

It doesn't have to be productive, and it doesn't have to be writing related. It just has to help you forget that your email is in some agent's inbox, being read or not. If you want to do something that could be helpful in your future writing career, you can read a ton or start your next book. Start a writing group. Offer to beta read for some friends now that you have some time. Share your experience in your community so others can learn from you, and you can learn from others.

But before you dive into writing your next book, consider this. If you're planning a series or a follow-up to your first book, whether it's fiction or nonfiction, *don't write the second book right away.*[‡] You may or may not sell the first book, even if you get an agent at this point. That's

---

* The answer to all of these questions is no.

† I absolutely know this is easier said than done.

‡ You can outline it or take notes if you must, but don't devote a ton of time to it yet.

normal. Many people do not sell their first book. If you write book two in your series and you don't sell book one, well, that sucks. Neither agents nor editors want to start a new relationship on the second book in a series. This writing is not wasted time—no writing time is wasted time—but it might not be the most efficient use of it.

Write something else. Something new. Something fun. Something you've always wanted to write. Something you like. This way, you'll have an answer to the question "So, what else are you working on?" when you have a conversation with an agent. And if you strike out with one book, you have another in the wings.

EVERYONE GETS REJECTED

The most universal aspect of writing, for all writers, is rejection. Everyone gets rejected, and everyone will get a rejection in the future. Even if you sell your first three books, that fourth one is not guaranteed. Even bestselling authors don't sell every book they write or pitch. You will get rejections.

You will get rejections for that project you just sent out. Some will come fast, and some may come months after you've already gotten an agent. When you receive a rejection quickly, it's not because the agent didn't read your work. It just means the agent knew in that time frame the work wasn't for them. Maybe they don't want that genre anymore and they never updated their website. Maybe they're feeling overwhelmed and don't want to take on much at the moment. Maybe they've taken on a lot of fiction recently and are looking for more nonfiction right now. All these reasons are highly probable, and none of them means your book is bad or unsellable. You can't control any of this. Try your very hardest not to read between the lines of a rejection.

Rejections that take months and months to come don't necessarily mean the agent was hemming and hawing over your work and you were *this close* to getting an offer. It's possible that it happened, but it's not more likely than that the agent was overwhelmed with work. A very wise agent told me once that *maybe equals no.* If I'm not wholeheartedly enthusiastic about a project (even if it needs revisions), then I'm not the right agent for it. Fast or slow, you want that wholehearted yes even if it means getting a lot of nos first.

BUT WHYYYYYYYYYYYYYYYYYY?

Writers are desperate to know why they've been rejected by an agent. Many, many writers have said to me, *But can't you just tell me what's wrong with my book?* And no, we can't, and there are several reasons why.

First, it takes a lot of time to critique a manuscript, and not even in a line-editing, several-page-long editorial letter way. You want more numbers? Let's look at these numbers: let's say I'm just reading query letters, not sample pages, and I know right away a project is not for me (wrong genre, let's say). It takes me three minutes to decide that, and I get 500 queries in a month. That's twenty-five hours of unpaid labor *just* reading queries and sending rejections every month. More than half a work week just doing that. See why agents can't send you editorial feedback? Even if I wrote detailed rejections for only 20 percent of those queries, that's still a full hour every workday of writing emails outside my other duties, the ones that pay my bills. I do not have that spare hour. This is why you get form letters. I know it feels cold and impersonal, but it's a necessity at this point.

The primary way to handle rejection is to remember that it's the agent, not you. When I reject a project, I'm not thinking *Woof, this is a real stinker.* I'm thinking *I don't think I can sell this. I don't represent this genre. I have something close-ish to this in the works already. I'm not looking for more memoirs right now. I am not enthusiastic about this idea.* My rejection does not mean your project is bad. It means *this is not right for me*. There are lots of books out there that I do not like that are published and lauded and award winning and bestselling. Someone else obviously thought differently. You just have to keep going.

Until you stop. There will be a point in your querying journey, whether it's this book or one down the line, where you have to decide to stop sending it out and move on. And we'll talk about that more in chapter 8. For now, let's focus on the positive outcome of querying.

WHAT TO DO WHEN AN AGENT LIKES YOUR BOOK

It started with the email requesting more pages or your full manuscript or proposal. You sent that on, excited but trying to keep your expectations in check. You get another email. (It's usually an email.) It says something like *Hi! I read your work and I think it's amazing. I'd love to set up a time to chat more!* It really could be as simple as that. It might include more specifics about what they liked or some questions they have, but this is commonly what agents write when they want to talk to a writer. It's not like getting Willy Wonka's golden ticket, but it's just as exciting.

What do you do? *You set up a time to chat!* It could be a phone call or a Zoom or whatever works for you two. There's nothing you can say on this call that will automatically take you out of the running (unless you are purposefully insulting or offensive, I guess). It's as much for you to see if you want to work with that agent as it is for them to see if they want to work with you.

On this call, an agent might ask you questions about your work like *What inspired this story?* or things about your background or experience in a *I want to learn more* way, not a *let me check if you're allowed to write this story* way. They might have some light editorial suggestions, just to make sure you're on the same page about possible revisions. (If they're like *Have you thought about making your main characters not tax accountants but instead unicorns?*, it's OK to say no to this or anything else!) They will likely tell you all about themselves and their agency and open the floor for any questions you might have.

You can ask any question you want. The *least* helpful questions are *Do you think you can sell this? What advance can you get me for this? Will it be a bestseller?* If we didn't think we had a decent shot at selling your book, we wouldn't have called you up. But that's as far as our predictive powers go.

Some common questions writers ask are: *What imprints or publishers do you see sending this to?* (Don't expect a full submission list.) *Do you foresee any revisions? What is your communication style as an agent? What have you sold in this genre before?*

One thing I love to ask, and love to be asked, is *What are you reading for fun?* I think this tells you a lot about a person, especially how they answer it (Do they get excited to share? Are they sad they have little reading time?), and I promise you agents are not waiting for you to say *I am reading Proust for the fiftieth time.* I would much rather hear about the fic you read on AO3 or your thousandth read through of all the Goosebumps books than have you try to impress me with some fancy book.

When the call is over, the agent will likely tell you what's next. They might say they want to think about things for a bit and will be in touch, or that they want to read something again. They might offer you representation right then and there! How exciting! You do not, however, have to say yes or no on the spot. You can think about it, read over their agency agreement, ask to speak to one or two of their clients as a reference, anything you want. You likely have other agents still reading, so it's OK to say so and let the agent know when you'll be in touch. If you're sure this is The Agent for you, you absolutely can say yes right then and there. Saying

I want to think about it a little will not make the offer of representation evaporate. Give yourself the time and space to make an informed decision. Maybe even drum up some competition with other agents! Wouldn't it be cool to have more than one to choose from? Don't forget the power you have in this situation too. It's not all in the agents' hands.

You've probably heard someone say *a bad agent is worse than no agent*, and I know you barely believe this. You might think *Just give me any agent, please!* That gives agents even more power in this already imbalanced relationship, especially at the start. But you have more power than you think, and you should remember to use it. You are interviewing them as much as they are interviewing you. In the end, you can say no! You can say *Thanks for your enthusiasm about my work, but I've decided to go in a different direction* even if that direction is *more querying*. Don't let desperation lead you to ignore red flags or someone asking you to fundamentally change your work in ways you don't want to do. I know it blows your mind to think you'd get all the way to talking with an agent and then turn down their offer, but you can, and if the vibes are off, you should.

When you get an offer of representation that you haven't said yes to right off the bat, the next thing you do is email all the other agents who haven't passed yet to let them know. You can simply write, *I have received an offer of representation. If you are interested in my project, could you let me know by [date].* Two weeks is a common time frame to let other agents catch up, maybe a little longer if those two weeks straddle a major holiday. The agent who offered you rep *will not be offended that you are doing this*. This is normal! This is expected! Our whole job is drumming up competition!

This email will often make the other agents sit up and pay attention. Things tend to look shinier when someone else wants them. Most agents will move your work up the queue and see if they need to read it right away or say no if they know it's not for them. They might like the sound of your work but can't drop everything to read it right then. Some agents will never get back to you. That's life. The ones that really want your work will make space for it, and you might be in the grand position of deciding between multiple offers of representation.

You cannot fake this scenario to get a faster response from agents. You cannot send out an email that falsely claims you've received an offer of representation just to speed things up. Doing this is highly unethical and dishonest. If I discovered this was how a client of mine got my attention, it would make me distrust them completely. What else are they lying to me about?

PICKING AN AGENT

If you have more than one offer of representation, or honestly even if you have just one, the way you decide is—your gut. I know! It's so unscientific! But there's no hard-and-fast way to measure who will be the best choice for your career than how you feel about them. You should feel comfortable talking to your agent, even if you're a little nervous at first, because you'll be talking to them a lot once you join forces. They should get your book the way you get it and not make suggestions that veer far from what you want your book to do.* Whether they're the head of an agency or just starting out, it's more beneficial to work with someone you feel aligned with. How your friend picked their agent will be different from how you pick yours and that's OK. If only one kind of agent were right for all writers, there would only be one kind of agent.

When you make your decision, tell the winning agent first, and then tell everyone else, even those who did not answer your previous emails.

* You may not *like* all their suggestions, but you should at least be able to see where they're coming from.

Let those agents remove your work from their queue so they can move on to others. Congratulations! You have an agent!

Your new agent will send you an agency agreement or contract that outlines the parameters of your agent-author relationship. Just like anything you sign, you should read it and understand it. You can absolutely discuss it with your agent, and they will be glad to explain it to you. Don't be afraid to ask questions. To prepare for that, though, here is an overview of what agency agreements cover, so you'll be ready when you read yours.

First off,* let's talk about the format your agreement might take. An agency might write their agreement as a letter, a list of responsibilities or services, or something that looks more like a standard contract, full of legalese. A document doesn't have to include *herewith* or *notwithstanding* to be a legal document, so any of these formats work. If it clearly outlines what both parties agree to, then however it's written is fine.

The agreement will be between you and the agency, which are known as the Parties. Take note I said *agency*, not the specific agent you're saying yes to. That doesn't mean you can be handed off to anyone else working there without your consent, but that does mean that if your agent leaves, your agreement isn't automatically voided and you won't automatically follow your agent to their new job. To follow your agent, they have to ask and you have to agree.

Next, your agency agreement will specify how long it will be in effect, or the Term of the Agreement. This tells you the minimum length of time your author-agent relationship will last. Don't worry! This clause is not generally used by agents to quickly ditch their clients. It is not a ticking clock. It doesn't say *If the agent doesn't sell your book in two weeks,*

* I am not a lawyer, and this is not legal advice. If you have any legal concerns, contact a lawyer with publishing experience in your area.

you're outta here. It's common to see a term of one year in an agreement, which means that if your project isn't ready to go and/or an agent doesn't submit your work to editors within a year of signing you up, then either party has the option to end the agreement. Some agreements are on a book-by-book basis; some say the agreement is in effect until it ends under the termination clause (see below) but in essence are intended to be for the author's whole career. I promise this sounds scarier than it really is. There isn't a mechanism at the agency where a red flag goes up and all clients whose books haven't sold are unceremoniously dumped. Contracts need a defined term, and this part of the agreement will stipulate how your prospective agency defines it.

You will likely find another section that defines the Agent Services, or things the agent will do for you. These seem fairly obvious when you read them and include developing/editing your work with you, sending your work to editors, negotiating deals on your behalf, exploiting (that's just a fancy word for "selling") foreign and subsidiary rights, reviewing royalty statements, and processing payments.

Every agency agreement will clearly outline what happens with the money, and it usually starts out by defining Commission rates. This clause will also tell you how quickly you can expect payment once the agency receives the money (usually seven to ten days).

Speaking of money, your agency agreement will also tell you if you ever owe the agency Reimbursement for fees or expenditures. Before we get into that, I want to remind you that if there's ever mention of an up-front payment to an agent—for a "reading fee" or "processing fee"—RUN. Reputable agents do *not* charge clients a cash fee for their work to be considered, sold, or any other service of representation, and the Association of American Literary Agents prohibits their members from doing so. The money flows from the publisher to the agency to the author. Not the other way around.

Your agency agreement may indicate that the agency can ask you to reimburse them for routine office charges like shipping or photocopying or buying physical copies of books to send to foreign coagents, and this clause will cover that too. Now that everything is sent via email or electronically, this is becoming very rare. It's a general practice that you're notified before any large expenditure is made, so you're not likely to get some big surprise deduction on your next check.

To me, the most important clause in the whole agreement is the Termination clause. This is the part that tells you the procedure for ending your relationship with your agent and how they can end it with you. It very often states that either party—that's you or the agent—can terminate the agreement in writing with thirty days' notice. That means you can send your agent an email that says *Thanks for everything, but I think it's time to move on* and that is that. Your agent may do that, as well. Termination is generally that straightforward but not necessarily that simple.

Even if you part ways with your agent, they are still the "agent of record" for any projects they have sold for you. This means they may collect commission and continue to send you statements and checks and anything else relevant, in perpetuity. If you part ways with your agent in the middle of a submission (which I would not generally recommend), and you later sell that book to an editor your now-former agent sent it to, they are entitled to commission. Since agents don't get paid until authors get paid, this is to protect them from authors who use their services right up until the book sells and then fire them, thinking they won't owe commission. I've never been in this situation, but as my boss and mentor Howard Morhaim has always said, "Contracts are scar tissue." If you see something like this in a contract, it's probably because it happened to someone somewhere.

Regarding termination, it matters too who is due commission on unsold subsidiary rights. Yes, I know that sentence is confusing, so let me explain. Let's say you amicably part ways with your agent after your first novel comes out. You sell your second with a new agent, and the new agent wants to see if anyone will buy the unsold audiobook rights to your first book. Can they? If they do sell them, do you owe your former agent commission? Your agency agreement will make this clear, and if it doesn't, it's important to do so. It doesn't have to be a contentious issue, but it is worth ironing it out from the beginning. Don't worry—your agent will not think *Why is this new client worried about what will happen if we break up?* They will give you kudos for advocating for yourself and thinking ahead. That's what contracts are for!

Some agency agreements have stipulations that if you terminate the agreement, you can't get another agent or send out any project you worked on with your now-former agent for a period of time, like six months or so. This is not in every agreement, but it's important to know if it's in yours. If you're ever in the position of ending your relationship with your agent (it happens!), be sure you understand your termination clause.

There are very often other, more contract-y-sounding clauses in agency agreements, such as a Warranties and Indemnities clause, which outlines what happens in the event of lawsuits; a Venue clause, which says which state's laws govern the agreement; and more. These are generally straightforward and a routine part of many contracts. If you have any questions about the terms, ask your agent.

The most frequent question I get about agency agreements is, *Can I negotiate any of this?* It's possible, but in all my years of agenting, I haven't had a client ask to. Whether that is a function of our agreement, my clients, both, or neither, I don't know. You won't get very far asking for a reduced commission rate, as 15 percent is industry standard. You won't get very far offering an *increased* commission rate either. But if something in the agency agreement doesn't work for your specific circumstances, or if you want something to be more detailed or clear, talk to your agent about it. We are here to answer questions and certainly understand the need or desire to tailor an agreement to fit the needs of the author. That's an agent's whole job! That doesn't mean they can or will say yes, but it's OK to ask. If you don't feel comfortable talking to your agent about it, look into the legal services provided by the Authors Guild to its members.

Contracts are meant to outline what each party can expect and to account for what happens when something goes wrong. Most times, contracts cover things that you'll never have to deal with, and you'll see this clearly when you sign your book contract. But it's important to understand what you're signing before you sign, and I hope this gets you at least some of the way there. When in doubt, ask questions. Your agent is there to answer them.

Your experience with an agent will be yours alone. What your agent does for your book isn't going to be the same thing they do for another's. Your friend's agent will answer emails faster than yours and slower than another's. You might not find an agent for this project, or the next. But keep trying. Agents *want* to find new things to read and sell. It's our whole deal.

Chapter Six

SUBMISSIONS, EDITORS, AND HOW BOOKS ARE SOLD

You wrote your book or proposal. You queried agents and landed a great one. You've edited it with your agent and now it's ready to go out into the world, for editors to read it.* Here we will go over the basics of how agents submit books to editors, how editors buy books, and how to weather the whole agonizing, long, and exciting process.

SUBMISSIONS

Every agent does submissions a little differently, but this is the general process. Agents research editors to submit books to in much

* If you haven't done these things, this chapter will help you understand the process to come and will make you sound smart next time you're talking about publishing with your friends.

the same way you research agents to query. We have many different sources of varying levels of reliability and no single, authoritative, always-up-to-date source, just like authors. Among those are our own in-agency database(s) of editors, self-maintained and not shared; the deals section in Publishers Marketplace; rosters of editors periodically sent out by publishers (and almost always instantly out of date as editors move around frequently); our personal, friendly, and professional connections; looking in the back of books to see who edited comps; going to lunch and talking about preferences and areas of interest; pitching books on the phone to see if that editor is a good fit; asking colleagues and other editors for recommendations. Sometimes it's one conversation with one editor two years ago at a lunch where you remember they said they like gymnastics that sells a book.* Most times, agents employ all or most of these tactics to come up with their submission list.

Agents also keep track of each publishers' rules about submissions, who you can and cannot submit to at the same time, and all matter of other industry news. Some publishers are organized into internal groups, and you can send to only one editor in each group. Some are not organized this way but still ask you to submit to only one editor (but as long as your two editors do not share an editorial board meeting, you can get away with sending to more than one). Some places ask you to tell them who else at the publisher has the same book, because they can (or cannot) bid against each other if they're both interested in it. Some publishers don't do certain genres at all. Some change what they're doing between the time you sign up a client and the time the book is ready to go. Some imprints close. Some reopen. Some editors change jobs the week before you're sending something

---

* True story.

out and are taking a month off in between jobs, and they're *perfect* for your book, so you wait. Some editors and writers have complicated histories. Some editors will not read books about children in peril or adoption or spiders. Some editors *say* they can acquire books that have four-color illustrations in them, but heck if you've ever seen them do it. Some editors are wonderful, smart, lovely, and hungry for books but never get back to you (because they are understaffed and overwhelmed). Some editors get back to you ASAP if they love something and very not ASAP if they don't. Some editors and agents click right away. Some editors really want to click with specific agents, or the other way around. Some editors and agents are BFFs but don't do the same kinds of books. There are a million different ways an agent can decide an editor should receive a submission. Some of it comes down to gut feelings.

Agents will do [*waves hands at above paragraphs*] and come up with their submission list. It might be seven or twenty-seven editors. Some genres, like adult science fiction, are only published by a handful of imprints, so those lists are only a handful of editors. Some genres, like picture books, have many editors interested in acquiring but only so many slots open on any one imprint's list. Your submission list might be much smaller than your friend's, even in the same genre. Your agent might send out to a few editors at a time, to test the waters. Your friend's agent might send out to a wider list so that everyone is on a level playing field. Another agent might send an exclusive submission to one single editor because they *know* they're the perfect person for it and that editor is going to respond gratefully for the exclusive submission (i.e., $$$$). All of these approaches are correct. No one is better than the other. One way could be right for your book and not right for another's. If you want to know why your agent chose the approach they chose, ask. They'll tell you. Some writers want to know how the sausage is made, and some don't. Some agents have very specific reasonings behind sending to each editor on their list, and some go *I just think she'll love it.* It works all kinds of ways.

Your agent should share the list with you before they send it out, in case you have questions, thoughts, suggestions, or all or none of the above. Many times, I share a list with an author, especially a debut one, and they respond *This looks great! I have no idea what any of it means!* And then we talk about it, lol. The author might not know these editors by name, but they still should be told where their book is going.

It can be tempting to google all the editors on your submission list. Some editors are active online and do interviews and write articles. And many others don't. Keep in mind that the information you find will pale in comparison to what your agent knows about them as editors. And if you feel the need to google your submission list, ask yourself if that impulse is coming from a place of curiosity or insecurity. Do you want to know if your editor is a *Real Housewives* fan too? Or do you feel lost and need more information about the people and process? If the latter, ask your agent before you start googling. Do you worry your agent isn't sending to the "right" people? If so, talk to your agent and ask more about their submission techniques and who those "right" people might be. These are completely normal questions to ask your agent. And you're allowed to ask them.

More seasoned authors may have lots of opinions about the editors on their list. *Oh, I worked with that guy before and no thank you!* Or *My friend had the best experience with that person, so yes, please!* An author might know an editor they want to send to, and their agent might have good reasons why they should or shouldn't get the submission. The list-building process can be as collaborative or not as suits the agent, author, and that specific book. All these ways are correct.

It's important to know who read your book, whether it sells or not. If your book doesn't sell, and you leave the agent who sent it out, now or years later, it may be important to know who passed on your book in previous submissions. Someone who's passed on it before cannot reconsider the same book again, even if sent out by another agent (and sometimes even if heavily revised; that's decided on a case-by-case basis). You should have your submission list and the outcome of each one in your files at some point in the life of your submission. I usually give my clients the submission list before it goes out (at which point we talk about it and adjust as needed) and then all the editors' responses (usually emails) at some point at the end of the submission, whether the book sells or not. Either way, the author knows who got their book and what they said.

Once the list is done, the agent will decide when to send it out. There are some commonly "bad" times to send out manuscripts to editors: the end of August, the week before Thanksgiving or Christmas, the weeks of the Frankfurt, London, and Bologna (for kids' books) book fairs, but each agent assesses this for each project. With every submission some editor will be on vacation, some will have sales conferences (big, all-day meetings) and will be away from email for four days, someone will have just gone on maternity leave or jury duty. There's always something because editors are people with lives. Agents adjust and accommodate as needed. There is no perfect time to send out a book. The only guaranteed bad time is never.

Editors have told me anecdotally that they get a lot of submissions on Thursdays. Some think it's because the agent hopes their book will be on the top of their reading pile for the weekend. I personally think it's because the agent meant to send it out on Tuesday, but life had other plans. I think many agents avoid sending things out on Fridays, maybe because in the before-times many editors worked from home that day to read or edit. Now many of us work from home all the days, so I think it's just a holdover. Maybe your agent sends out books *only* on Fridays. There's no one way to send out a book.

These submissions are almost always—I think I can safely say *always*—sent by email. The agent may call the editor first to pitch the book, or not. They may just send the email. They may have already talked about the book at lunch or in a previous meeting. Some agents send a pitch and say *Do you want to see this book/proposal?* And some agents just go ahead and send the materials attached to the email. This is personal preference, and all ways work (and editors feel differently about each way too!). Personally, I always go ahead and send the manuscript or proposal, but I think this depends heavily on how you were trained. Agents who wait to send might feel this is a more courteous way to go, or that it gives the editor a chance to quickly say *You know, this one isn't right for me. You should try my colleague.* This, too, is fine. There's no one right way to send out a book.

Once your submission is with all the editors on your submission list, you wait. And wait. And wait and wait and wait. This is the toughest part; one you know well from sending queries and every other step of the process. There is no fix for this. It takes what it takes.

HOW TO SURVIVE WHILE ON SUBMISSION

Just like waiting to hear back from agents was hard, so is waiting to hear back from editors. You might have established good coping strategies back then, and if not, now's the time to do so.

Agents approach how they keep clients updated on submissions in different ways. Personally, I do not forward clients every rejection as it comes in. My clients know they can ask for an update at any time but that if I haven't contacted them with good news, all we have is rejections. This saves them from seeing my name pop up in their email, getting excited and then instantly deflated when they realize it's a rejection. And it's going to be a rejection more often than an offer. Of course, if any client wants their rejections as they come in, I'm happy to do that, but so far few have asked.

My own agent, though, sends me rejections as they come in. LOL. I could easily say *Michael, please don't do this, it's too depressing*, and he would! But the writer in me wants to know whatever information is out there the minute it's available, even though the agent in me knows better. Yes, this is contradictory to how I work as an agent! This just goes to show that every agent and every writer (even when that agent is a writer) is different. If I or any other client wanted something else, all we'd have to do is ask.

Either way, here are some ways to avoid making the whole thing harder for yourself.

COMPARISON IS THE THIEF OF JOY

It's hard to watch your friend get a book deal just days after their book went out. And someone else will tell you about a six-way auction for a six-figure deal mere hours after it went on submission. Even when you hear about someone who finally sold their book after four rounds of submissions to a buzzy new press, it isn't easier. You *want* to be happy for them, but it's easier said than done.

It's hard to stay optimistic in the face of emails that never come, offers that never materialize. Professional jealousy is part of almost every author's life—mine included!—and we have to be vigilant about not letting it take over. The answer isn't to ignore, deny, or hide from these feelings but to name them in the light of day. It's not that we want our successful friends to be less successful; we just wish we had that too. We're sad we didn't get that agent, deal, or great review (yet). We're scared it's never going to happen to us. We're worried there's something fundamentally wrong with us, our work, our book that is preventing our own success. So much of publishing is out of our control, and happening at such a remove, that these feelings make perfect sense.

The balm to those feelings is not to focus on what others have and what we don't but to remember that no one is getting a book deal *at* you. It's OK to drop out of the chat or mute people on social media for a bit while you regain your equilibrium. Focus on the people in your life who inspire and support you, not ones that drive your competitive instincts. Be kind to

Writers' Coping Strategies

Whether you're waiting for answers, the muse, or your kids to go to bed so you can have five minutes to yourself, being a writer takes a lot of coping strategies. Here are some you might employ.

Buying Shit

The lure of a new gadget or journal or *whole computer* that will solve all your problems is very strong. Capitalism is designed this way! Buying things is fun! But stuff will not take the place of sitting down and writing. Unfortunately, this is my coping strategy of choice. Hold on, I think the UPS guy is at the door with a new notebook that's totally going to change my life.

Giving Up

This is a viable strategy! You do not have to write your book. Chances are, no one is waiting for you to write it unless you already have a book contract. (If you do, you probably have to give the money back.) If this floods you with relief, don't write the book! If this fills you with yourself and prioritize what makes you feel better. When you've processed those feelings, you can move on with whatever you have or want to do. Write more, read more, edit more. Do not spend your time on submission counting the days between your friend's book deal and your own. Your future is another, different, unwritten thing that will happen only to you.

momentary euphoria and then an aching sadness, then you really do want to write your book—you're just stressed about it. If you would regret not writing your book, for any reason, find a way to cope with the—fleeting, temporary—anxiety and just write.

Complaining to Writer Friends

This is the best coping strategy. All writers want to bitch about writing! Be sure to tell your inner circle you're just looking to vent and don't need any suggestions.* Sometimes you need to air your frustrations, and then you'll feel better. Check Reddit, social media, and the like. There's always a writer somewhere willing to listen and kvetch.

Doing the Actual Writing

I hate to admit it, but this is the most effective coping strategy if you actually want to write a book. I know! It sucks! Writing *anything*, even *[tk something big happens and then the hero dies]* can be the foothold you need to get back to work. How does he die? When? What happens next? You can't edit what you haven't written.

* Highly recommend doing this for all people in your life.

DON'T STALK EDITORS ONLINE

Maybe you only did cursory googling when your agent gave you the submission list. You saw that many had social media profiles, but you didn't do more than peek. Publishing professionals are allowed to be online! Editors might post funny TikToks or thirsty Instagrams or repost important news articles. That's their choice and not (usually) a direct function of their day job as an editor. But do not monitor their social media to predict what will happen with your book. Avoid thinking *Oh, they had time to go to a music festival this weekend and not read my book? Harumph.* Or *They didn't post all weekend, so that has to mean they're reading my proposal.* Or *That vague post about being happy must mean they love my novel!* Don't do this. Nothing good can come from it, and it's very, very creepy. Under NO circumstances should you contact an editor directly to ask about your work, via email, social media, or any other method. That's your agent's job.

EDITORS AREN'T TAKING A LONG TIME AT YOU

Editors are not reading slowly to personally make you suffer. They are juggling dozens of tasks as well as their own lives, and as we've discussed, they're reading submissions outside their normal working hours. Cut them some slack. They aren't looking at their Kindle and thinking *Yeah, I'm not going to read this jerk's submission just to spite them.* They're looking at their Kindle and thinking *OMG, which one of these is most on fire?* Sometimes that's yours. Sometimes it's twelve other ones. Try not to take this personally.

DO LITERALLY ANYTHING ELSE

Just like you did when you were querying, do literally anything else that will keep you occupied. Write, or not. Read, or not. Play video games. Visit your grandma. Take in a museum. Lie on the floor. Anything other than check your email fifty times a day. I know it's hard, but this effort is worth it.

WHAT AN EDITOR NEEDS TO BUY A BOOK

This is what an editor has to do while you're waiting for an answer. Many people think that if an editor wants a book, they just do some math, call up the agent, and make the deal. Unfortunately, it's much more complicated than that. Each imprint at a publishing house does it a little differently, depending on their size, structure, and what the boss likes. I talked to many editors about what they need to buy a book, and I got a slightly different answer from everyone. These, however, were the most common elements they needed to have, create, or secure before they can make an offer on a book to an agent.

A MANUSCRIPT OR PROPOSAL

It seems obvious, but editors need a book to buy. It occasionally happens that a publisher will buy a book from a celebrity or someone who's gone viral before anyone's written a sentence. But even then, someone somewhere has to decide what the book will be about, who its audience is, how many pages it might be, and if there will be any illustrations in it.* The editor needs something to buy so they can say *I like this, and I think readers would too.*

* Ninety-nine percent of you won't be in this situation, but if I say it *never* happens, someone will post that their friend got a book deal on one sentence and, ugh. Yes, that happens. Some people win the lottery. It most likely won't happen to you, or to me, for that matter.

SECOND READS

When an editor likes a book, they often (or are required to) share it with colleagues to get their opinions. Andrew Eliopulos, a former children's book editor, said that he would post the projects he wanted to take to the acquisitions meeting to an internal shared folder and, at one time, four members of his team had to approve its inclusion on the agenda for the acquisitions meetings. At other publishers, an editor can meet with their direct manager, usually an editorial director, and get approval to buy a book from one meeting. Most times, though, editors will ask their colleagues to take a look at a project, both as a gut check, a second opinion, and as a way to gather support from different departments (sales, marketing, publicity) to buy a book.

PITCH MATERIALS

These go by many different names at publishing houses across the industry, but many editors said they needed documentation of how they would pitch the book to sales, to marketing, and to readers. Sometimes called TI sheets, or title information sheets, these are basic fact sheets about books that get used throughout the publishing process. They include title, author, genre, format (hardcover/paperback, etc.), page count, if it has illustrations, and other information, either actual or proposed depending on when the form is being used. It also includes positioning information, which defines the book's target market, as well as selling points. Does this book cover a groundbreaking scientific development, or is it the true story of the first something to do whatever? Is it the second novel by a bestselling author? Is it an exciting debut? That goes on the sheet. It also includes comps, both of the *we think it will sell this many copies* variety and the *we think readers of X book will like it* variety. Any interesting and/or relevant author bio or marketing information (big social media following? huge tour planned?) is also included. There's a lot of information here, and it's not quick to put together. And don't forget, the editor hasn't even bought the book yet.

P&L STATEMENT

We talked about P&Ls in chapter 4, and here you can see how they're actually used. The editor has to create a budget for the book, to show everyone else that if they make it a certain way, and it sells a certain amount of copies, and they pay a certain advance, the company will make money.* Some P&Ls may represent the *highest advance* the editor wants to ask for, and others might be the *please let me just have this much I love this book so much please* advance level the editor wants to offer the writer. You'd think the editor would just ask for the most money all the time, but someone in the finance department (among others) has to sign off on the P&L, and they will bring the editor back down to reality with their numbers. Former children's book editor and current freelance editor and packager Leila Sales told me that no one could pull a fast one on finance. She said they'd notice if you described the book as lush and full of color illustrations but put cheap paper and black-and-white illustrations on the P&L to make the numbers work. P&Ls are based on many unknowable factors (future sales, licensing income, comp title sales), but they aren't wholly fictional documents.

A LOVE LETTER

Many editors will write a love letter, so to speak, to the author/agent about their vision for the book, what edits they see making to bring out its true artistry, the production bells and whistles they hope for, and the blowout marketing campaign they'd want to help plan. They might describe their

* Don't forget, this is the editor's actual job.

personal connection to the work, if applicable, or how the book made them feel while reading it. Have you ever heard of, or written yourself, a letter to the owners of a house you're trying to buy? This editor love letter is a bit like that. It's sincere, but it's definitely an emotional appeal for the author to pick them. Sometimes this is included in the editor's pitch materials so that it might also sway the other decision-makers on their team.

Editors have told me that it takes anywhere from two to ten hours to put these materials together, depending on the project and if they have the support of junior staff to help them seek out sales figures and comp title information. On a book they haven't even acquired yet! Frankly, I didn't even realize it took as much paperwork and form-filling-out as it does until I started researching this book. As much as I would like them to, publishers don't let me see their P&Ls or sit in on their acquisition meetings. But I sure would love to!

WHAT IS INTEREST?

While an editor is doing all the homework, they might call the agent to ask questions and say they are *interested* in the project. The agent may then tell the others on the submission list that someone is *interested* in the project, which might move things along. But all editors and agents have been in the situation where we've read a few chapters of a book and reached out before we're done and said *Wow, I'm really liking this!* only to fall out of love with the book by the end and not be interested in pursuing it further. That needlessly gets the author's hopes up, so after doing that once or twice, most of us hold off saying anything until we're really sure we want to go to the next step. But still, interest is just that. No guarantee of more.

An editor might say *I really enjoyed this and am taking it to my editorial board*, which is the first step in the acquisitions process. This is great news!

It's not a guarantee of an offer, and no, I do not have any statistics on how many of my books get this kind of note and go on to sell. It's probably closer to fifty-fifty than you really want it to be. Sometimes agents will tell the rest of the submission list when someone else is taking a book to their editorial board, to let anyone know they should hustle if they want it too.

Personally, though, I do not shop (i.e., tell editors about) interest very much. Taking it to ed board is not a strong enough indicator that a book is going to get an offer for me to spend this capital. I feel like the more I pester editors, the more I might wear out my welcome, especially if I'm not following up all this *interest* with a notice of an offer.

You might think *What if my agent just* told *everyone there was interest, even if there wasn't? Who would know?* Oh, the editors would know. It gets out. An agent's reputation is precious to them, and if they become known for exaggerating interest or lying about offers or anything else unethical like this, they're sunk. They'll become the agent who cried *interest*, and editors won't trust them ever again. (Really.) Some agents will shop various levels of interest, and that's OK. It's an individual decision, and it could even vary from book to book. Personally, I like to wait for confirmation that an editor is going to make an offer or actually makes the offer before I call around to editors to say I have interest. That way when I do it, editors know I'm not bullshitting them and if they really want the book, they should get moving.

THE CALL BEFORE THE CALL

When an editor calls your agent to say they're interested in your book, they might ask to speak with you too. This is a good indicator of interest but not a guarantee of an offer. This kind of phone or Zoom call might sound terrifying to you, but I've found them to be casual, low-pressure, getting-to-know-you calls. The editor won't make you say yes to any offer on the spot and isn't out to ask you *gotcha* questions to see how you react. They usually just want to ask questions and maybe pitch themselves a bit.

For a novel, an editor might ask what the inspiration was for your story or if it came from personal experience—just something to get the conversation going. There may be talk of possible revisions, not because you have to say yes or no to their ideas immediately but to see if their vision for the book lines up with yours. All books need editing, and the editor will have some ideas, maybe even notes to share. They might say things like *The beginning is a little slow* or *I think the end needs work* or *I wasn't as convinced of the stakes in the middle*. Sometimes more, sometimes less. This is all fine. You won't be forced to make changes to your book to get the offer (unless there are legal reasons behind this), and every editor I know absolutely works together with their authors to better the book. Editorial comments are not a sign they want you to significantly change your book.

Most likely, your agent will be on the call and jump in any time they think you need a hand. You can employ what I call the McKean Punt: my client says "Oh, that's an interesting question. What do you think, Kate?" and that's my cue to jump in. They rarely have to use it, but I think it makes them feel better to have a lifeline.

Like any type of meeting, both parties are studying the chemistry and vibes, and it is absolutely OK to take vibes into consideration when you pick an editor. You can also ask them questions much like you did when you first spoke with your agent. *What's your communication style? What kind of revisions do you think the book needs?* But you can also ask specifics about your book like *Do you see it being initially published as a hardcover or paperback?* Or *What publishing season* do you see this coming out?* Editors

---

* Publishers release books in seasons, usually three a year: Fall, Spring, and Summer. Some publishers do a Winter too. It varies from publisher to publisher.

may have general ideas at this point or detailed specifics, but either can be information you use to make your decision. If you've always dreamed of a hardcover, and their imprint only does trade paperback originals, that's a good thing to learn up front.

I know it's been a good meeting when I've done none of the talking. If I feel like I have to lead the conversation, that could mean the editor wasn't that enthusiastic about the project or something else was off. I can just tell, too, when an editor *gets* the book the way the author does by how they talk about it and the questions they ask. I don't have a checklist for what makes a good author-editor call, and what makes an editor right for one author might not work for another. Everyone, including the editor, is going off their gut, and that's OK. My primary concern during this call is to figure out if the editor sees publishing the book the same or close to the way the author wants to see their book published, and we use that info and the offer to find the best fit.

ALL TOMORROW'S MEETINGS

Once an editor has decided they're interested and have done the necessary paperwork, they go to a variety of different meetings of different sizes and staffed by different levels of colleagues to get approval to buy the book they want. It varies from publisher to publisher, imprint to imprint. Here are the different kinds:

SMALL TEAM MEETING

Some editors meet weekly or periodically with the editors on their team (either the whole imprint or a part of their imprint) to talk about the books they want to acquire. They may pass around materials for reads, or discuss comps, and even advance levels. It may be that there is no group meeting, and the editor goes straight to their boss (usually the editorial director or publisher of the imprint) and talks about the project. With a green light here, they likely go on to do paperwork and a P&L, and sometimes go to an additional meeting before they can make an offer.

EDITORIAL BOARD MEETING

Some imprints are structured so that all the small teams in an imprint meet together to talk about all the books various editors want to buy. This may or may not include staff from other departments, like sales, marketing, publicity, or finance—it depends on whether there is *another* required meeting after this one. If it's the last meeting before the editor can make an offer if approved, there might be even more senior staff there such as the head of sales or marketing, or whoever is the editor's boss's boss. This team of people will likely have had access to the manuscript, P&L, and other pitch materials prior to the meeting, and their level of familiarity with all of it depends on the structure and policies of the imprint and publisher. A former children's book editor told me that their group was once expected to have read at least a bit of each manuscript on the agenda for an editorial board meeting, *on top of* their own editorial work, *on top of* submissions, *on top of* reading to be familiar with the market. My eyes are tired just thinking about it. This editor said they changed that policy because it became untenable, and I'm so glad they did. Regardless, some editors will go to a second, bigger meeting to discuss the book they want to buy.

ACQUISITIONS

Some editors must then present their books to the acquisitions committee, often just called acquisitions, for the final say on what they can buy. At HarperCollins, in the children's group, editors told me that they would present to a team of senior management in editorial, sales, marketing, publicity, and finance in a conference room, and for them this meeting could be hours long. The senior staff stays in the room, and the editors are called in when it's their turn. Sounds fun, huh? I'm an extrovert and even I am intimidated by that process. But editors need to buy books, and if this is how it's done at their house, this is what they have to do.

You think that after all that, the editor can finally take the offer to the agent and the author, who will then say *huzzah!* and the process is complete, right? No. The agent will invariably ask for more money and higher royalties and want to retain different subsidiary rights for their clients, which throws the editor's P&L all out of whack, and they have to redo it and get it approved by finance and whatever chain of command is above them, and while they likely do not have to go through the whole two- or three-meeting process again, they do have to get approval for whatever has changed. Editors, thank you for all this hard work! There'd be no books without you.

Once the editor actually makes an offer, the first thing I do is call/email the author so we can celebrate. YAY! The deal's not done yet of course, but this is the news we've been waiting for, and it's exciting! There are many exclamation points and sometimes screams of joy. When my agent called me to say we had an offer on this very book you're reading, I put my head down on my desk and said a string of expletives. (Happy ones.) I was in shock. It wasn't that I was shocked we sold it, but it's never a given (even for agents!), and it had been a long road to this point in my life as a writer. I hope you get a call like that too.

WHEN AN EDITOR LOVES A BOOK, HYPOTHETICALLY

All this is pretty abstract and nothing happens exactly like anyone plans it, and it doesn't even cover things like auctions, pre-empts, or other offer requirements an agent might set, so let's look at a hypothetical scenario for how a book might sell.

Let's say editor Angel Neverwrong receives an email from agent Hasthe Beststuff at 4:45 p.m. on the Friday before a long weekend.* The email subject line catches Angel's eye and she scans the pitch letter and loads the manuscript on her e-reader before she runs out the door. She remembers talking about the book over their last lunch, in between miso soup and spicy tuna rolls.

She's in luck! There's a subway train waiting in the station for her commute home. And she gets a seat! Soon she realizes why. This train is delayed and has been sitting in the station for fifteen minutes already. Other passengers abandon ship. Just as she is about to get up to take another train, the doors close and she's trapped. And she knows it'll be a trip of stops and starts all the way to Brooklyn.

Angel pulls out her trusty e-reader (the Wi-Fi in the tunnel won't connect her to her crossword puzzle app, so might as well read, she thinks). Right on top is Hasthe's submission. She dives in.

Before she knows it, she's in Coney Island. She blew right past her stop and is at the end of the line! The book is so good she barely noticed. (Except she gets out of the train, has a hot dog and a beer on the boardwalk for dinner, and makes her way back to Park Slope. Field trip!)

---

* I'm exaggerating here because it'll be funny to publishing nerds. It would be super annoying to send an editor a submission at this time.

Angel read the manuscript all weekend. (On her own time! For no extra pay! God bless editors.) She spent her spare minutes while brushing her teeth and walking her dog thinking about how to pitch this to her team. At her publisher, BigAdvancesForEveryone & Sons, their process is this: once an editor knows she wants to go after a book, she first contacts the agent to see if she has any "plans." An auction? Best bids? Any interest from other publishers? Does anyone else at BAFE & Sons have the manuscript too? Angel is trying to get any information about the process she can, so she knows how quickly she needs to act. If the agent is planning a best-bids auction for the next Friday, she better get moving if she wants to participate. If it sounds like she's the first one to respond so far, she *might* have a little more leeway.

This, of course, is on top of all the other things Angel has to do that week. Marketing meetings, editorial meetings, meetings about having fewer meetings. Phone calls with authors. Following up with design about covers. Three more lunches with agents. A book launch on Tuesday night. Oh yeah, and editing the books she already bought. And that's just work! Angel also has a life.

Lucky for Angel, Agent Hasthe BestStuff is a straight shooter. She doesn't oversell the "interest" she has from other editors on a book, but she also isn't going to say *Lol, you're the only one who likes this weird book so far!* She tells Angel, because it's the truth, that she *thinks* there will be an auction, but plans are still firming up.

Angel can breathe just a little easier. She has time to pass the manuscript around for second reads and to ready all the other materials she needs before her next editorial board meeting, a week from Wednesday.

And she's lucky. At BAFE & Sons, she just has to pitch the book to her colleagues, they discuss it a bit, and the boss makes the final call on whether she can buy it or not, taking in all the discussion and materials and Angel's pitch and a finance-approved P&L.

Hasthe knows how Angel's editorial board meeting works (but always forgets how they do it on the children's book side of BAFE & Sons), so she knows it'll be at least a week before she hears more. As other editors call and email and ask questions about the project, she says she does already have some "interest" in the project but doesn't oversell it. There's no telling which way Angel is going to go yet.

Meanwhile, the second reads from Angel's colleagues are coming back positive, so she ramps up her research and number crunching for a P&L. She watches her email like a hawk, worried someone else is going to scoop up this project before her meeting.

Oh no! There's a rumor that the editorial board meeting will be pushed back because of some mandatory all-company safety training about static electricity and stepping on staples! But, whew, her boss says they can all watch it in the conference room after, and they'll cater lunch. The meeting goes as scheduled.

And it's unanimous! Everyone loves the book, and Angel is cleared to make an offer. The boss compliments her P&L, and good ole Jimmy in Finance agrees. The offer is approved, and Angel sends it to Hasthe that afternoon. What's in the offer itself? We'll talk more about the details of deals in the next chapter.

GETTING THE CALL

When I got the call from my agent that there was an offer on the proposal, after the string of happy expletives, I talked over the details with Michael, slipping easily into agent mode, and he went back to do what he does best. Over the next day or so, the details were finalized and it started to sink in. We'd done it. We'd sold the book. This very one you're reading. I would finally not be the only one in my book club without a book on the way.* I could finally say I was going to be a published writer. I could finally put my money where my mouth was, after all this time.

This sounds dramatic, and it was for me. It was the culmination of my lifelong dream. I'd only ever wanted to be one thing—a writer—and I have always been one, regardless of the validation of a book deal or not. I've had other things published, in print and online, but I always wanted to write a book. In the next days and weeks, I found I didn't know what to wish for at 11:11 anymore. I had to—got to—find new dreams to aspire to. I find that invigorating, not daunting, luckily. You may have all, some, or none of these feelings when this happens to you. That's all normal. However you feel is normal. This is just how it felt to me.

But let's go over in detail what happens after an editor makes an offer to an agent.

After I call my client about the offer, I notify all the other editors reading the proposal. I say *Hi, we have an offer on the table for this one. Where are you with it?* Just like you did if you got more than one offer of representation. My note means basically *Hey, if you want this book, hop to it.* Some editors will quickly respond with the rejection they'd been meaning to write for a week and will get out of the way. This is good! We want only the really interested editors in the game, and that won't be everyone.

Getting an answer from the other editors might take an afternoon or a week. It depends on where they are with their reading and the hoops they have to jump through to make an offer. There's nothing to do but wait, and I keep the author updated as any new information comes in, like another offer.

* Really!

But don't worry. Offers do not evaporate.* An editor made to wait will not think *Geez, this author must not want to work with me.* The editor wants the book (if they didn't, they wouldn't do all that work to make an offer), so you are in the driver's seat at that point. Does an editor *wish* their offer will be accepted right away? Yes, because that means there probably won't be other offers driving up the advance and they won't have to go back to their boss and ask for more money, and when all is said and done, their boss might even say *Nice work! You got this one for a song!* But that is a *them* problem, not a *you* problem. It is not the author's job to worry about the editor's boss. I'm serious; do not worry about offers going away. In my experience, the only time an offer went away between the time the editor made it and when the author had a chance to say yes or no was when that (small) publisher went out of business.

AUCTIONS

Your agent might, either before an offer comes in or after there's good indications of a lot of interest, set up an auction. An auction is just what it sounds like, except the agent doesn't stand at a podium and talk really fast, and it doesn't happen in person. Many authors are disappointed to learn that book auctions mostly take place over email or the phone. I know, it's much less exciting that way.

There are roughly two kinds of auctions: round-robin and best bids.

In a round-robin auction, the agent takes offers until a certain time (Wednesday by noon, say) or until everyone's weighed in, and then orders

* Some offers come with a timer, where the editor tells the agent they need to hear back in a matter of hours. But this is a special case usually involving a preemptive offer, and you'll know if you're in that situation.

the offers from lowest to highest. Then the agent says to the low bidder, *Hey, editor, you are the low bidder of X number of bidders. The high offer is Y. Let me know your next bid.* The low bidder has a chance to go back to their team and strategize their improved offer; they'll come back to the agent with that number when they can or according to the schedule the agent dictates. If there's no schedule, it could be the next day when they submit their next bid. The next-highest bidder has a chance to beat that new offer, and so on until no one's bidding any higher. Sometimes that means there's a clear winner, and sometimes there are two (or more) close bids, and the author gets to choose. (The way I run auctions, the author gets to choose regardless of the amount, so if they really want to work with a certain editor but their offer isn't the highest, they can choose that.) From my experience, whatever the most annoying, complicated outcome there could be, that's what'll happen. The editors do not know who they are bidding against (though I'm sure they can guess), but they often know how many bidders there are. Every major publishing house has some kind of rule about what imprints can and can't bid against each other, but your agent will have worked all that out before the auction starts.*

Round-robin auctions can take a lot of time. This is the primary downside about them, in my opinion. It's not uncommon for them to take a week to wrap up, depending on what the editors have to do to get a higher offer approved. There is less chance, too, for an editor to wildly increase their offer, not even to just get the auction over with.

None of that is fun, but it's also not necessarily bad. The good thing about round-robins is that they really show what the market will bear. These auctions rarely lead to editors overpaying for a book or having bidder's remorse. I think, too, that it breeds a lot of goodwill between agent/author and editor, because the process is pretty transparent.

---

* This is another reason why you want an agent.

Bids usually increase by a few thousand dollars at a time (hence how long they take) and every editor is trying to pay the least for the book they want the most (this is true all the time). While this might yield less cash, the author is much less likely to be saddled with the outsized expectations that come with an overblown advance. Author and former editor Andrew Eliopulos said he thought authors should want their book to do as well as editors projected on a realistic, not inflated, P&L, because then he'd "get to sign up your next three with almost no discussion at the acquisitions meeting." Otherwise, if an author got a huge advance they had no hopes of earning out, it would be hard to argue that the publisher should buy their next book, since their first one lost the company considerable money. And if the editor could buy the next book, it would likely be at a significantly lower advance, which no one likes to offer or receive. Of course, most authors can't or don't want to turn down the big bucks if it's offered to them. YA author and senior editor at Alcove Press Jessica Verdi said she didn't know anyone, including herself, who would turn down a hefty advance, "but at the same time, I think it is a weight. I think it is a lot of pressure."

Eliopulos said that at his former company, the salespeople doing the selling to bookstores weren't even aware of a book's high advance, that they were just told that everyone had "high hopes" for the book. If you fail to make back your advance, you don't owe the publisher any money. But that doesn't mean there aren't other costs of not earning out.* Everyone wants the big, splashy advance because they think it signals a lot of investment, faith, and, well, high hopes for the success of their book. But it's useful to think about your future books, not just your debut.

---

* This is what we call it when an author sells enough books to earn back their advance. We'll talk more about that in chapter 7.

The other kind of auction, best bids, does have the chance (but not the guarantee) of higher payouts. I know you're thinking *If one gets you more money, why would you ever do the other???* But trust me: if one way guaranteed more money, we'd just do that all the time. There are trade-offs with each kind of auction, and every agent makes an informed decision about which tack to take for each individual book.

In a best-bids auction, the agent says to editors, *Get me your best bid by noon on Wednesday*. And that's it. The editors are flying blind. They don't know how many people are bidding for the book or whether their competitor is coming in at $10,000 or $100,000. If they really want the book, they better come in big, right? But what if they make *too* big an offer and their P&L is a lost cause and they greatly overpay for it?* A best-bids auction doesn't automatically yield the big bucks. It might yield crickets.

The benefits of best-bids auctions are definitely speed and the potential for a big payout. In the best-case scenario, you know all the offers for your book by noon on Wednesday and all you have to do then is choose one. But best bids can also potentially scare off interested editors. If they don't think their $25,000 offer will fly in a best-bids auction, they might not make an offer at all. To agents and authors, one $25,000 offer is better than no offers at all. (I see you all nodding enthusiastically.) In a round-robin auction, that $25,000 might even get bid up to $35,000 or $40,000 with a few not-scared-off editors.

Sometimes, an agent will set a two-round, best-bids auction especially if there are a lot of players in the field.† They might say *Give me your best bid, and the top three advance to the next round.* The editors sweat over their

* The author doesn't necessarily care about this—they're all *Show me the money!*—but the editor is hyperaware of it.

† It takes the *best* out of best bids now, doesn't it?

bids, shoot their shot, and cross their fingers. And if they're lucky, they have one more chance to improve their offer against two other bidders.

Some agents set a best-bids auction for every book, especially those who represent a lot of celebrities or high-profile clients. Editors eventually figure out, though, the agents who cry *best bids* every time and the ones who have the goods to back it up. If every project is a *big deal you can't miss out on—this is going to go so fast*, then eventually none are a big deal. This is why most agents pick the right method for each book.

What I've heard from editors is that some agents are not as, uh, scrupulous about auctions. I've heard all kinds of tomfoolery about making up offers, and one-round best bids turning into surprise two- or three-round best bids. Maybe it's just gossip, but the fact is reputation is everything for agents, with editors and authors. If an agent pulls shenanigans to get ahead, it will be found out, and editors will look at all their future submissions with skepticism. Tricks do not sell books or get higher advances. An ethical agent will earn you more money in the long run than one willing to cut corners.

Personally, I usually wait until there is at least one (but better yet, two) offers on the table before I set an auction. My thinking is, I don't want to throw a party I'm not sure anyone's going to come to. That doesn't mean I never set auctions from the jump or plan best-bids auctions, but I like making a decision with a little more information. This has worked for me for a few decades, but I sense things are changing. The round-robin auctions do take soooooo long. The most important thing, for me and for you and your agent, is to make the best decision for *your* book with the information you have, not the flashiest decision or the one that will trick anyone into offering more money than they think the project is worth. You and your agent have to look the editor in the eye after the auction is over and work with them for several more years! No one likes to be tricked.

IF YOU GET AN OFFER, SHOULD YOU SAY YES?

When all other editors have passed or the auction is done, it will be time to say yes to the dress—or not. Just because you got an offer doesn't mean you have to take it.

Your agent and editor will negotiate the finer points of the offer until everyone's happy and/or that's the best the editor can do. If you are happy with the terms, all you have to say is *Let's do it*, and your agent goes back to the editor and says *We have a deal*, and there might be more excited phone calls or emails and vague posts on social media about some upcoming "big news." And that's it for now. It'll be weeks before the contract is ready for you to sign (and it won't evaporate between drafting and signature either).

But how do you know if you should take the offer? The reasons are too numerous and too specific to go into every case here, but here are some litmus tests I apply to offers I'm considering myself, as well as with my clients.

Do I feel like the editor gets my book? You may not have spoken to any potential editor(s) very much, or at all, but it's likely that the editor communicated to your agent how much they loved the book and if they thought it needed editorial work beyond the norm. It's very normal to hear feedback at the offer stage like *OMG, I loved this book so much! The ending could use some tweaking* or even more detailed things. Does that feedback sound reasonable to you? Do you agree with it in principle, even if the details could use more fleshing out? Or does it feel like they want your book to be something completely different? It's OK to say no to an offer if you don't agree with the editor's vision for it.

Is this how I want to publish my book? If you wanted that hardcover and the editor who offered can do only a trade paperback, is that OK with you? Did the editor keep calling it a mystery, but you don't really see your book as that? Are your expectations reasonable, or do you need to realign them to take advantage of this opportunity? Only you (and your agent) can answer these questions, and they are important ones to ask.

Can I afford to do the book? Especially with nonfiction, books can be expensive to write, including travel, research, supplies, photography, specialized editors or artists, etc. Your deal might cover some of these expenses; for example, you might have a photography budget, but many times that is paid to you *after* you deliver the photographs. And the photographer you hire is not going to wait until then to get paid. There's no guarantee that the publisher is going to pay for your proposed book about healing your depression through five-star-hotel stays in the Mediterranean.* It will take weeks for the contract draft to come through, another few weeks (or more) of negotiating the contract, and then another several weeks for the first check to come. Few authors make more money than their advance† on their whole book. Many authors reap benefits of publishing a book outside of money from the publisher, such as general publicity that can lead to an increase in their business (whatever it might be), speaking engagements (sometimes for pay), freelance writing opportunities, subsequent additional book deals, tenure, new jobs, and more. Sometimes it takes years for these benefits to come. It might be worth it to not turn a profit on this specific project in hopes of potential future gains. But if you have to take out a huge loan to complete a book, I would think twice. If it would put you and/or your family in dire financial straits, it might not be worth it. Only you can make that call. Your agent can talk you through it, but they don't have a crystal ball.

Most advances do not replace the income you'd make at a full-time job, so the "afford to" calculation doesn't work for everyone. I would also

---

* Take me with you.

† As we'll talk about in detail in chapter 7, the advance is the money the publisher pays you up front, and after your book earns that much in sales, you get royalties.

resist calculating your "hourly wage" when you get an advance, because it will not be good. Writing can be a job, but the pay isn't great.

Would I make excuses for this publisher? This might not be clear to you until you've been in publishing for a bit, but one test I apply to new opportunities is how many times I have to say *but* while explaining it. *They're a really small publisher, but . . . They don't do a lot of fiction, but . . . It's only in e-book, but . . .* None of those things is inherently bad. Small publishers are amazing. Being the first on a new fiction list is fabulous. E-book-only projects are read far and wide. But if it's not what *you* want, if you feel the need to justify your decision to others or yourself, then it might be a sign this deal is not for you.

Is the book I'm selling the one I want to write? In the flush of getting an offer, it's easy to breeze past any editorial comments and say *Yes, yes, of course I'll do that, yes, kill off the love interest, whatever you want, just buy my book!* And then you sit down to write or edit and you're like, *Wait, what did I agree to?* If your editor says things like *What if this is a fantasy novel?* when you haven't written a fantasy, or *Have you considered making your main characters not gay? Could your book be less political?* take a beat. I'm exaggerating here, but it's my advice that you should not say yes to a deal that asks you to fundamentally change the concept of your book in a way you do not want to. At the end of the day, it's your name on the cover. You alone have to stand by your work.

Do you want to do the work of being an author in this genre? You might think it's fun to write a quick children's book, but do you want to be a children's book author? Do you want to do the necessary promotional duties that go with this genre, like school visits or talking to librarians or interacting with kids? Or do you just want to say you wrote a picture book? Ask yourself questions like that and try to think about what it will feel like the day after your book comes out, not just the day of.

Only you (and your agent) will know if you should take an offer. You can say no. The editor won't be mad at you. They won't say *You'll never work in this town again.* Writing a book is a years-long endeavor. Be sure you understand what you're getting into.

OFF TO THE RACES!

After you say yes, it's time to get started on the book. Yes, you can do this before the contract is signed. I know that doesn't fly in many other industries, but it does in publishing. It is 100 percent OK to start work on your book, talk to your editor, schedule interviews, start research, and more before you sign the contract.

You actually want to get started, because the publisher will not automatically extend your due date by the length of time it took to get the contract to you. The clock starts ticking when you agree to a delivery date. Can you get a deadline extension? Often, yes. But it's best to use your time wisely, starting now.

WHAT IF THERE'S NO OFFER?

No agent sells every project, and that's no fun for anyone. Remember, your agent doesn't get paid until you get paid. There aren't any tricks an agent can do to make an editor buy a book they don't want to buy. I always say you can't make someone take you to the prom.

Just like with calculating your query chances, many writers want to ask agents for their sales batting average. How many books do we send out and how many do we sell? It's an easy question with a complicated answer.

I could count the submissions I sent out last year and tell you how many I sold, but that wouldn't be all the deals I made. Not every book I sell is the result of a submission. Some publishers hire my clients for illustration or work-for-hire projects. Some editors buy more than one book at a time. A book could be on submission for a week or a year, which makes any sort of number hard to track.

It would be nice if there was a tidy number to use to rate and rank agents, but there's not. Publishers Marketplace has lists of Dealmakers on their site, ranked according to reported deals per genre over time. But that's only the *reported* deals. I have six deals right now that we're not ready to report that aren't counted toward my Dealmaker rankings. That's OK—it's not something I pay that much attention to. Keep that in mind, too, if you're looking at this or any other place that lists agent deals.

But what happens if your book doesn't sell? Your agent might send it to more people. Your agent might help you edit the book or proposal according to feedback from editors (if any). It's possible an editor mentioned revisions in their rejection and offered to read it again if you make those changes.* You might do any of these things and see what happens. Eventually, it will be necessary to stop sending something out and call it a day. This point is different for every book. Remember, it's not *any port in a storm* when it comes to editors, either.

You might get mad at your agent when your book doesn't sell. Believe me, we understand. If you have a specific grievance, please do talk to them. They have insight that will help you process this information, and sometimes they don't know you need to hear it unless you tell them. Of course, you should not use your agent as a punching bag, but we do understand how hard these feelings are.

---

* This is called a revise and resubmit, or R&R.

It's possible for a rejected book to find a home down the line. I've seen it happen. Your agent won't likely keep sending it out to editors here and there for many years. They will likely run out of viable places to send it before that happens, and they have other clients to work with too. There comes a point in all authors' lives when they have to put a book to rest and acknowledge that it isn't going to work. That's OK. Every single writer I know has *several* unsold books in their trunk, so you are in good company. It's a rite of passage.

Process your feelings the best you can, the way that suits you best. Feel your feelings. This sucks! But come back to the page soon. It will be waiting for you.

BUT WHAT ELSE COULD HAPPEN?

Your book could also *almost* sell in two very annoying but not bad ways.

GETTING CLOSE

Getting close is wonderful and painful. Your agent said five editors took it to their editorial board or acquisitions meetings and you had Zoom calls with two of them. The whole time you were thinking *Are they going to make an offer? Have they made an offer? When would it come, if it's coming?* And then, it doesn't come.

This could happen several times, even with multiple books! What does that mean about your book? Good? Bad? Hopeless? ¯_(ツ)_/¯ You may never know. What I take it to mean is that there's something about this author or idea or prose that was beguiling and eye-catching to the editor, but something got in the way. It could have been the market, a similar book already on the publisher's list, a difference of opinion at the editorial board meeting, platform concerns, internal issues at the publisher, budget problems. So many things that have nothing to do with you. But getting close is a good sign even if it is frustrating to experience.

EDITORIAL NOTES

You could receive editorial notes from an editor, a Revise and Resubmit, which you might be familiar with from your querying days. This can be a really good thing! An editor may have fantastic insights about what could make the book sing, ones you and your agent didn't see. Huzzah! As with agents' revision suggestions, you don't have to take them. You can talk them out with the editor and/or your agent. You can think about it, noodle around with them, consider them from all angles. You might be able to say yes to some and hold off on others. Just because someone gives you editorial feedback about your book doesn't mean you have to take it.

If you do end up accepting the notes, you'll very likely have to make those changes before the editor will consider the book again. That might mean revising your proposal and sample chapters, or your whole novel. I know you're thinking *Why can't I just agree to the changes and get to the offer already?* Just because an author says they will change something doesn't mean they can do it in a way that improves the book. Unless you've worked with them many times before, editors need to see evidence that you can follow through with the editing work. But most of the time, you'll have to go back into the manuscript or proposal, at least to show a sample of the whole.

Being on submission might give you flashbacks to being in the query trenches. Luckily, you'll have your agent there to help you through it, as well as your writing community. But I hope you get to go through this annoying process over and over, because that means you've written a lot of books.

Chapter Seven

HOW TO READ A BOOK DEAL

If only I could be Oprah and say AND YOU GET A BOOK DEAL! AND YOU GET A BOOK DEAL! AND YOU!!!! When it's your turn, I hope it's as exciting as that. This is the good stuff. Money! Contracts! Numbers with percentage signs after them! I understand these things don't necessarily bring joy into the hearts of all writers and publishing professionals, but over but the years, I've come to love them.

WHAT'S A BOOK DEAL?

A book deal is the agreement between an author and a publishing house for the exchange of money (usually) and publication and subsidiary rights to a book property. Every book deal is unique, but we will talk about the most common aspects in this chapter. Your deal might have other things, but these are the high points, the salient details, the things that make a deal a deal.

ADVANCE AND PAYOUT

This is the money! This is how much the publisher is going to give you in exchange for the publication (and other) rights to your book. When people say *I got a $100,000 book deal*, this is the number they're talking about.

The money you get in a book deal is most likely an *advance* against future sales. Unless you are doing a fee-based or work-for-hire project, then the money the publisher gives you as an advance is what they think your book would eventually earn in sales (for you, not them) in the first year or so. They are giving you this money up front, in advance, and a percentage of the money from your book sales goes back to the publisher to recoup their investment in you. Anything over that, you and the publisher share. These are called royalties. If you do not earn back the whole of your advance in sales (what we call "earning out"), you do not owe the publisher your advance back. You basically only owe the advance back if you break the contract, don't write the book at all (non-delivery), or turn in a cookbook when you said you'd write a picture book (non-acceptance).

Your advance is paid out over time, in portions tied to the publication process. You'll receive an amount after you sign the contract, which could take many weeks to arrive after you accept the deal (signing). You'll get another portion after you turn in *and* complete the edits to your book to your editor's specs. This is called your delivery and acceptance payment (D&A). Next you may receive a payment on your book's publication (the publication payment) and sometimes another one after that, often tied to the paperback release of your book, typically twelve months after first publication.

So, how much money will you get for your book? Whatever the publisher is willing to spend and what your agent is able to negotiate for you. I know you want numbers, like an average book advance or a ballpark range. Unfortunately, there aren't any useful numbers here. Advances vary widely, though some books fall in a higher range than others. Full-color illustrated books tend to be on the lower end of advances because they are such expensive books (for the publisher) to produce. Debut novels can get a lot of people excited, which can drive up the advance. You will likely have a conversation with your agent about advance expectations when your book goes out. If your agent is conservative about your potential advance, don't interpret it as a lack of faith or enthusiasm. We all want six figures all the time. *Should* authors get paid more for their work? Yes. But *should* is not a strong bargaining tool.

You might have the chance to do a work-for-hire project, where you're fulfilling a specific job for a specific amount of money, or a flat fee. In some cases these are called IP projects, because you're often dealing with someone else's intellectual property, like writing a *Star Wars* novel. These gigs are hard to get, and publishers often contact agents to help find the right people for them. Some come with advance and royalties, instead of flat fees, but those royalties are very, very low. And because they are work-for-hire projects, the author does not retain the copyright to this work.

A handful of publishers, large and small, pay their authors through a profit-sharing relationship. This means you get no advance, but you do get a greater percentage of the royalties when the book goes on sale. This type of deal tends to benefit those writers who can afford to get no money up front or can otherwise support themselves until the royalties start coming in, if they come in. You probably can't tell editors you'll take a profit-sharing deal to make them more likely to sign on, but if this appeals to you otherwise, talk to your agent and see if your book is right for that kind of publisher.

TERRITORY AND LANGUAGE

Your book deal will include what language and territory rights the publisher wants to acquire. *Territory* means where the publisher can sell and ship the book, and *language* means in what language(s) the publisher can publish in, translate to, and/or license the same for the book. Yeah, I know that sounds complicated, so we'll look at some typical territory and language offers, and it'll make more sense.

A publisher might make a North American English offer for your book. That means they can sell your book in North America (US, Canada, not Mexico, but also the Philippines and other US territories like Puerto Rico and Guam*) in the English language only. No Spanish. They can't sell the French translation rights to anyone, even the French arm of their own company. The author controls all the rights not specifically granted to the publisher.

Another common territory and language offer is World, All Languages. It means the publisher can publish, sell, license, and/or distribute the book anywhere in the world, in any language. They can license the World Spanish rights to a Mexican publisher and English language rights to a UK publisher, separately from the English publication in the US. They can publish the book in another language through their own company or license it to someone else to publish. It would make sense that a company like HarperCollins, with HarperCollinses all over the world, would take a book they bought in the US and just, like, publish it themselves all the places they can. But they do not do this. Just because a book is published by a publisher in one country doesn't mean it will be published by a sister imprint elsewhere. Every single book market in the world is distinct and different and separate from one another. Make no assumptions about where your book would sell well.

You might sell World English rights to your book, which means your publisher can ship the English-language version of your book anywhere

* Why the Philippines? Because of the global American military presence. Fun!

in the world there's a market for it or license the rights to another publisher to sell it in their home territory, such as a publisher in the UK. But only in English. They can't translate it or allow others to either.

So what's the difference in all these configurations? Apart from the practical difference of who is in control of what, the main difference is how the money works out. If your publisher controls translation rights, then their in-house subrights team handles this. When they license your rights somewhere, you share the money with them, according to the agreed-upon splits in your contract, maybe 50/50, 75/25, 80/20, with the higher amount in your favor. That money goes into your royalty account. Subrights can make up for a good chunk of earning back your advance, so you might get royalties faster, but every book, and every publisher, is different. If your publisher sells the French translation rights for $5,000 and you split that income with them 75/25, then $3,750 goes into your royalty account and they keep $1,250. And you're now $3,750 closer to earning out your advance. You do not, however, get a check for that $3,750.

If you retain these rights, your agent's subrights team, either in-house or a group of associated agencies in other countries, sells those rights for you, and that's when you get a check directly. These deals are commissioned as per your agency agreement (most often it's 20 percent in foreign territories, split evenly between them and any foreign co-agent they might work with). You get the money as soon as it's available if your agent sells your foreign rights, because it doesn't go through the US publisher first. If your agent's foreign co-agent sells the French translation rights to your book for $5,000, you get a check for $4,000,* and your agent and their co-agent split a $1,000 commission. Your French contract will have a payout schedule just like your US one, and you'll get the payments according to that.

* Don't forget about taxes, foreign and domestic.

Which is better? It varies book to book, author to author. There are some genres (graphic novels, picture books) where it is standard to sell world rights, all languages to the US publisher because the books are so expensive to produce and the publisher uses foreign rights to recoup their investment. You'd have a lot of trouble retaining those rights without a lot of leverage (say, you were already a *New York Times* bestselling author). You can always ask to retain any rights, but the publisher can always say no.

Some genres and books just do not translate well. A million years ago, in 2009 and 2010, I had two *New York Times* bestselling books of cat pictures with funny captions in bad (English) grammar from the website I Can Has Cheezburger. They sold like hotcakes here! But translating them into other languages was almost impossible, at least as compared to the potential foreign market. You might be shocked* that there are very "American" topics or issues that other countries do not care about. And conversely, just because your book prominently features the people or the culture of another country, or your background is of another country or culture, doesn't mean there is automatically a market for your book in that related country.

ROYALTIES

These represent the percentage you earn on the sale of each book, and they vary from format to format. The royalties on a hardcover book sold in the US by a US publisher are different from the paperback, e-book, audiobook, large print book, etc. There is clause after clause about royalty rates in your actual book contract. In your offer, they'll cover the major ones: hardcover, paperback, e-book, audio. The industry standards

* I.e., not shocked.

for these vary from genre to genre, and sometimes publisher to publisher. But generally speaking, hardcover royalty rates for adult fiction and most nonfiction are 10 percent of the retail price for the first 5,000 copies, 12.5 percent to 10,000 copies, and 15 percent thereafter. If your book costs $25.00, you earn $2.50 per book of the first 5,000 copies sold, $3.12 per book for the next 5,000, and $3.75 thereafter. Remember, this is after you've recouped the advance. A simple example would be if you got a $10,000 advance and your book costs $25.00, you would have to sell about 4,000 hardcover copies to earn back your advance and start collecting royalties.

Some royalties are calculated on the retail price of the book, whatever's printed on the back cover. Some royalties are calculated on the net costs of the book, which is the retail price minus the publisher's costs to produce it. You'll know from your offer if the royalties for your book will be retail or net. Costs vary greatly book to book, publisher to publisher, but as a rule of thumb, we calculate net royalties as 50 percent of the retail price, until we see otherwise on a royalty statement. So, if your book costs $25.00 retail, the estimated net price would be $12.50. If you earned 10 percent royalties, you'd have to sell roughly 8,000 to earn back a $10,000 advance, at $1.25 a book. Retail versus net royalties makes a big difference.

The bulk of US publishers send royalty statements twice a year, covering a sales period of six months. These sales, or royalty, periods vary from publisher to publisher, and sometimes from book to book, and you will typically receive a statement a few months after the close of the royalty period. For example, you might get a statement in April that covers sales from the previous July to December, and another in October that covers the sales from January to June. Yeah, it's confusing. I'll give you a minute to read it again.

It takes publishers several months to create statements that include data that's over six months old when it reaches you. I know! It's baffling! But not when you remember that they are creating these statements for sometimes hundreds of thousands of books and authors. And it's not like publishers are investing in the latest, highest-tech, fastest royalty accounting software. The publisher will either send these to you directly or you will get them via your agent. Some publishers even have an online portal where you can download them yourself.

SUBRIGHTS

The offer from your editor will hit the high points of what subrights they want to buy from you. In the contract, there are many more listed, but they're often not contested. You're not going to withhold large-print rights from your publisher. It's industry standard that the publisher gets those.

What Are the Major Subrights, Then?

- **First and Second Serial:** First serial rights are the publication of an excerpt of your work in a magazine or periodical *before* the book is published, and second serial is the same *after* your book is published. It's not likely that you will independently sell the first serial rights to your YA novel. There just aren't places that publish that. But this might be very important for your political exposé. If you're a journalist, your work might have already been published in some places, or your employer might have rules about this. Commonly, these rights are controlled by the publisher, though.
- **Audiobooks:** These days, publishers almost *always* acquire the audiobook rights from authors. I've had deals come down to the fact that if the publisher couldn't have audio, they wouldn't buy the book. Audiobooks have become incredibly popular in the last several years—outselling e-books in

adult nonfiction in 2023—and it is a big part of how everyone makes money now.* If, for some reason, you are able to retain audio rights, your agent can likely sell them for you, just as they would foreign rights. Of course, there are stronger and weaker audio markets according to genre. Cookbooks don't sell well in audio, for example, but publishers have sold the audio rights to several of my clients' picture books. Go figure.

- **Movies and TV Shows (Dramatic Rights):** Ninety-nine percent of the time, you will retain your movie/TV rights. You *should* retain your movie/TV rights. Large, traditional publishers do not routinely ask for those rights, and if they do, say no. There are some publishers who insist on it, and we agents know who they are, and your agent might avoid them for this reason. There are some genres, like comics—even creator-owned ones, and not Marvel and DC—where it is industry standard that the publisher retains dramatic rights.* But if you do any negotiating yourself, don't give the publisher your movie rights. Will your book get made into a movie? Almost certainly not. But it is industry standard for the author to retain those rights, and if your book *does* get made, it's a lucrative deal.

- **E-books and Multimedia:** Like audiobooks, the publisher is going to acquire the right to make an e-book of your book. Readers expect an e-book to be published simultaneously with the print book, and the print book publisher is usually the best one to do that. But what about all the other *electronic* things your book could be? Have you ever heard of *enhanced e-books*? (Lol, you probably haven't.) They were a thing lots of people in

* Booooooooo. I hate it.

publishing thought readers would want one day. Like e-books with videos and links and who knows what else. But video doesn't work on all e-readers, and it turns out, most people who buy books want to . . . read books.

We agents make sure that publishers do not retain broadly defined "multimedia" rights to a book because who knows what that even means. This can also extend to apps and games. Is your publisher going to make an app of your book? Probably not. They are incredibly expensive to produce. So publishers shouldn't automatically get the rights to do that, just in case someday they might want to.

Funny story: When app rights were just coming on to the scene, I got into a heated debate with an editor whose boss was adamant they keep software/multimedia rights. Book-related apps were going to be the next big thing! But the book we were talking about was a YA novel about teen pregnancy. "What's the game," I said, "dodge the sperm?" I won that negotiation.

- **Commercial Tie-ins, Merchandise, and Paper Products:** These rights cover T-shirts, plushies, journals, calendars, notebooks, and things like that. There are certain cases where these rights are very important to a book, but most of the time, no one is making a T-shirt out of your literary novel.* Keep these.

- **Other Stuff:** There might be other rights covered in the deal: graphic novel adaptations, picture book adaptations, video and/or board games, theme parks (yes, really), something vague

---

* The Sally Rooney bucket hat that got a lot of media attention in 2021 was marketing swag for the publication of *Beautiful World, Where Are You*, not merchandise rights.

called "derivative works," which is purposefully vaguely defined so that if something new and cool comes around, the publisher can make your book into it. This will vary from book to book, publisher to publisher. What is important for your book will vary from book to book, publisher to publisher too.

DELIVERY

Your book deal will include *what* you are delivering to the publisher—an 80,000-word novel, a 32-page picture book, a cookbook with 175 recipes and 250 full-color photographs, a 286-page graphic novel, fully inked and lettered—as well as *when* you will deliver. This is a contractually binding description of the work you must deliver, so pay attention to this language.*

You'll also negotiate the delivery schedule, and it usually starts with the publisher saying *How about this date?* Your publication date sometimes dictates the delivery date, and if you're aiming for a specific pub date, you might have to reverse engineer this. There are many months of production after delivery, not including editing time, and the publisher can't just do those things real quick to accommodate your late delivery or preferred publication date. An accelerated delivery and production schedule is called "crashing" a book, and it takes a lot out of everyone involved in making your book. Think of it like asking your editor to run a marathon tomorrow with no notice. Your pub date is often twelve months or more after your delivery date.

Why so long? As soon as you have an edited manuscript, your marketing and publicity team springs into action. Everyone needs to read your

---

* The publisher won't care if you deliver a 79,817- or an 89,817-word novel, but they will care if you deliver 41,000 or 241,000 words.

book to figure out the best way to design, market, publicize, and sell it. If your book has to go from your hands to the store shelf in the blink of an eye, all those people who so greatly contribute to the success of your book will have nanoseconds to figure out the best way to do so, on top of all the other books they're working on. Publicity won't have time to contact long-lead media, like print magazines, so there goes your chance at getting in *Town & Country*. Eager indie booksellers who could potentially hand sell dozens of copies of your book—or more—won't have time to build that enthusiasm if they have only a matter of weeks to consider your book. This is why your publisher can't just make the book real fast, just for you, just this once. It costs too much in everyone's time, effort, stamina, and potential lost sales.

This doesn't even take actual production timelines into account. Your book may be printed domestically, but it also may be printed overseas and shipped back to the US on a container ship. The technology to print and ship things quickly may exist, but that doesn't mean those are options available to any or all books.

The more materials you deliver (photos, etc.), the more detailed your delivery section will be. This will let you know what the publisher expects you to pay for (said photography?) or what they will provide. Make sure this part is clear when you negotiate your deal, so you're not left footing the five-figure bill for that photographer and food stylist you thought the publisher was going to pay for.

OPTION

Most book contracts contain an option clause. This gives the publisher first dibs on your next book. The publisher wants your option book idea as broadly defined as possible, like your "next novel" or your "next memoir." You and the agent want this as narrowly defined as possible, like your "next novel in this series" or your "next how-to book on knitting." You'll also negotiate when you'll be able to share your option project with your editor, usually either after the delivery and acceptance of the first book, or after its publication. A narrowly defined option can leave room for you to do other books with other publishers (as long as they won't compete with each other), so this clause can really affect your career. Your agent might be able to strike this language from the contract or the offer, depending on your circumstances. The option language is not always included in the offer, but I like to bring it up then.

MISCELLANEOUS

An offer answers the question *Who is paying for what, and how much?* If you're doing a graphic novel, will the publisher provide lettering, flatting, and/or coloring? If you're only writing the script, how are the overall earnings from the book split? Every book has different needs, and your offer may look very different from your friend's in another genre.

Your offer might include bonus language, which is a financial incentive as your book reaches certain milestones. These might be sales-based, like a $5,000 bonus if your book earns out in the first year on sale, or award-based, like $10,000 if your book wins a Newbery Medal or hits the *New York Times* bestseller list the first week on sale. Tbh, I don't put a lot of stock in bonuses. They're a nice thing editors like to give when they can't raise the advance any more. Truthfully, there's little the author can do themselves to reach those benchmarks. Most of the time, these are "additional advance" bonuses, not "here is extra cash" bonuses. So if your advance was $20,000 and you reach a $5,000 additional advance earn-out bonus, you get a check for $5,000, but now your advance is $25,000. If you reach that point, you'd probably get that money in royalties anyway, making the bonus moot, but that's just my opinion.

Nonfiction writers take note: publishers do not pay for fact-checking. It's not standard in this industry. If you are a journalist accustomed to being fact-checked, you will not receive this from your publisher. If you want that, you're on the hook for it. Publishers also do not pay for permissions, so if you want to open each of your chapters with nine lines of Beatles song lyrics or a photograph by Diane Arbus, you have to secure permission, negotiate the contract, and pay for it yourself.

NEGOTIATING

On to negotiating! Your agent will answer all your questions and discuss their negotiating strategy going forward. Maybe there are more offers coming and there's an auction brewing, or this is the last stop on the train and you're going right into it with the editor. What happens next? It depends on the agent, editor, author, publisher, book, astrological position of Mars, and day of the week.

Your agent probably can't go in and demand triple the offered advance, unless you have a lot of leverage. There are very few *Show me the money!* moments in publishing. Do I ask for more money 99 percent of the time? Yes. Do we always get it? No. The key to negotiating, I think, is if you say you're going to walk if you don't get X, Y, or Z, you have to be willing to walk. If you aren't willing to walk, then you have to be willing to negotiate. No one gets everything they want in a negotiation. A friend said to me once: "Everyone was a little unhappy with the deal, so it must have been fair." I love this.

If you're negotiating your own deal, ask for more money. Always. Unless they specifically say so, it's rare a publisher opens with their best offer. Don't be scared. It won't make anyone mad or make the offer disappear. Ask for more money.

But here are the things you're never going to get in a book deal: marketing and publicity commitments, a specific publication date, promises of how many copies they're going to print, financial guarantees outside of the advance/royalty rate/bonus, bestseller status, bookstore placement, absolute control over the cover and title, and more. The publisher isn't going to promise to do something they can't fully control. We all want those things, but it's just not going to happen.

THIS BOOK DEAL WILL CHANGE YOUR LIFE __________

By now, you won't be surprised when I say that getting a book deal will not change your life overnight, or maybe ever. Your life may change because you reached a personal goal, because you got to express and share your art, because you accomplished something impressive and sought after. But you're still the same person with the same friends, same bills, same weird cowlick as you were the day before. You will not get recognized on the street. You will not get a better seat at that restaurant. Your middle school bully won't reach out and apologize for how they treated you. You will not get to quit your job and write full-time (right away or maybe ever). Yes, this is not fun to think about. Yes, it is true.

You might expect the world to look different the day after you get a book deal, and maybe it does, through your own eyes. For me, things were a little brighter, the normal petty agonies of daily life were easier to bear for a couple of days. Then, life went back to pretty much normal—except I had to write this book! So, as you are sitting there, working and yearning for your first or fifth book deal, remember that you will be the same person the day after you reach your goal as you were the day before. You might have some money coming your way, but it's rarely life-changing money. You will suddenly have a lot of homework. But try not to hang all your hopes on what will happen when the book deal comes through. Being a published author might change your life, but it's a long, slow process.

You also might be battling some disappointment when the big news comes to you. You got the offer! But it was not what you were expecting. Maybe it wasn't the editor or imprint you were hoping for. Maybe you had your heart set on a hardcover, and the editor really wants it to be a paperback original. Maybe you were hoping for another zero at the end of that advance number. (Aren't we all?)

It's not going to be perfect. You're not going to get everything you want. It's OK to be happy that it happened and still feel disappointed with one or more of the details. It doesn't make you ungrateful. It doesn't make you picky. You're allowed all the feelings you want, messy or not. I would go as far to say that it's common to be disappointed with an aspect or two of your book deal(s). Why would it be perfect? What's perfect? Nothing.

Feel your feelings. Talk to your friends and/or agent to get some perspective. Maybe you were expecting something that was never going to happen, and you just didn't know. Maybe it's something that can be addressed.* If you're prepared for imperfection, for surprise, for complicated feelings, you'll be better off than if you expect perfection. But isn't that true all the time?

Be careful not to get caught up in professional jealousy too. As you immerse yourself in the writing community, you're going to be around a lot of, well, writers. Someone you think is a hack is going to get a huge book deal. Someone you think is amazing won't. You're going to hear about someone who seemingly waltzed into a book deal for something you could have written in your sleep. Someone's going to get an offer for a book on the same subject as yours, while you've been languishing in the

* Unless it's money. The publisher isn't going to give you more money just because you want it, or even because you deserve it. Believe me, I've tried.

slush pile for years. One or more of these things are guaranteed to happen to you at some point in your career.

Letting these things consume you just takes up the time you could be writing, reading, or staring off into space. It will not take that deal away from that guy or get your query read faster. It will only eat you up inside. It is impossible to avoid these feelings completely, but when they do pop up, try to remember that no one is getting a book deal *at* you. Just like any success you find is not directed at anyone else.

When it comes, though, be sure to enjoy your good news. You got a book deal! It's wonderful and amazing and you are allowed to enjoy it. The publisher is not going to change their mind and say *Just kidding!* You will not spook the good news away by looking at it dead-on and saying *I did it! I achieved my goal! I got a book deal!* Put on your best lipstick and go out and celebrate. Stay in and binge *You've Got Mail* and *Misery* and *The Proposal* and *Bridget Jones's Diary* and *Julie & Julia* and *Wonder Boys* and *Elf* and all the other great publishing movies in your coziest socks and mute your phone.* Revel in your success for a bit, but then get to work. The clock starts when you say yes to the deal, not when you sign the contract.

If you are reading this chapter before you've had your good luck, your offer, your deal—stay strong. I know it's hard to watch others get what you want. That was me for *years*, and getting people book deals is my *job*. It's hard to have little control over this thing you want so badly. It's hard to think about the work you've done that hasn't yielded results. You are not alone. Here's to hoping good news is coming your way.

---

* Yes, *Elf* is a publishing movie.

Chapter Eight

IT'S A REAL BOOK!

You thought you were done when you typed *The End.* You thought you were done when you sent out queries and then when you got an agent and then when the book went on submission. You thought you were *really* done when the book sold. You were so far from done. In fact, there is no *done.*

FIRST, YOU HAVE A MANUSCRIPT

Before it's published, many people call their book a manuscript. This becomes a book through the editing and production process. Your manuscript may have a different editing process than your friend's or your next book or your last book. A cookbook is built differently than a novel than a graphic novel. You may have collaborators or photographers or colorists or fact-checkers working with you. Your specific editing journey will be your own. But generally speaking, this is what you can expect.

EDITING

You will turn in a complete draft of your manuscript to your editor, and they will edit it. They will read your work cover to cover and ascertain what needs to be done to make your book the best expression of itself. They do not "fix" books or make them "correct" or "perfect." They also won't rewrite your book for you—whether that makes you disappointed or relieved. They will look at your book on the macro and micro level and make suggestions about structure, pacing, organization, stakes, theme, and also grammar and language. I know people love to say that editors don't edit anymore, but I know from personal and professional experience they do. When you get a document full of Track Changes bubbles back from your editor, tell me again that editors don't edit.

Yes, most editing takes place using Word, and yes, there are better programs out there. No, your editor cannot use Google Docs or whatever newfangled program has come out whenever you're reading this book. I'm sorry that Track Changes is cumbersome, unintuitive, and confusing.

You may have one or more rounds of editing, depending on your schedule, editor, and scope of needs. You might have a first round of editing that addresses structural issues, followed by a line-by-line edit of the next draft. There will be a few more chances for you to review your book before it goes to the printer, but this is the time you do the most editing and moving things around. After you've addressed everything you can, your editor will send it to copyediting. This is often when the delivery and acceptance portion of your advance is released, so huzzah! Money!

The Hard Side of Editing

I wish that editing was as simple as *your editor reads your book and tells you what to change*, but of course it's not. Besides the difficult task of moving things around the page, the editing process involves a *lot* of feelings, and here are some ways to deal with that.

Editing with your editor is not your first editing rodeo. You edited your own book or sample chapters as you wrote it. You probably got feedback, of varying levels of helpfulness, from friends or loved ones or your critique group or a paid editor. Then you may have gone through a series of edits with your agent (or not). You might be thinking *Editing? Pish, I am an editing expert.* And you might be.

Editing with your editor after the book deal hits differently. Your editor is a lovely person, I'm sure. But some writers take this stage of editing like a personal attack. Your editor is not editing your book *at you*. They are working with you to make it the best it can be. By this stage in the game, though, you're getting tired. It's the last few miles of the marathon, and you are ready to cross the finish line.

And then here comes this editor, who thought the book was so good when they bought it, asking questions like *Whose POV are we in right now? Chapter 2 is not as clear as it could be; let's restructure it (again).* And *I'm not convinced your main character would do that.* You want to be like, *Excuse me? I did all that already!* Or *Someone else told me to structure chapter 2 like that!!!!* Or *I do not wanna!*

These are all normal feelings. You've cleared so many hurdles to get to this point, and someone wants you to keep working! You're tired! I know! But don't take it out on your poor, overworked editor. They are trying to help. They are a *professional editor*. It's their job to help make your book do what you want it to do in the best way possible. It is natural to feel resistant to doing work. I mean, wouldn't we all rather not?

Your editor is *probably* right, though. Not all the time! But if they are saying chapter 6 is a little slow, it's probably a little slow. They will be open to all the various ways you can speed it up. If you're feeling resistant to their suggestions, ask yourself why you feel like that. Are you tired and just don't wanna? Are you nervous about making the necessary changes because you've been avoiding it this whole time and now someone has come right out and said *This part needs work*? Are you sensitive to being perceived as wrong, and it feels like you just got an F on your book? Is the editor off base and you need to speak up about it? Think about why you're reacting the way you are and then decide your course of action. If you need to vent some frustration, do so with your group chat or your agent.

You can say no. You can say *That's not the direction I want to take this story; how about this?* Or *I'm not willing to make that change. Let's find another approach.* Or *I'm thinking A and B about that change; can you tell me more about your thoughts?* You might have another way to address the issue that is more genius than your genius editor's! You might have a very good reason not to make a change, and your editor agrees! You might be wrong, but it's your book and if it's not a legal issue, maybe your book will just be this way! You do not have to take all changes your editor suggests as gospel. You should not reject them out of spite, but you are allowed to say no. Be professional and clear, and it will work out.

You may also be looking at your pile of notes and hundreds of Track Changes bubbles and the lovely, thoughtful edit letter and be thinking *OK, but how?* You agree with your editor about almost all their edits, and you're ready to dive back in, but it feels like that huge ball of tangled yarn from when you were first editing your book. This is how I felt when I started my first big edit of this book. My editor's notes were amazing: smart, thoughtful, clear, and absolutely what I was anticipating. Remember in chapter 2 when I talked about printing out my edited manuscript and color-coding the changes with sticky notes? Printing it out grounded me, made me realize the idea of editing was bigger in my head than the actual work would be. Don't be shy to approach your own edits in creative ways—whatever your brain needs to make sense of the mess.

By the end, I was ready to stop looking at this book! And there will come a point where you will be ready to stop editing too. You'll need to stop tinkering so things can move on to production. Remember, you're not striving for perfection. There will be a typo somewhere and someone will say *They didn't have cotton candy in Gilded Age New York*, and you will think *Ugh, I shouldn't have named that character Jayden*. But it's OK. Your book will have its own life in the minds of readers, separate from you. Let your reader learn and grow and get mad and fall in love and find insight and make connections in your book that you didn't even know were there. That's why we read books. They become ours when we do. Don't hold on so tightly that you deny readers this essential experience.

Now that you've managed your own feelings, should you worry about your editor's? You should in terms of being a kind human in the world, remembering they're on your side and have the same goal as you: a great book. But if you say you don't want to do something they suggest, you are not hurting their feelings. They will not be *mad* at you. They'd rather you be happy with the work and come to the best resolution about a change than you take their suggestion without question. Do not worry that your editor will have a reaction to your reaction, as long as you are being kind and professional. Your editor is in charge of their own feelings, like everyone else on earth.

And once you're done with all that, it's time for your book to move into copyediting, which comes with absolutely no feelings whatsoever.*

COPYEDITING

Your editor will not copyedit your manuscript. Professional copyeditors will do that, and make it conform to the publisher's house style—i.e., the rules about grammar, punctuation, and usage the publisher has decided to adhere to company-wide. You know how *The New Yorker* puts umlauts over everything, like *coöperation*? That's their house style. Your copyeditor is the person who will catch all the times you used the wrong there/their/

* It comes with feelings too.

they're. They will put the commas in the right places since you (and I) can't remember all the rules anyway. But more than that, copyeditors will remind you that you said it was night in the beginning of the chapter, so it can't be noon already. I have a good friend who is a copyeditor, and the details she catches astound me. She once looked up the phases of the moon in an almanac to make sure that it was a full moon on the date that author said there was, a hundred years ago! The dedication! The knowledge! The time investment! Copyeditors, we salute you!

Whatever you do, thank your copyeditor in your acknowledgments. Even if you think they are being overly pedantic and fussy. That's their job! I know it feels like they're pointing out all the ways you're wrong, but they aren't. They aren't copyediting *at* you. They're saving you from mistakes that might impact reader comprehension. They're saving you from looking foolish. They want the reader to focus on your content, not your commas or your weird writing ticks.*

The secret (and don't tell my friend) is that you can STET your copyedits. STET is copyediting shorthand, from the Latin for *let it stand*, that tells the production team *Hey, I know the copyeditor says there shouldn't be a comma here, but I like it, so keep it.* If you meant to do a thing that the copyeditor thinks you shouldn't, guess what? It's your book! You can override the copyeditor. You should not do this because you are annoyed at their changes—they're just doing their job, and they're probably right anyway—but you can do it if it's important to your book. My sister overrode the copyeditor on her novel *The Secret Lives of Dresses* (shameless plug) who said Kleenex should be capitalized. It should, according to the publisher's house style. But my sister is a lexicographer (look it up), and she knows that words like Kleenex and Dumpster and Google are

* Apparently, I write "lol" at the end of a lot of my sentences, just like I do in text messages.

proprietary eponyms (look it up) and can be lowercase, as kleenex. And in her book, it is.

If it isn't offensive, if it doesn't impact meaning, if it's not going to get anyone sued, your editor and copyeditor are not likely to fight you too hard if you want to stet some commas and stuff. And as you look through the manuscript stetting or not stetting, remember you don't automatically get an A if you have few copyediting changes or an F if you have many.

PRODUCTION, DESIGN, COVER

When you have a clean manuscript, after you've stetted everything you wanted to, your editor will send your manuscript to production. This department in the publishing house turns the manuscript into a book. They typeset and design the pages, make sure there aren't any widows (a single word or short phrase left on its own at the top of a page or column) or orphans (the same, but at the bottom of a paragraph). That chapters always start on the verso (left side of facing pages) or recto (right side of facing pages), or however your book is designed. They'll design any dinguses that separate sections or drop case letters that start a chapter. (You know, when the first letter is really big and "drops" down into the first few lines—that's drop case.) They'll see notes from your editor and copyeditor about headers and sidebars and text boxes—anything unusual your book needs—and create a clear and cohesive design.

Your manuscript might be very design heavy and include hundreds of photographs or illustrations. It might have tricky footnotes or numerous charts. It might be a graphic novel or a picture book where the design *is* the book. In any case, you will see a sample of your proposed interior before production puts your text into the overall book design. You might get to see a selection of fonts to choose from, different dinguses, different effects for the page headers, numbers, and the title page. If your book is design heavy, this will be a whole process before you're even done writing it to make sure you create all the elements you need for the book, and that there's space enough to fit them.

Your editor and production team will finalize the trim size (dimensions of the book), whether it's hardcover or paperback, or paper over board (a hardcover without a dust jacket), and the type of paper used, though you may get to voice your opinion about these things, with varying influence depending on the book. If the whole team, sales and marketing included, think your book will sell better in paperback, at a paperback price point, you'll need a really good reason to convince them it should be a hardcover, and *because I've always dreamed of a hardcover* is not likely reason enough. The publisher does not want you to hate the design of your book, but there are economic and market realities to face. Don't forget, publishing is a retail industry, not art patronage. Make your feelings and preferences and opinions (kindly) known. But you might not get everything you want.

And before copyediting, too, you will likely see the design concepts for your cover. This is when things start to feel real! Your book has a face! A cover to greet the world! And it comes with a *lot* of feelings on both sides.

I like to prepare my clients for this by reminding them that a book cover is like a cereal box. It has to sit on a shelf and entice people to buy it. The publisher wants the cover to be visually interesting while also telling them what's inside. Is it for kids or grown-ups? Is it a bran cereal that's good for you or is it full of marshmallows and cookie bits? Does it also have added vitamins? Does it want you to guess so you'll pick it up and look at the back? Does it want you to think it's like the other oat circles, but different/better/new? Your cover is sometimes the only chance your book has to communicate with the reader, sitting there on the shelf or passing them by as a thumbnail while they scroll. It has to yell out what it is, not whisper. This is what the publisher is trying to do with your cover.

Unfortunately, the author wants the cover to be a work of art (it is/can be!), visually distill the heart and soul of their prose, and also accurately represent the physical characteristics of the main characters or subject matter.* Sometimes it matters that the person on the cover has brown hair, and sometimes it does not. The biggest disagreements I've seen between authors and publishers regarding covers happened because neither side communicated what they wanted the cover to do, and it turned out they both wanted opposing things. Before you see a cover draft, you will likely have a conversation with your editor about what you want/hope it to be, and you may even send them pictures, other book covers, fonts, etc., to give the art department as inspiration. *Do not* create your own mock-up cover in Photoshop and send that. If you're a professional designer, remember that you're probably not a professional *book* designer and it's a different thing. If you're a graphic designer, can you design a car? Probably not. Use your experience to communicate what you want, and then let the professionals do their job.

There is a chance, of course, that you will hate your cover. It happens! You are allowed to not like your cover, even if you know the art department worked very hard on it. People have different ideas of *good.* If you hate your cover, the first thing to remember is don't panic. You can voice your opinions and preferences and your publisher will listen. That doesn't mean you'll get everything you want, but your publisher really doesn't want you to hate your book cover. The second thing you should do is talk to your agent. You can be honest and unfiltered with them, and they can translate your *Are you kidding me with this hideous thing?????* to *We were expecting a different direction.* I personally have a lot of opinions about cover design and love talking this part out with editors and clients, and

* I was on the rowing team in college and, boy, do I like to snark on book covers that use the wrong kind of oars.

your agent may make suggestions to guide the conversation too. This may happen on the phone or over email. If you have big feelings about your cover, use your agent to convey them calmly and rationally to your editor.

You may get one cover option or you may get several. You might get one primary design but a few options for the title treatment/font/color. You can say *no* to a cover design, but that doesn't mean you will get infinite additional options. You can't keep sending your burger back to the kitchen. And there may be a point where your editor says *Sales really thinks this is the direction to go* and that might be it. In your contract, it's likely you only have the right of cover *consultation*, not *approval*, and that is industry standard. This may surprise you. But it goes back to the cereal box. Your cover is a big way readers decide to buy your book. Listen to the input of the people who design book covers for a living.

There are also special things the publisher can do to the cover for extra oomph (often called specs). The text or images can be embossed (raised) or debossed (recessed). Elements could have a spot gloss (shiny) or matte effect. The cover could have texture or die cuts to reveal something underneath or be a paperback with French flaps (literally flaps built into the paperback cover, resembling a jacketed hardcover). That thing when the pages are unevenly cut so it's not all smooth and uniform when you close the book? That's called deckled edges. The hot new thing as of this writing is sprayed edges, which means that the edges of the pages are sprayed an eye-catching color. Popular choices are black, gold, and purple. All these different effects cost money. Your book may or may not get these treatments depending on the budget, retail price, and prospective orders. Sometimes these things are decided mere months before the book's release date, and can depend on how preorders look, or if a retailer decided to take a large quantity of books for their stores. These are icing on the cake. I wish sprayed edges for you all (or whatever the next big thing is).

FIRST PASS/SECOND PASS

OK, back to the part of production where you have to do things. At some point after copyediting, you will get an electronic document that's called First Pass or 1P. This is a fully designed and typeset version of your book that *should* incorporate all the changes you and the copyeditor made. You get to review the First Pass to make sure the charts are in the right place and they didn't capitalize kleenex and the right version of the newly added second appendix made it in. This is the time to point out errors. This is likely the *last* time you can make little, tiny, necessary changes to your prose.

You really can't rewrite things in 1P. If you change a lot and production has to go back in and fix all the new widows and orphans, no one is going to be happy. Of course, if something is wrong, correct it, but if you are just swapping one adjective for another, it's time to stop tinkering. In fact, if you make too many changes at this point, the publisher may charge you for it. It's in your contract. But also, in twenty years, I've never seen this happen. Remember, no book is perfect. You will have to let the book be as it is at this point. Channel Elsa and let it go.

There may be 2P or 3P, but there are not infinite drafts before the book is locked and sent off to the printer. Focus on errors and corrections in these passes, not rewriting. And don't forget it's *your* book. You might be the only one who notices that a photo got flipped or that chart is in the wrong chapter. Don't be afraid to speak up if you see something others may have missed.

GALLEYS, ARCS, BOUND MANUSCRIPTS

At some point, somewhere around copyediting or 1P, you'll get a galley or ARC, which stands for advance reader's copy or advance review copy. These are paperbacks (even if your book will be a hardcover), and sometimes they have the cover printed on them and sometimes they are plain. Either way is fine. (There are even ALCs: advance listener copies of audiobooks!) These go to reviewers, long-lead media (like magazines that plan issues far in advance), and readers who might offer blurbs (endorsements) of the book. You will likely get a few copies to send to friends and family, but keep in mind these are primarily for marketing purposes, not to send to all your second cousins and that English teacher who never thought you'd amount to anything. Save a few of your finished copies for that. At some point you'll be asked to make a list of your professional contacts who will, hopefully, talk about the book, and your publisher will send them ARCs. Don't forget: these are for *marketing purposes*. The cost comes out of your marketing budget. Use them wisely.

Sometime before galleys, the publisher may produce bound manuscripts, which are very basic, non-fancy galleys for review purposes. Sometimes they're just printed-out manuscripts that are quickly bound together. This is OK. Everyone knows they're supposed to be basic.

There will be mistakes in your galley/ARC. This is OK and normal. Reviewers know that if they want to quote from your book, they will need to check that against the finished copy. It literally says this on the cover. Do not freak out about this. They won't make an ARC from a manuscript that is way, way, way far away from being done. It's usually the draft right before copyediting or 1P. This is normal and fine, and anyone who has a copy knows this and anyone who does not know this will look like a goof. Galleys are exciting. Enjoy it.

INDEXES, ENDNOTES, AND, OH YEAH, A TITLE

Some books need extra elements like endnotes or an index. Every book needs a title! Here's how those things work.

INDEX

If your book needs an index, one may be provided for you. But the cost usually comes out of your advance or is charged against your future royalties, which comes as a shock to some authors. This is outlined in your contract, but it's easy to overlook or forget it. In most cases, your publisher will handle all of this, and you will see it in 3P. Creating an index is a specialized skill, and your publisher will likely hire someone to complete it. You don't want to make your own index, I promise. Let the professionals handle it.

ENDNOTES

If you cite a lot of sources in your book, you'll need to create endnotes for them, using the Endnote function in Word.* Your publisher will let you know what style to use (mine followed the *Chicago Manual of Style*), and you'll want to be sure they're accurate. Someone suggested I use AI to generate mine, and while that sounded easier, I didn't do it, for many reasons. AI isn't accurate! It makes stuff up! Do your own endnotes, friends.

* Your publisher might use footnotes, like this one right here. If you're not sure, ask!

TITLE

By this point you will have likely discussed the title of your book with your editor. You might have come up with the best title the very first time you sat down to write, or it may have been *Untitled* for the last four years. Titles are tough. Personally, I love them and love brainstorming them, and this book had *many* titles before we landed on this one, including many in the proposal stage. Those included:

- *Newsletter Book*
- *Ask an Agent*
- *Fuck the Cat, Save Yourself**
- *Write On*

The subtitle, too, went through many iterations. My brainstorming list here included:

- *Your Guide to Publishing, Books, and the Creative Life*
- *A Real-Talk Guide to Publishing and Writing Books*
- *Direct Advice on Books, Publishing, and the Creative Life*
- *Navigating Publishing, Books, and the Creative Life*
- *How to Navigate Books, Publishing, and the Creative Life*
- *The Truth About Publishing, Writing, and the Creative Life*

This book's current title came to me while I was finishing the first draft. I turned it in and said, *Sorry! I came up with a new title!* I knew it might not stick, but I liked it and wanted to try. Titles are like book covers—they have to be informative and enticing and match the book's genre—and many departments weigh in on the title for every book. I got lucky that they loved it, and then we worked together on the subtitle. Your

* This makes more sense if you're familiar with the book *Save the Cat!: The Last Book on Screenwriting You'll Ever Need* by Blake Snyder.

title may change several times over the course of your project, and that's normal. Your publisher wants you to like your title, but they also know a lot about how titles work in the marketplace. Listen to them. According to your contract, you may have approval or consultation of your title.

Titles are not copyrightable, so it's not illegal to have the same title as another book, but it could be confusing or detrimental if it's easily mistaken for something else. It would have done no good to title this book *Moby-Dick: How to Write Books and Stuff.**

TO THE PRINTER

And then, at some point, your book will go to the printer. Wave bye-bye! It's off to be made into a real book, to be printed on paper, bound, and boxed up to be sent to stores. You're done! You did it!

That doesn't mean, of course, that it's perfect. Books are made by humans and will contain errors. Everyone works hard to make the number of errors as close to zero as possible, but no one can guarantee perfection. It's OK. Readers should (I'm looking at you, people who like to email authors to report typos) forgive small mistakes as evidence that a person, not a machine, made this book. Revel in the imperfection! It's fine. If you find a typo in your book, tell your editor, and they will create a reprint correction. If you get an email from a reader that says *Hey, you idiot, you used the wrong* there *on page twenty-nine*, just forward that to your editor and they will take care of it. Typos can be fixed immediately in the e-book version of your work, but the hard-copy changes will have to wait for the next printing. Sometimes there is not a second printing, and you

* Copyright is different than trademark, and you can't use someone else's trademark.

have to wait until the paperback. It's OK. The publisher is not going to recall and pulp (i.e., destroy) all print copies of your book just because a comma got left out. Say it with me, humans make typos.

Your book has a specific time slot at the printer, and missing it is a *big* deal. Publishers use all the same domestic printers, and there aren't very many of them anymore. They also use overseas printers, especially for color printing, and shipping can take weeks or months.* There are lots of flexible points in your book's production schedule. You can be a little late on your manuscript deadline or ask for a few more days with your copyedits. But as you get closer to the end, there's much less flexibility, and your book has to make its slot at the printer if it's going to be published on time. The more time you take to do your part means less time for everyone else on the team to do theirs.

FINISHED COPIES

A few months before your on-sale date, you'll get a box from your publisher with the finished book in it. Your contract stipulates how many author copies (i.e., ones just for you to give away for fun, not for resale) you get, and most authors find they end up with too many. If you need a few extra, though, your publisher will give you some. Enough to give to a few more cousins; not enough to send one to your entire graduating class, just to rub it in their faces.

Holding that copy brings up some big feelings. It has your name on it! It's got all the words you wrote in it! You should take a few moments to savor it (and then reenact it for an unboxing video for social media). You did it. You wrote and published a book. Congratulations.

---

* Remember when that boat got stuck in the Panama Canal? Publishers and bookstores certainly do!

There may be imperfections in the final book too. They are made by machines run by humans. You might see an ink splotch. You might see a wonky jacket, misfolded a bit. If you see a BIG problem—like the cover is right but the insides are for a completely different book (it's happened! I've seen it!), or if it was bound upside down (also seen it!)—tell your editor.

If readers contact you with complaints about the book, such as *I thought the paper would be nicer* or *I don't like this sticker on the front. Why can't I take it off?* just nod and say *Thanks for buying my book!* If someone has a really messed-up copy, for whatever reason, they can likely exchange it where they bought it. Most people just want to complain. You cannot do anything to make those people happy.

When you get finished copies, that means books are in the warehouse or will be very shortly. That means stores will be getting their copies to sell pretty soon. That means your publication date is coming up fast.

Display your book prominently in your home or office (unless it has a *lot* of spicy content and you're hiding your pseudonym from your family/coworkers). Post about your book a lot. You wrote a book! Sing it to the heavens.

WHAT YOU DO AFTER YOU'RE DONE

There are other things you need to complete, write, and/or solidify after your book itself is done, and these include:

AUTHOR QUESTIONNAIRE

Every publisher has a form called the Author Questionnaire that they ask you to fill out about when you turn in the first draft of your manuscript or before. You might type your answers into a document or through your publisher's online portal. I'll be honest with you—it's not a quick and easy form. It's an in-depth and detailed questionnaire that will take you a chunk of time to complete. It definitely took me several hours over the course of a few days.

The point of the form is to tell the marketing, publicity, and sales departments anything you can to help position, market, and sell your book. They'll ask for your hometown and alma mater so the sales team can tell area bookstores you're a "local author." If you're a nurse or a teacher or a veteran or something like that, there might be awards, organizations, or other marketing opportunities related to those fields. You might be connected to other like-minded authors at the same imprint or publisher for group publicity opportunities. The form asks for the names of people who'd be good to blurb your book, whether you know them personally or not. Or influencers you're aware of who are active in your genre. Or editors, journalists, or media personalities you know.

You won't have perfect answers for every question. Some you may even leave blank. I sure did. I didn't have an answer to a question about specific awards I wanted to be considered for. ¯_(ツ)_/¯ But put everything and anything you can think of on there. Set aside time to work on it. Don't just brush it off.

And it's likely you'll get asked these questions again. You'll get an email from your publicist asking if you know any booksellers or have a favorite indie bookstore, and you'll be like, *I put that on the questionnaire!!!* in your mind. Just answer the question politely and remember that your publicist is working on dozens and dozens of books and you putting your answer in an email might be a big help to them. Give everyone some grace, like you hope they will do for you when you inevitably ask them for the fifteenth time when the preorder link will go live.

CATALOG AND COVER COPY

Publishers produce a catalog of their books every season, and this goes out to bookstores, retailers, and foreign publishers for subrights sales. They're mostly digital now, but they used to come in the mail and soon we'd have a stack of them knee-high. I'd go through them to get an idea of what each house was publishing to better tailor my submission lists, and I still do this today, except I can view or download catalogs off publishers' websites. You can too!

Each book gets a page or so, and includes the cover, a description, rights information, publication information, and book specs, like format, trim size, and price. Your editorial team or copywriters will write the catalog copy and share it with you for your feedback and notes. Sometimes catalog copy is similar to the summary you'll read on the back of your book, but not always. Remember that the point of the copy is to accurately portray your book *to booksellers and librarians* and not really to the general public. You want it to be clear, thorough, informative, and enticing. And artful, yes, but mostly those other things.

The cover copy—either for the flaps of the hardcover jacket or the back or both—will probably be shorter than your catalog copy.* Your editorial team will write this and give you a chance to review and comment, and yes, it'll be difficult to get everything you want to say in there. Plot points will get left out. It might feel more salesy than you wish it did. But think of how you judge a book by the back cover copy. If it says, "a haunting and moody story of loss" and you wrote a beach read, your reader will be confused. The point of this is to get the reader to buy or borrow the book. It's not your application for a MacArthur "Genius Grant."

---

* About 350 words for hardcovers and 250 words for trade paperbacks.

EARLY READS AND BLURBS

Once there's an almost-done manuscript, your team will start talking about early reads and blurbs. Blurbs are endorsements from other writers about your book. Impressive blurbs on the back of an ARC can really help a book get attention from booksellers and retail accounts, like Barnes & Noble and Amazon. An early reader or blurber for your book could be a writer you know (personally or professionally) working in the same genre, a bookseller you're friendly with, an expert in your field, a colleague or professional contact, that famous writer your agent also represents, or a fellow writer published by the same imprint. You and your team will come up with a list and cast a wide net in the hopes of catching a few live ones. It takes a lot of time and energy to read books and offer blurbs, so don't be offended if someone you had high hopes for doesn't have time. Sometimes readers have six to eight weeks to respond to these requests, and while it's possible to read a book in six weeks, could you do it tomorrow, with little notice, on top of all your other work and family obligations? Yeah, it's tough. Be thankful for every blurb you get and remember how people helped you when others come knocking for blurbs. Return the kindness of their time and labor with what time and labor you can spare.

MARKETING MAILINGS

Your publisher might put together a package to send early readers. These usually include the galley, a letter from them or you, and maybe a little bit of swag—a postcard, sticker, tchotchke, or similar—intended to get the attention of a bookseller who might order your book or an influencer who might post about it to their many followers. The big, fancy, decked-out special mailings are few and far between, so don't worry if your book doesn't get sent around with a candle, water bottle, and bucket hat all with your book cover printed on it. Author Silvia Moreno-Garcia said her publisher didn't send out one of these big, flashy influencer boxes until her *tenth* book, which was also after her big success with *Mexican Gothic*.[1] So don't assume your publisher doesn't care about your book just because your mailing is a heartfelt letter you wrote and a copy of the book. That could reach just the right person at the right time. Marketing budgets for books are small, and swag is expensive and doesn't always turn into comparable sales.* But you may be asked to write something for or come up with ideas for this kind of thing.

SUPPORTING ARTICLES OR STORIES

You might be asked to brainstorm and write additional pieces in support of your book that you can place, or your team may be able to help you place, on blogs, websites, newspapers, or magazines. Your publisher isn't going to be able to get you instantly on the front page of your local paper, but they may be able to connect you to outlets active in your genre. If you have connections that will help you here, speak up! It's a good idea to keep a running list of ideas as they pop up, so you have a well to draw from when the time comes. There are more opportunities to do this for nonfiction writers than for novelists, and more for writers for adults than for kids, but the latter aren't completely out of luck. Think broadly about the topics related to your book and look around for publications where that would fit. Your team will help you, but you know your content best.

Many years ago, I wrote a piece for the Electric Lit website that was admittedly a little clickbait-y titled "10 Novels Agents Have Already Seen a Billion Times."[2] And it got a ton of traffic. Newspapers in France

* And how many mugs can one book influencer have?

and Italy contacted me to license and translate it. It was very exciting. Then when I was in the middle of writing this book, the editor contacted me again and asked if I wanted to update it. It'd been seven years since it ran, and it was still one of their most popular posts. I could have immediately come up with ten YA novels agents have seen two billion times or something like that but instead, I asked if they were willing to wait until closer to the publication of this book, so I could tie it into my promotional plans. They said sure! Maybe this time I'll do nonfiction. Nora Ephron said "Everything is copy." But when you're writing a book, *everything is promo.*

ONCE MORE, WITH FEELINGS

You're going to have a whole host of feelings as you complete the editing and production process of your book. You'll be wowed that so many people are working diligently on it. You may be underwhelmed by your cover or overjoyed at some fancy things like deckled edges or French flaps. You may be nervous about getting it right or how readers are going to react to it or panic with *OMG, it's real, how do I get off this train?* feelings. I've seen it all. Your agent has seen it all. Your editor has seen it all. They're all there to help you, though keep in mind none of them are licensed mental health professionals. You can absolutely vent, rejoice, worry, mull, question anything and everything with your team. But they're not going to be able to fix your abandonment issues or chronic anxiety. It can be hard to navigate this, but such is life. You won't be alone, no matter what you're going through.

Chapter Nine

I WILL TEACH YOU TO LOVE SELF-PROMOTION

Are you hiding under the covers? That's what most writers do when it's time to talk about self-promotion. I get it. It's hard to talk about yourself and your work, full stop. It's hard to do this in a way that doesn't sound like bragging or begging. We're all cringing all the time when we have to self-promote. It's OK. You're not alone.

Or you're fine with talking about yourself and your work, online and in person, but you want to make sure you're doing it effectively and learn how to avoid pitfalls whenever possible. Maybe you've tried one way in the past and it didn't work and you don't know what to do next. Maybe you're excited and just don't want to fuck it up.

In this chapter we're going to talk about why you have to do self-promotion, what you can actually do, and how not to crumble into a pile of dust or annoy all your followers every time you suggest people read something you wrote. I promise you can get to an OK place about this or at the very least a neutral place about it. Because if you don't want to talk about your own work, who will?

HOW TO MAKE PEACE WITH SELF-PROMOTION

To start, let's recognize that promoting yourself brings up complicated feelings. I mean, *I* love to talk about myself, as an agent and a writer, but that's because I am the youngest child, a natural ham, and a Leo Moon. Also, I've gotten used to it over the last twenty years of my career because I've seen what good it can do for me and my clients. Whether you're dreading it or cautiously optimistic about it, here's how to integrate promoting your book into your writing life.

IT'S NOT ALL SOCIAL MEDIA—JUST MOSTLY

As we talk about self-promotion, let's admit that we're mostly, but not exclusively, talking about social media, however that exists when this book comes out. This is where most writers start because these have the lowest barriers to entry. They're right at our fingertips, on our phones and computers. Social media sites, however, are not neutral places. They can be unsafe for some, especially marginalized communities, and can adversely affect anyone's mental health. If you are unsafe on any platform, *you do not have to be there*. If one makes your life noticeably worse, *get off it*. Your health, safety, and sanity are more important than posting "Buy my book!" Everyone will understand if this is the case for you. There is no evidence that says *You will sell [x] fewer copies if you're not on all the platforms*. You'll find what works, safely, for you.

If you merely hate a specific platform, you also don't have to be there! If you are loathe to make short videos, then you do not have to be on TikTok. In fact, you shouldn't be, because hate will make you create bad content, and bad content will not help you promote your stuff. It's OK to factor in your personal preferences and skills when it comes to self-promotion. As I finished this book, I contemplated making Reels or TikToks as part of my promotional strategy. I absolutely did not want to do fifty takes or spend hours a week editing just to get one thirty-second video. I mentioned this on my newsletter, and my helpful readers reminded me that many of these kinds of videos don't show the creator's face and can be more, shall we say, loosely edited. This was a big relief! While on a long flight, I experimented by making a Reel of me writing out a query tip on my tablet. I put some music behind it. That was it! It took me about six takes and forty-five minutes to do the whole thing, but it was more fun than I thought it would be and much lower stakes. I just might even do it again! You don't have to do any specific form of social media, but you do have to do something. It's very hard to ignore self-promotion altogether.

Most people are on several platforms, with one or two taking the lead. Don't worry that you're overloading your followers if you cross-post the same stuff to Instagram and TikTok. Why? Because no one sees *everything* you do to promote yourself and your work. That might sound depressing—because why do it if no one's going to see it?—but it can also take some of the pressure and anxiety out of talking about yourself online. You can say *buy my book!!* three or four times more often than you think you can, and no one will notice the increase. Because of algorithms and the fact that some (smart) people are not glued to social media all day, no one is going to see every single one of your posts. Your followers might be on the other side of the world, where it's night for your morning. Some followers only check stuff once a day for fifteen minutes and are not going to see all the posts that happened since the last time they checked regardless.

And frankly, most people are not paying that much attention to you, or me, or anyone else but themselves. It's true! Hasn't someone said to you before, when you're worried about your hair or your outfit or that pimple on your nose, that no one is looking at you? It's kind of deflating at the time, because many want to be (positively) noticed out in the world, but tbh, isn't this also an example of how we're all focused more on ourselves than on anyone else? It's the same with posting about your newsletter, latest article, picture book, or career milestone. The people who matter will notice. The rest will go about their business as usual. Very few people are actually thinking *Gah, will that person shut up already?* And if they are, they are not your core audience and they can hit the bricks! Talk to those who want to listen and ignore the ones that don't. Try to remember this every time the old anxiety creeps in, because it will, even after you've really absorbed all my good advice. It gets easier, but for most it's never painless.

WHY CAN'T THE PUBLISHER DO IT?

I talk to a lot of writers, especially first-timers, who are surprised by the amount of marketing and promotional work they need to do. Their comments come with varying levels of bitterness, depending on the success of the book. Most writers think that their job is to write the book and the publisher's job is to print and sell the book and that's it. But this is false. It's a team effort the whole way through, from the editor's notes to the sales team's pitch. There are some things the author does best, like write the book. And there some things the publisher does best, like design and sell the book, and together those things create things readers want to buy.

This goes double for marketing and promoting a book. The publisher is better at getting trade reviews and convincing booksellers to stock a book. The author is better at speaking directly to their readers (via social media or in person or otherwise), and that's why the author does more marketing and promotion than they expect. They're better at it and they don't even know it. Readers do not want to listen to a publisher say *Look at all these great books we have!* It's like listening to Old Navy say *You don't have enough pants!* You'd much rather listen to a friend or famous person say *These pants are great.* See how that works? When it's your turn to promote your book, remember you're better at some things than the publisher is, and that's why you should do it.

People do read book media and reviews, and publishers are good at getting that stuff. Unfortunately, books coverage in mass media is on the decline, and it's getting harder and harder for anyone to get coverage. The *LA Times* laid off their book editor between drafts one and two of this book. And only so many books are reviewed in *The New York Times Book Review* a week. Maybe a dozen? And how many books are published a week? Tens of thousands. With a few exceptions for journalists and other media personalities, the publisher is likely better than you are at getting your book reviewed somewhere notable for your genre. But you are better at posting for the people who already follow you, who know who you are, who specifically signed up to hear from you. You can't call up the *Today* show and ask to get on the second hour to talk about your book, but the publisher can. The publisher cannot grow your personal online platform because followers are looking to *you* for that content, not to publishers.

It feels like you're doing more promo than the publisher because you don't really see much of what the publisher does. Librarians that read the *Publishers Weekly* review that your publisher solicited may order your book for their collection and then come and follow you on

Instagram. Another librarian that follows you on Instagram because you post interesting stuff will see your book announcement and make a note to order it for their collection. And those library sales can really add up! This is how your efforts dovetail with the publisher's, whether you notice it or not.

If you're already established in your specific market, especially if you're writing nonfiction, you are way better at getting to the readers in your specific genre or specialty. You're probably already talking to other writers who might help promote or blurb your book. You may be involved in specific organizations that could include your book in their newsletters or conferences. You may already have your own newsletter about your topic and can promote your book to your fans directly.

Publishers do not know every niche interest group for every niche topic, because that's impossible. This is not a ding against publishers. Hopefully, this doesn't make you think *Well, then, what's the point if they don't know how to market my book?* They do know how to market your book, to the venues they can reach, which you likely cannot. There is never enough time, personnel, or money to fully promote every single book, and that is capitalism's fault. Not to let publishers too much off the hook (love you, publishers) because there are many ways in which they fall short in promoting books. That's why you have to do a lot of it yourself and why you might be better at it than the publisher. It would be nice to only have to write the thing and then magically watch it make a glorious debut into the world. But that's not the book market we have. Your book deserves promotion and accolades. You have to work together with the publisher to get them.

THE DIFFERENCE BETWEEN PROMOTING FICTION AND NONFICTION

There is a big difference between how publishers see platforms and self-promotion for writers of fiction and nonfiction, and if you think about how you buy books, it'll make a lot more sense.

When you're buying a novel, you might narrow down your choices a few ways. You might have specific genres you prefer to read: science fiction, mysteries, graphic novels. You might want to read whatever was reviewed in *The New York Times Book Review* last week, what's on the front table at B&N, or what you heard about from a friend or on a podcast. You might have some authors who are auto-buys, and you seek them out by name.

Do you see what's not there? You aren't saying *I only read authors who have 50,000 followers on Instagram. I only read authors whose TikToks are funny. I only read authors who post regularly.* In fact, I read a book I saw on the *New York Times* bestseller list recently, and it was only after I was done that I realized I had seen many of that author's TikToks. This doesn't mean the author or the publisher did a bad job of marketing the book. It means that readers will find books in many ways and pick them up for many reasons.

You don't read authors because you have vetted their social media and it has reached a certain level of visibility. You know about a book because their social media (or book placement or reviews or word of mouth) put that book in front of your face and your brain said *Oh, that looks like something I might like.* A novelist's social media increases the chances that a reader may be aware of their name or their book. Larger author platforms may correlate to more name recognition or awareness, which may lead to more sales. (And it is absolutely correlation, not causation.) But editors and agents are not looking at novelists and thinking *Welp, they don't have enough Instagram followers, so they don't get a book deal.*

I personally believe readers are more drawn by genre and subject when it comes to novels, not necessarily name recognition, though the big names take up a lot of space, literally and figuratively. Fiction readers are much more likely to take a chance on a debut novelist if they like the genre or subject (or title or cover or what their friend said about it in the group chat). Platform is just one way a fiction writer reaches a reader. More is better, but less is not the end of a writer's chances for publication.

Now think about how you buy a nonfiction book. You are probably driven a lot by genre and topic. You might want a history of Black New Yorkers in the Gilded Age. You may want a guide to smart investing. You may want a memoir about divorce. If you don't have an author already in mind, you're going to scan the shelves and pick up whatever catches your eye and look at the back of the book. The publisher has likely incorporated into the back cover copy something about the author's credentials, authority, or name recognition. *From Pulitzer Prize–winning author of . . . From Harvard professor and chair of the whatever whatever . . . From TikTok sensation . . .* The book you're looking for might not have a famous author, but whether you're aware of it or not, you're looking for some indication that this person knows what they're talking about and that you can trust them. You might think Harvard is the pits and put that book down. You might see someone's list of publication credits and think *Oooof, I do not read that website. No thanks.* These might be conscious decisions or not. But you spend more time vetting the author of a nonfiction book than you likely do for a novel.

If the author doesn't need a special degree or publication credits to get your attention or to be an authority on a subject, you're still looking for books where you can say *Oh, wait, I know that guy.* Maybe you're looking for a diet book, and you recognize the buff trainer on the cover from that TV show. That one might look better than one from someone you've never heard of. Again, these might not be completely conscious decisions, but your brain is definitely doing this work.

Even if you are not at a bookstore or library scanning the shelves, you are still influenced by the author's platform. You might have read the author's articles in a magazine for years and now they have a book out. You might have read an excerpt from it in a magazine last month and didn't even realize it was from their book. You might have heard an interview with them on the radio last year that really stuck with you. Their existing platform might have gotten them that interview, which may have piqued the interest of an agent, who reached out to them about a book, and then a year or two later, you're checking it out of the library.

We vet nonfiction differently, just as a function of being human. We want to be able to trust what we're reading, and even if we know it's biased, it's a bias we agree with, that whatever we aim to learn from a book is coming from a source we can put our faith in. The way that agents, editors, and authors assess this kind of thing is an author's credentials—maybe a degree or previous publications or specific experience. Like we talked about before and will again later, how the reader ties the name and the credentials together is platform, or how they've heard of this person. If you have none of those things, the reader is going to think *Who's this guy?* and move on. Even if you've never heard their name before, you might think *Ohhh, this person went through that? I did, too, so I know they know what they're talking about.*

As you learn how readers interpret your platform and self-promotion efforts, I hope it'll take some of the stress out of it. No one is looking at everything you do. There isn't one right way to do it, so you're not doing it wrong. Everyone feels like they're not doing enough and that the publisher should do more. Everyone feels like it's an additional full-time job, on top of everything else. All you can do is find the best way to fit it into your life, for your book, and not let it take up more psychic energy than it should. Spend that energy on writing your next book.

HOW TO BUILD A PLATFORM

And now for the nuts and bolts of building a platform. This is not an exhaustive list of every possible place you can build your platform, online and off, but it's a lot of the big ones. Your specific genre and area of expertise may lead you to places I don't even know about. Add those to your list.

ONLINE

Social media. Twitter/X, Facebook, Instagram, Threads, Bluesky, LinkedIn, TikTok, Tumblr, and the site that launched between the time this went to the printer and was shipped to stores. The ones you should be on depend on your audience, genre, and preferences.

It is not *if you build it, they will come.* Simply being on these platforms will not magically make your platform appear. It takes time and effort. You'll be frustrated, confused, annoyed, and baffled by what works and what doesn't. And then the platform will change its algorithm, and you'll have to relearn how it works all over again.

Do not make your social media handle the name of your book, especially before it's bought by a publisher. Your title can change multiple times over the publishing process. And what happens when you write your second book? Will you change your handle to that? It's best to use your name—professional or preferred—whatever works for you. If you have a very common name, there's nothing wrong with creating a unique handle and using that. It's not uncommon for a publisher to put "by Juan dela Cruz, aka @yourfavoritewriter" on the cover of a book, if that's a big selling point. But consider how that will look if your handle is @YankeesSuck4Eva or something.

You can keep your personal and professional social media feeds separate. You can keep your personal ones private, or just private on Instagram and public on TikTok. It's your choice. I do not generally suggest an author maintain two (or more) fully separate social media accounts for your writing personas, like one for your adult books and one for your children's books. Or even one for books written under your real name and another under your pseudonym. (Obviously, if there are safety reasons to do this, do it. Your safety trumps all my advice here.) It's just a lot to maintain. And frankly, your audience probably doesn't want two of you. They want you all in one place, even if that's the same place for your space-opera science fiction news and your 🌶🌶🌶🌶🌶 spicy romance news. Use your judgment on whether separating things might be best for your particular career. But I don't feel it's a good reason to maintain multiple personas because you think it'll be easier. It's not. In fact, I think it's more difficult.

NEWSLETTERS/BLOGS

Remember blogs? For those of you who don't, they were like newsletters, but they lived at a specific URL and weren't emailed to you. You followed a lot of blogs on what was called an RSS feed, and it used to be great fun to check in with the random people you followed, whether you knew them IRL or not. People also used LiveJournal or Tumblr for things like this. But I digress. There are still blogs, and if they're connected to another network to publicize them (i.e., alert readers to new posts via social media), they can be a fun and effective way to build a platform.

Newsletters have taken over the blog space because social media sucked up everyone's attention and Google stupidly killed Google Reader. Sorry, I have strong feelings about blogs and their demise. Now that readers need to be brought the content instead of seeking it out themselves, email newsletters have become The Thing. I mean, mine got me this book deal, so I'm not complaining.

Like social media, you don't *have* to do a newsletter/blog, and you should not if writing it feels like pulling teeth. You could do one about a defined subject, like books and publishing like I did, or a broader one that may cover several of your interests. If you're just starting out, I suggest focusing on a clear topic so you can bring in readers interested in that, and it goes without saying that the topic should be related to what you ultimately want to be known for. If you're writing fiction, you might review books in your genre or something like that. A newsletter that's full of your random thoughts and pictures of your cat might be fun to write, but unless you have an excellent voice or are very funny (and you're trying to build a humor platform), it's going to be hard to pull in an audience. What's in it for them?

Most often, a newsletter is or becomes its own thing, outside of what you'd put in a book. It has to, or you'd just be writing your whole book in newsletter form. Casey Johnston, author of the newsletter *She's a Beast*, found success in newsletters in the face of a crumbling media landscape.[1] After getting laid off, she took the concept behind her popular column "Ask a Swole Woman" and reinvigorated it in a newsletter about weightlifting and more. No, she wasn't starting from scratch like many authors, but she took her expertise and passion and let it evolve organically. Now it's her main gig, and it's brought her more opportunities than just in the book world. How has that happened? Because of the quality of her work. She said, "I get a small, sustainable amount of organic growth just from people sharing my work with other people, and from my work getting covered, or people asking me to come on podcasts, things like that. But that happens not because of some complex, high-volume, flood-the-zone marketing strategy, but because . . . the work is good." It's not magic. It's work. Your newsletter doesn't have to become a paying side hustle, but it does have to give readers something for their time and/or money. Start one because you have something to say, not because you think you have to.

I do not suggest serializing your novel in newsletter/blog form. People do it, and yes, I've seen some book deals come out of it (OK, maybe one). You should avoid this not because publishers will feel like everyone's already read your book for free (though this can be part of it), but because it's hard for readers to catch up. Unless they follow you from day one, they'll have to go all the way back to the beginning to understand what's going on. And who's got time for that? You could do other kinds of fiction work in newsletter form—flash fiction, haiku, short stories—but novel-length projects are hard to get off the ground in this format.

You can monetize your newsletter or not. You can host it yourself on your own website (if you have those skills), or you can use a newsletter network like Beehiiv or Substack. The reader doesn't usually care where you host it, as long as it's easy for them to get.

I'm hoping newsletters are still around when you're reading this, but maybe we'll have cycled back around to blogs. Maybe there will be something called norfs we're all writing, delivered to us by passenger pigeon. If so, I thought of it first.

PITCHING ARTICLES

Instead of posting it to your blog, you might pitch your article to a website, newspaper, or magazine. This can help get your name out, especially if you concentrate on a specific area related to your book/genre. The key to pitching, though, is actually reading the publications you want to submit to. That way, you have a better idea of what they're looking for, so you're not pitching listicles about office-appropriate fashion to *Outside* magazine. It's a lot of work and much more useful for nonfiction writers, but it can really help build your platform. If it makes you nervous, just remember: the worst thing that can happen is they say no. Which is the same answer you get if you never pitch them anything. Like with agent queries, you're going to get more rejections than acceptances. That's OK. Everyone else does too.

Also, don't work for "exposure." Get paid. You aren't going to get rich writing online or print articles (no, not even in the big, glossy magazines and world-famous newspapers), but they can cough up at least a little money. Whatever you're offered, ask for 25 percent to 50 percent more. Don't be scared! If they can't afford to pay you, maybe you can't afford to write for them.

PODCASTS AND VIDEOS, YOURS OR OTHERS'

You might be a writer, but that doesn't mean you can't traffic in audio and/or video content. You can create your own podcast, short videos like on TikTok, or longer ones like on YouTube. If you listen to or watch others' podcasts or videos, and you think you have something to say that would be useful or interesting to their audience, reach out and ask if you can be a guest! This will be harder before you have *any* established platform, but if you're an expert in something or have unique experience to share, it might work. You're not going to have much luck cold emailing *This American Life* or *We Can Do Hard Things with Glennon Doyle*, but there are many more niche venues with wide viewerships and listenerships that can help you get your name out there.

You can start your own too. Widely available apps and tools, not least of all an iPhone, make the learning curve for this easier than ever. But videos and podcasts are a lot of work, and some audiences expect high production values. Like all things platform, these take time to grow, but if you have a particular interest in these mediums and the skills to back it up (or the enthusiasm to learn), they can become big parts of your author life.

IN-PERSON EVENTS (COMMUNITY > PLATFORM)

You can build your platform offline too. I know, we sometimes forget we can connect with people IRL and not just through our screens. This is what could be called old-fashioned networking, but if that makes you cringe, you don't have to think of it that way. You might attend conferences and sign up to give a talk or organize a panel related to your topic. You might just attend and meet people and form connections that pay off later. You might find places to teach a class or get more involved in professional organizations related to your field. You might take or lead workshops, organize book clubs, start a writers' group. These areas take the longest to develop, but I think the potential rewards justify the time investment. People like to make a personal connection, and getting out there in the real world is a great place to start.

Another way to look at this, which my conversation with Yahdon Israel made me see, is to think of it as building a community, instead of a platform or network. Writers often approach their platform as a collection of people and resources they can call upon when they need something down the road—a blurb, preorders, reviews. This transactional approach might work. You might create a network of people you can ask for blurbs one day. But are you giving just as many blurbs too? Why not? But what if you found that instead of a platform, you became part of a community?

What if you learned how to start a writers' group at the library or found experts to teach a whole bunch of like-minded people? How can you pool resources to share with others, instead of finding things only you can use? Israel said: "The subtext is that writers are supposed to be selfish and solitary, so they only think about themselves. And the advice that I give writers in understanding what community building looks like is that they have to see community as standing outside of their craft and not as an aid to it. When it comes time to ask for blurbs and preorders, you'll have a community to call on, and not just a network. And they'll have the same in you."

ABOUT NUMBERS AND TIME

I've said it before, and I'll say it again. Building a platform takes time. Heck, I had more than 30,000 followers on Twitter before I started my *Agents & Books* newsletter, and it still took me several years before I reached 10,000 subscribers. The next 10,000 happened in half that time. I'd taught classes at NYU and at various conferences, universities, and writers' workshops across the country too, but I don't think I could have sold this book without that newsletter. And I've been an agent since 2005.

There are no shortcuts. Going viral won't help you jump the line.* You might get a bunch of followers, but are they there because they want to hear about your graphic novel or because you posted a video of a duck where a duck shouldn't be? There are many companies out there willing to sell you followers or secret tips or other magic beans that promise to build your platform overnight too. Don't waste your money. You might get the numbers, but you won't have a platform.

What are those numbers, you ask? There are no specific numbers that equal a book deal or constitute a platform. I once sent out a proposal for an author who had 80,000 followers on Twitter, and in hindsight,

* The only time I've gone viral was with a tweet about email, lol.

we probably sent it out too early. It wasn't long before their account reached several million followers, but there was no way we could have known. And it varies widely from genre to genre. Ten thousand followers on Instagram might be great numbers for a debut romance author, but it's a drop in the bucket for someone trying to write a parenting book. I know you want goalposts and end points and a way to organize things that allow you to say *OK, I'm going to work on my Instagram until I hit 20,000 followers and then I can stop.* But it doesn't work like that. It's not a task you start and eventually complete. It's something you maintain regularly and watch grow. It's not so different than writing a book, honestly. You have to build it one sentence, one follower, at a time.

Chapter Ten

FAILURE IS THE BEST WAY TO LEARN

It is always my impulse to start with the worst-case scenario. When you're prepared for that, you can handle anything—or at least the bad things that come your way. There's this other thing, though, that can happen. It's called success. And it too can happen to you.

What is success? It can be whatever you want. It could be finishing your first draft. It could be getting a six-figure deal. It could be writing ten books or seeing your first one still in print ten years later. You'll have various amounts of control over these things, but it's OK to define your own goals, big or small.

The truth of the matter is that most books don't "work." No writer sells every single book they write forever and ever. Everyone's got a manuscript in the drawer. Even when your book is published, very few books hit the bestseller lists, get a ton of attention, or make it into the celebrity book clubs. This is normal and fine and true for everyone. Your book does not have to sell a certain number of copies to be a "success." It can be a success because it exists at all.

If you do find success, it's important to enjoy it! Eisner Award–winning author and illustrator of *The Magic Fish* Trung Le Nguyen said that he'd tell his past self to "figure out how to chill and enjoy" success, if he could. He said success feels amazing "while somehow also feeling a little bit like the moment right as a Looney Tunes character looks down and realizes they've run out of solid road under their feet and will shortly plummet down toward a canyon floor." *New York Times* bestselling author of more than twenty novels Madeleine Roux said that "success to me now is finding satisfaction and meaning in the work." I know that's easy for her to say, after getting so many book deals and hitting the list, but really, once you reach that goal, you have to find other things to strive for. Roux emphasizes that "there are so many factors that are out of your control in the publishing world, but I can absolutely control how much effort I'm putting into each book, and how much I care about developing as an artist." However and whenever you succeed in your writing, celebrate it. But remember that each of those successes doesn't have to come with a deal announcement.

If you aren't celebrating yet, don't worry. There is not a writer alive who has succeeded at every aspect of their writing life. Most writers do not sell the first book they write, or even the first book they try to sell. That project may have failed in the sense that it didn't cross the publication finish line, but that alone does not make it a failure. You learn something with every sentence you write. You gain something from every project you try to launch. You will carry with you the lessons every book teaches you, regardless of whether it ever hits the shelves.

I know this is cold comfort for the fresh sting of rejection. It isn't going to make anything feel better immediately. But like all hard-won life experiences, in a little while, you'll be able to see the gifts of this rejection (and the last one and the one before that) and you'll think *Gah, I was so lost back then! Now I see!*

BE MAD, THEN

If you're thinking *Kate, there's just no way. I will never get over not getting an agent/a deal/a starred review.* Well, you might not. You can decide not to get over it and be mad forever that those bigwigs in New York did not see your genius. It's much easier to worry that stone than to sit with discomfort and attempt to look objectively at yourself and your writing. (And honestly, there are going to be times when it's not you, and it is those bigwigs in New York.)

I've told you already about all the books I didn't sell before this one: the quickly outdated YA novel, the middle grade/chapter book series I wrote before I knew enough about the genre, the timely picture book we got scooped on, the literary adult novel that was probably too quiet. This is the one that worked. It's not lost on me that all my longform fiction hasn't worked—so far!—and my nonfiction that has. Does that mean I suck at writing novels? Maybe! That won't make me stop trying.

HOW TO LOVE YOUR FAILURES

You know what I *feel* about those books that didn't sell? Fondness. I haven't reread that YA novel in years, but I bet if I did, I'd probably pat it on its head and say *Aww, you tried so hard!* I absolutely can recognize how the diction was too high for my middle grade/chapter book project, especially now that I've read seven hundred chapter books with my kid.* It's a little harder to look my literary novel in the eye, because I love it and worked so hard on it, but it probably is too quiet and my stature in the industry (lol) didn't matter maybe quite as much as I kinda thought it might (though, ugh, I can't believe I really

* Remember, kids' books are not easier just because they're shorter!

thought that). The other picture book was a stunt, an effort to capitalize on something, anything, just to *get published*. Boy, is that a bad idea. There're no shortcuts, friends. Even for me.

But you know what I'm going to do when I'm finished writing this book, besides sleep for a week? I'm going to write another book, because that's what I did after all those other books didn't sell. Yeah, I know, it's easy for me to do that on the heels of this book, but I do not think it'll be a sequel. (Though I have ideas, Stephanie! Let's chat!) I was 50,000 words into another novel, very aware of making it not "quiet," when this one sold, and you know what? I've learned things about writing *this* book that will apply to *that* book, even though they could not be more different. But it all adds up, all the attempts and failures and successes and abandoned projects. There's no wasted writing. Every sentence is a rep that builds a muscle. After a while, you'll be jacked.

IT WAS YOUR BOOK, NOT YOU

The other near impossible thing to remember while you're treading water in the sea of rejection is that it was your *book* that was rejected. Not you. Yes, yes, we fill our books with our essential selves, parts of our lives and hearts and experiences. If you wrote a memoir or a book based on your life, it can be hard to not take that personally. Really hard. But even then, you are not your book.

If an agent or publisher rejected your book, they rejected your book. You were not passed up for prom queen. You were not voted off the island. You did not get left at the altar. You presented a book to a commercial enterprise, and they decided, for whatever reason, one you'll never know for sure, that they couldn't make money off it. Yes, it's crass and harsh! Publishing is a retail industry, not art patronage! Countless worthy stories are rejected every day. Editors hate to do this! Agents too! I know it's tempting and easy to think *If I were younger, if I were cooler, if I were a different [something], if I went to [school], if were thinner, if I were richer, things would be different.* But would it? I don't know! Neither do you! There are people with all the [things] who don't get what they want, and then there are people who know a guy who seems to get everything. That is the world. I cannot fix that, and you probably can't either. The only thing you can do is get off that mental track and write your next book.

WRITE ANOTHER BOOK

Because you do have other books in you, I know it. That last book wasn't the only good idea you'll ever have. You might have some false starts, some ideas that die on the vine. Everyone does. You may research for months and find out someone just published the super-obscure factoid you discovered. You might finally get to that idea from a while back, only to find out the market has dried up. You might chase after a sure thing, only to find it leaves you feeling empty and bored. You can do *all* these things and still write another book!

Yes, it will take a long time. All writing does. Yes, you will feel like you're losing momentum or that your agent is going to forget you or that your editor doesn't want your next idea or that everyone else is publishing their next and next and next book, and you're being left in the dust. It's not a race. You are not behind. I'm going to be forty-six years old when this book comes out. My first book! I thought I was going to publish my first book when I was in my twenties! I have so many journal entries that emphatically say this. I was incredibly stressed when I turned thirty and still wasn't close to publishing a book. I didn't publish a book back then because I was not writing! And when I did start writing, it took some time to put in the reps, find the right idea, be there at the right time. These feelings are hard to quash and avoid, but try not to lose yourself in them. They won't help you.

HOW TO PARSE WHY

I said my literary novel didn't work because it was "too quiet." How did I know that? My agent and I talked about that after all the editors responded and we read between the lines of their remarks. We can do that because, combined, we have almost fifty years of publishing experience,* and we know that when editors say things like *I just don't have the vision for it* or *I just didn't fall in love with it*, they mean *This was fine, but it didn't stand out.* There could be more specific reasons, like maybe my dialog was stiff or my characters weren't fully developed, but editors didn't say things like that, and they don't have to. The editor or agent who passes on your project is not obligated to give you detailed editorial feedback on why they don't want to publish or represent your work. It's nice when they do! But they don't have to. Remember that calculation of how much time it would take me to offer feedback on queries? All those unpaid hours?

Editors at publishing houses are paid a salary, and they do take more time to craft a response to the agents who send them projects, most of the time. But sometimes there isn't much to say. Sometimes it's just a feeling that's hard to quantify, so they rely on vague fallbacks like *I don't have the vision for this one.* Sometimes they want to say *Oh my god, why did you think I would like this?* But they can't because they want the agent to keep sending them projects. Sometimes editors are so busy they do not

* Michael, omgggggggggg.

have time to write more than a kindly generic rejection, and as an agent, I completely understand. It's never fun to write rejections, for anyone. About as fun as it is to receive them. If you *must* try to figure it out, here's how to glean whatever little bits of information you can out of your rejections, without driving yourself bonkers.

Look at comments in the aggregate. If only one rejection mentions not loving the characters and there's not a hint of that anywhere else, then you can put characterization low on the list of things that might have been The Reason. There's going to be a comment that really sticks in your craw—try not to let it get to you. Treat it like an outlier. Consider the comments as a whole, not an enumerated list of everything you've done wrong. If a few mention pacing, that might be something to revisit in your work or pay attention to in the next one.

Don't take anything as gospel. These are only a handful of opinions from a handful of people. Are they important people? Yes. Are they standing in the way of you getting what you want? Er, yes. But these are still only opinions. A rejection does not mean you are a bad writer. A string of rejections doesn't mean you are hopeless.

Understand they will contradict each other. Someone is going to say they loved your voice, and someone else will say they didn't connect with your voice. So which is it? ¯_(ツ)_/¯ It's both and neither. Some people like voice-y things, and some people don't. As above, one single rejection is not gospel. No one has the exact same opinion.

Take the compliments to heart. No one has to say anything specifically nice about your work. Editors and agents will be kind in their rejections, but coming up with specific, detailed, true, helpful, nice things to say about your work takes time, and no one has time. If you do get detailed praise in any rejection, frame it and put it on your wall. (I actually did this.) When someone goes out of their way to say a nice thing, the most appreciative thing you can do is listen.

You aren't going to please everyone. You may have written a really great book! I'm sure you did! But it might appeal to only a small set of people, and maybe publishers aren't sure they can get to those people. Or there aren't enough of them out there to justify the investment. It sucks just as much to be rejected for this reason as it does if you'd just written a crappy book. There's nothing you can do about the perceived size of your potential reading public, except try to reach them yourself and prove those hardheaded publishing people wrong. The more you try to please everyone, the more you'll please no one.

Don't read too deeply into rejections. If one rejection says that an agent is passing on your project with "great regret" and a different one says they're just passing with "regret," that obviously means the first agent loved the book much more than the second and you should ask if they want to see a revision, right? No. That is not correct. Rejections are not written in a secret code you have to break. Their true feelings are they didn't want to work further on it, and that's it.

Take what you need and leave the rest. You aren't going to make every change every editor or agent suggests to you. Some might take you away from the heart of your book. Some might be a cool idea but not what you were going for. Some might be so genius you can't believe you didn't think of it yourself. You get to pick and choose what advice you listen to and what you fully ignore. Editorial comments are not a prescription for what to do to this book or the next.

GET BACK ON THE HORSE

Once you have assessed what you might revise or take with you for future books, the next hurdle is to find your confidence again. Not reaching the goal you set for yourself is a blow, and you have to tend to the fallout.

You have to feel your feelings and lick your wounds. Brushing it all under the rug just means you'll find it again eventually. However you best deal with disappointment (wallowing, distraction, therapy, exercise, friends), do that for a while and get it out of your system. You may be dealing with more than just disappointment at the end of this particular road, and if you need more than a few binge watches or yoga classes, seek further help, however you can. It's OK. You're worth it.

When you've reached a point where you're feeling more like yourself (or even not, because sometimes faking it until you make it actually works), write again. Anything. Lists. Journal entries. Short stories. Dirty limericks. Poems. Comics. Screenplays. Whatever you want! For no one's enjoyment but your own! Show yourself you can put words on the page again, and then doing something bigger will feel more doable. Who knows? Maybe the thing you do for fun will turn into your first published book. That's what happened to me.

EVERYONE GETS REJECTED

Remember, too, that everyone gets rejected. EVERYONE. Of course you've heard stories about all the editors who passed on *Harry Potter* and music execs who turned away the Beatles and whatever. It's hard to relate because those things went on to be world-changing cultural moments. Most of us would settle for a book deal if we can't take the world by storm. Even those writers with more modest success rates have piles of rejections under their belt. Beloved Golden Girl Rue McClanahan once said, "Every kick's a boost." Every writer you know has gotten a kick. But not all have used that as a boost.

It will come back—your confidence. The sting of rejection will lessen. I promise. I have gone through this too! Not selling my novel felt like a kick to the stomach. But then it was a boost. Because I did have at least a little control over the whole situation—I could write another book. There was always going to be the chance I'd never achieve my goal of a traditionally published book. Coming face-to-face with that actually made me more comfortable with it. It's always there. I might never publish *another* book, and that's OK. I've met this particular scary truth, and there's nothing I can do about it but keep going. The idea of never writing again is worse than the idea of never being published again.

WHEN TO CALL IT

There's going to be a point when you have to call it, either for your current book or another later down the line. Sometimes you will find yourself with no one left to send to and that may just be that. It might not be a conscious choice. That's OK. You've reached a natural stopping point. You can put this one aside, for now, and try something new. That book might have life again at a later time. I've seen stranger things happen. For now, though, move on to your next book and get excited for the journey ahead. You already know how to do it!

Chapter Eleven

HOW TO WRITE ANOTHER BOOK

You're going to do it! You're going to write another book! Whether it's the second in a series or a new genre or your second attempt at your debut release, it's time to do it all over again! Yay!

Yay?

Yay.

Start off by taking what you learned from your first (or most recent) attempt at getting published and apply it to your next project. Writing is a cumulative skill; each book builds on the one before it, whether you're writing a series or not.

Then remember that this new project is not your previous project. You are not rewriting your old book. You are not writing a *response* to your previous book. You are not taking whatever feedback you got and saying *Too slow paced? OK, I'll show you how not slow-paced I can be.* You are not going to write another book *at* the people who rejected your previous book. That kind of revenge is boring. No one cares as much as you do that your book didn't get picked up.* The only thing writing a revenge book feeds is your own ego. Let the last book be what it is and was and move on to something else.

But also, while we're at it, writing a book to avenge anything is not a great idea. Be it fiction or nonfiction, for adults or kids—I call these axe-to-grind books. Mad that person didn't take you to the prom? Don't write a YA novel about it. Pissed you got fired from that job and want to write a how-to book on dealing with a toxic boss? Maybe not. Most writers do not have the perspective necessary, usually born of time, to write objectively about these situations, and so the stories come off as one-dimensional. In your YA novel about the wrongful prom snub, your main character (quasi-you) will read as all good and the snubbing-other as all bad. The truth is probably that the person was a jerk and you wouldn't have had a good time anyway! Or something else! Take it from a person who has seen thousands and thousands of axe-to-grind novels in the query pile—we can tell, and it's not as interesting as exploring the nuance of multidimensional characters with thorny new problems.

Can you use this experience to inspire you in future works? Of course. But instead of writing a thriller where an angry author gets their revenge on a hapless literary agent, maybe give your main character something big to lose and channel your feelings that way. In my graduate school writing program, Frederick Barthelme would say "If you're full of love for the sea, say something nice about the bath."[1] It's a little opaque as far as writing advice goes, but I've always taken it to mean the bigger your feelings are about something, the better you can convey them on a smaller scale. Or a little goes a long way.

* Not to be harsh, but it's just true. You *should* be your book's biggest fan.

WHAT NOT TO WRITE NEXT

And speaking of what to not write next, if your first book in a series did not get picked up, I would not advise writing the second book next, if you're still aiming for traditional publishing. Just like we talked about when you were querying.

With your new project, start fresh by looking back at what did and didn't work for you with the previous book. Not just what didn't work in the *story* but also the physical creation of it. Did you write better in the mornings, even if it was hard to get out of bed? Did you find your outline was actually more of a hindrance than an aid? Did you wish you'd used Scrivener from the jump instead of halfway through? Make a list of things that worked for you production-wise and post it somewhere you'll see it often. You'll want to remind yourself of what you already know, as our brains tend to go blank when faced with another empty page.

Remember, too, what *felt* good about writing that last book. Remember how satisfying it was to do that last edit. Remember how proud you were when you crossed 10,000 words. Remember how great it felt to finish the whole book proposal. Remind yourself that you have done this hard thing once already (or maybe even more than once!) and you can do it again.

Every writer I've ever talked to says they have a moment at the start of a new project where they feel like they've totally forgotten how to write. They stare at the cursor or their blank outline or their notebook and . . . *nothing*. If you are experiencing this, too, you are just like all other writers! You can get ahead of this and write yourself reminders that you *do* know how to write a book or proposal and any specific things you found helpful along the way last time. For me, that would be to remember the panicky feeling about 20,000 words in—that I'll never finish, that fixing whatever I already know doesn't work in the first bits will take forever, that the end is so far away and I don't know how to get there—is normal for me. There's another feeling, about 20,000 words from the end, where I feel like the middle is too slow and boring and maybe the end I'm planning isn't that great after all and editing is going to take *so* much work. These are my anxieties and fears, and they come up at roughly those points. Even with this book! By now I can recognize them—*Oh, hi; you again. Right on time.*—and move on. I can't stop the feelings from happening, but I can prevent them from totally derailing me. Just a little derailing.

Coming fresh off rejection can make it really hard to muster the confidence to keep going in the face of anxiety. We all worry that no one is going to care about this one if they didn't care about the last one. I don't know a writer who doesn't have that feeling deep down inside, regardless of how many books they've written. That's just fear and anxiety. Not truth. Say hi to it when it rears its ugly head. It's probably one of your oldest friends. Look back at your list of things that worked or that you accomplished and keep going.

WRITING IS HARD, AND THAT'S NORMAL

I mean, some people have an easier time than others, and bully for them. I actually consider myself in that latter group because, when I know what I'm going to write, I can draft very quickly. With my experience as an agent and a writer, I am comfortable with how hard it'll end up being. If it's not the drafting, it's the editing. If it's not the editing, it's something else. If writing books were so easy, just think of how many *more* people would do it. But you've already done that hard work once before, and you can do it again. Don't forget—you can do hard things.

DON'T TAKE THE EASY WAY OUT

Don't let self-doubt, which we all have from time to time, tempt you to take the easy way out on the road to publication. Try not to fall into the trap of thinking *I'll just write a ______ book! That'll be easy and sure to be published!* People tend to fill in that blank with *picture book* or *romance novel* or *self-help book* or other perceived "easy" book to write, and guess what. Those are some of the hardest genres to get published in because everyone thinks they're easy. There's no slam-dunk genre that will get you quicker to *published author*. Other times, writers want me to give them an idea so they can just write it and be published. They think I must know exactly what editors want, so I can just tell them, they write it, and we both profit. Sometimes I do have ideas that are a good fit for a current client, or I will go out and look for someone with specialized experience to do a job. But I'll also tell you a secret: 98 percent of those ideas don't go anywhere or are so changed by the end that they barely resemble my original idea. And this is good! Why? Because the author should make the book their own, even when they're given the seed of an idea. And it's very hard to write a good book when you're not excited about the idea. It's like writing an 80,000-word essay about the kinds of shoes Charles Dickens gave his characters or some other not obviously interesting idea.* There aren't secret sure-thing ideas that the publishing industry is withholding from you. We'd actually like to hear what you have to say instead of listening to ourselves talk, tbh. Yeah, I'm sure you know someone else who was handed an idea from a book packager (i.e., a company that comes up with ideas and hires writers to do the work) and everything was sunshine and happy-face-daises, but it only looked that way on the outside.

---

* I don't know, maybe the shoes in Dickens *are* interesting, but you get what I'm saying.

They, too, had to contend with the fear of the blank page and tricky edits and waiting and uncertainty. There is no easy path to publishing, so you might as well write the book you want to write.

FIND JOY IN THE PROCESS

You could—and I know this is radical—find the joy in the process. Joy! You could approach all the uncertainty and anxiety and say *Wheeeee, isn't this fun! Look, it's my dumb feelings again! I must be doing something right!*

Remember you get to make up *characters* and have them do your bidding! Or tell your story exactly the way you want to without worrying about what your mom or your English teacher or your ex thinks.* You know what can be fun? Writing! I'm having fun right now. So can you.

Having written a book before doesn't always make the second one easier. Easy is not the goal. It's never easy. It may be less hard because you learned things from your previous experience and will avoid making the same missteps twice. Or you'll catch them before you send anything out to editors or agents or beta readers or whomever. That it is not easier the second or third or fourth time around does not mean you are doing anything wrong. That's just how it goes. For everyone.

It may not be easier, or faster, the next time around. Experience may make you faster at some things, like editing or outlining or whatever, but it may not make the overall project time line faster. Like easy, faster isn't always the goal. It's just that hard and slow are annoying, and we'd all like those to not be part of our creative life, thank you very much. You don't know if anything is faster or easier until you're done anyway. So get moving and find out.

---

* They can think what they want! They're in charge of that, not you!

BE A BEGINNER AGAIN

If whatever you're doing or whatever you did is just not working, be willing to be a beginner again. Maybe what you did last time didn't work at all. Maybe you need a new approach. Maybe you need to outline when you didn't before. Maybe you need to try pantsing it. Maybe write chapters out of order or write the ending first. Maybe research *everything* before you get started or take it piece by piece. Finding out how *this* book needs to be written, regardless of how the last one was written, can be part of the process of any book. You must meet each book on its own terms and do what that book needs, judging what path to take based on your previous experience. Feeling like you're starting over (you are!) doesn't mean you are a skill-less beginner, a noob. You are beginning again, on something new, not on the whole of all writing. Be open to learning each lesson.

HAVE AS MUCH FUN AS YOU CAN

Before I leave you to your next project, try to remember the most important lesson of all. Try to have as much fun with this writing stuff as you can. It's hard, often thankless work, so make it enjoyable. Eat the good snacks while you write. Listen to your favorite music or white noise or fake coffee shop sounds. Give yourself the gift of the right ergonomic setup at your desk or the most frivolous comfort device. I have a heated footrest and it is wonderful! Use the pretty journals you have been saving for years. (I see you. Use them!) Explore libraries or coffee shops or parks or make your own writing retreat at a friend's house or a bed-and-breakfast or even your local corporate chain hotel.* Say *I can't chaperone the class field trip/bake the cookies/help clean out your garage/walk your dog* or other nonessential task because you are working on your book. Even if it never gets published! You can still make the time and space in your life because you *want* to. Your desire to create in this way is worthy, important, and a priority. It's OK to act that way. Have a sense of humor about the hurdles you will absolutely meet and have as much fun as you possibly can. No one's going to have it for you.

Good luck, my friends. I hope all your publishing dreams come true.

* I love an anonymous corporate chain hotel. I get some of my best work done in those.

ACKNOWLEDGMENTS

Thank you to my agent Michael Bourret for being the agent so I could be the writer. I couldn't have done it without you. Thank you to the whole team at Dystel, Goderich, and Bourret, especially Michaela Whatnall and Jim McCarthy.

Thank you to my editor, Stephanie Hitchcock. I'm so glad this book found its home with you and that we've gotten to work together as both agent-editor and author-editor. I've learned so much about this process from you—and your masterful way with an edit letter—I feel like I could write a whole 'nother book just about that. Thank you, too, to Karina Leon for your insightful comments and Track Changes cheerleading.

Thank you to the whole team at Simon Element: Richard Rhorer, Jessica Preeg, Francesca Carlos, Grace Noglows, Erica Siudzinski, Patty Romanowski, Benjamin Holmes, Julia Jacintho, and Zoe Norvell. You have all made this process seamless, painless, and dare I say it—fun. I'm proud to be on this team with you.

Thank you to Brandon Kelley for designing the beautiful logo and visual assets for the *Agents & Books* newsletter, and your years of friendship and support.

Thank you to all my loyal readers at *Agents & Books*. You have kept me afloat, emotionally and financially. Your thoughtful comments and gracious notes have buoyed me when I was low and given me buckets of inspiration. You make writing a weekly newsletter a joy, and I wouldn't be here without you.

Thank you to Mary McCarthy's The Group Chat: Katie Fee, Cristin Stickles, Maggie Lehrman, Marisa LaScala, Alison Williams, Sara Brady, Chandra Reilly, and Annie Bressack. Thank you for being the best wartime presidents a girl could ever ask for. I love you all.

Thank you to the Good Art Friends: Glynnis MacNicol, Jen Doll, Maris Kreizman, Michelle Ruiz, Carolyn Murnick, Jo Piazza, and Casey Scieszka. Your advice on these pages and steadfast encouragement have kept me going, all the way to the finish line.

Much gratitude to the Spruceton Inn (www.sprucetoninn.com) for picking me for the 2023 Artists Residency. I did some integral thinking on a hike in the Catskills during this time, and I'll be ever grateful for the peace and space to finish this book.

Thank you to the brilliant writers and publishing professionals who talked to me for this book: Katie Adams, Andrew Eliopulos, Yahdon Israel, Casey Johnston, Anna Sproul Latimer, David Levithan, Trung Le Nguyen, Madeleine Roux, Leila Sales, and Jess Verdi.

Thank you to all my smart and helpful colleagues at the Howard Morhaim Literary Agency, including DongWon Song, Kim-Mei Kirtland, Eric Showers, and especially my assistant, Nina Richner.

To Howard Morhaim, thank you for almost two decades of unwavering support, for always believing in me, and for explaining the Open Market to me again and again. Every success I've had is rooted in what you've taught me.

Thank you to Erin McKean, every other Friday at 10:00 a.m. Eastern.

Thank you to my husband, Josh Landon, for your support while I sequestered myself in my office to write. Knowing you were there to take care of things gave me the headspace to write this book. Knowing you're there beside me gives me strength to do anything. I love you.

And to Quinn, thank you for keeping me company in my office while I chipped away at this project. I hope you look at it one day and think *Wow, my mom did that* with the same pride I look on everything you do. I love you too.

NOTES

CHAPTER THREE: All About Literary Agents

1. "The Association of American Literary Agents 2023 Membership Survey Report," Association of American Literary Agents, accessed September 13, 2024, https://aalitagents.org/wp-content/uploads/2023/09/AALA-2023-Membership-Survey-Report-Final.pdf.

2. "Canon of Ethics," Association of American Literary Agents, accessed September 13, 2024, https://aalitagents.org/canon-of-ethics/.

3. "Membership Application," Association of American Literary Agents, accessed September 13, 2024, https://aalitagents.org/membership/membership-application/.

CHAPTER SEVEN: How to Read a Book Deal

1. Michael Cader, "AAP Annual Stats Show Trade Unit Sales Falling 8.1 Percent in 2023, Balanced by Price Increases," *Publishers Lunch*, August 24, 2024, https://lunch.publishersmarketplace.com/2024/08/aap-annual-stats-show-unit-sales-falling-8-1-percent-in-2023-balanced-by-price-increases/.

CHAPTER EIGHT: It's a Real Book!

1. Silvia Moreno-Garcia (@silviamg.author), *Threads*, August 28, 2024. "After I had a big hit for *Mexican Gothic* I've had things I didn't have before. The most visible ones are that for my latest novel (and only my latest, which is number 10) my publisher sent a PR 'box' to influencers with the book and some print material, and I did a three-city tour on my publisher's dime (I normally have paid for my own travel and avoid book tours instead going for book festivals and such; tours can be lots of wasted money)."

2. Kate McKean, "10 Novels Agents Have Already Seen a Billion Times," *Electric Lit*, November 9, 2017, https://electricliterature.com/10-novels-agents-have-already-seen-a-billion-times/.

CHAPTER NINE: I Will Teach You to Love Self-Promotion

1. Casey Johnston, "She's a Beast," accessed September 13, 2024, https://www.caseyjohnston.website/newsletter.

CHAPTER ELEVEN: How to Write Another Book

1. Frederick Barthelme, "The 39 Steps," FrederickBarthelme.com, https://www.frederickbarthelme.com/nonfiction/the-39-steps/.

APPENDIX 1

Query Letter Examples

Below are seven examples of query letters for various genres. They were written by me to show you different ways they do and don't work, and I'll discuss those things after each. Yes, it would be *so* funny if you used one of these for real and got rejected by an agent (even me!) or *funnier still* if it worked and some joker agent requested the manuscript! So funny!

Don't do this. It's not funny.

Dear Agent,

THRILLS AND CHILLS is a thriller for fans of DAVID BALLDUCCHI and JAMES PATTERSON. It is 158,000 words long.

What if your plane was hijacked by terrorists and you were the only one on board to stop it? What if you tried to stop it, but it didn't work and now you had to make friends with the terrorists to gain their trust and thwart their plan another way? What if the girl you loved was on bored and she couldn't know what was going on because she had a serious heart disease and would die from fright?

All those questions and more are answered in THRILLS AND CHILLS.

I am a retired homicide detective in Lansing, MI. This is my first novel, but I have been writing stories since I was 5 years old. Many were published in my school newspaper and I won an English award in the 12th grade.

Please let me know what you think of my novel as soon as possible.

Best,
K. Lamar
100 Main St.
Lansing, MI 48901
KMLamar@fake.net

This one takes the *What if?* rhetorical device too far. It is attempting to draw the reader in with suspense and intrigue, but there isn't enough context to get the reader invested in what's happening. And 158,000 words is on the long side for this genre, and the lack of salutation, light typos, and bio that features writing credits from high school together say to me that this author hasn't done quite enough homework about querying and publishing. Unless the included sample chapters were extraordinary, I'd pass on this one.

Dear Agent,

AN OCEAN AWAY is my middle grade novel for every kid who's had to move away and dreams about running ***back*** home. Benedict did just that—except his family had moved from Nigeria to Canada for a better life and better jobs. But they had to leave his grandmother behind.

Benedict and his grandmother Amo were very close. ***ARE*** very close. Even though they can text and sometimes call, there's no replacing their long walks and hours spent talking in the kitchen. Benedict knows there's so much in Amo's mind that will be lost when she dies, and he wants to make sure that he's the one who gets to carry all that knowledge on into the future. He's been trying to write it all down, but bits and pieces keep slipping away. Benedict knows that it's very expensive to take a plane back to Nigeria, but so many ships leave port in Halifax and ***one*** of them has to be going to Lagos. To Benedict, there's only one way to find out.

AN OCEAN AWAY was my master's thesis at The New School's program for Writing for Children, from which I graduated in 2013. I worked with author and editor David Levithan and editor Susan Van Metre, both who expressed interest in this work. My day job is in accounting, but my first love is writing for children without voices in the larger publishing landscape.

Best,
Z. Zipkin
100 Main Street
New York, NY 10010
zzzz@fake.com

This is a great query. The story shows strong stakes (the kid wants to stow away on a ship!) and a lot of heart. The author studied at a well-known writing program and worked with great teachers. The proof will be in the pudding, but I'd likely request the full manuscript of this.

Dear Agent,

STUFF MY KIDS SAY is a collection of the funniest stuff my kids say, straight from the horse's mouth. It is destined to be as popular as SH*T MY DAD SAYS, but for a more family friendly crowd. (I would never want a curse word in my title.)

Some examples:

6 yo: "GET ME MORE LEGOS NOW OR I'LL KILL YOU!!!"

8 yo: "I'm going to marry Harry Styles. I can just feel it."

16 yo: "What do you mean you're not going to pay for college? You're the worst parents ever!"

As you can see, my kids are snarky, funny, and out of this world. Everyone will enjoy reading what they have to say about being grounded, grades, snacks, what's for dinner, are we there yet?, grandparents, Christmas presents, allowance, clothes, and their future. Sometimes sad, sometimes happy, this collection will appeal to parents of all ages and types.

I've been tweeting the things my kids say for the last month and now have 103 followers. It's just a matter of time before this takes off and takes over the world. Be the agent who catches the next big thing right before it happens.

Regards,
M. Nielson
100 Main Street
Gainesville, FL 32712
gatormom@fake.com

This author acknowledges that they don't have a strong platform, and it's an interesting gambit to entice agents to get in on the ground floor here. Unfortunately, it doesn't work this way. The humor genre relies heavily on platform but also novelty. There have been many iterations of *kids say funny stuff* books, not to mention countless memes going around social media all the time. The average reader probably sees enough of this on Facebook to not need to buy a book of it, unless the author was very, very well known. (Also, these aren't funny!) Pass.

Dear Agent,

There are times in our lives when we must fish or cut bait. Bernina was at just such a point in her life.

After 9 years earning her PhD in organizational psychology, her life was in chaos. Her apartment was a disaster and her landlord was starting to notice. Her boyfriend stopped talking to her months ago, and she was oddly fine with that. Her parents were threatening to ***not*** bail her out, one more time. She wasn't a helpless child anymore. She was over 30. It was time to get her shit together.

But instead, she sold all her belongings and left town in the middle of the night before her thesis defense and drove to Badlands, South Dakota. She'd gotten an email a week before. It read, simply, "It's that time. I need some help." She knew what it was about and she knew what she needed to do. She just hoped she wasn't too late.

SHIFTING LANDSCAPES is the story of Bernina and her escape from her life in order to save a friend in need, and herself. It is literary fiction in the style of Lorrie Moore and Aimee Bender. I am a graduate of the University of Iowa Writers' Workshop and have been published in ***Glimmer Train***, ***Tin House***, ***The Iowa Review***, and ***Ploughshares***. I have a story forthcoming in ***The New Yorker***. Please find the first three chapters attached.

All best,
Q. Rasputin
100 Main Street
Iowa City, IA
qar@fake.edu

This one would probably get a full request from me, especially if I liked the sample chapters the author provided. There's intrigue here (*What happened? Is she too late???*) and an indication of spare artfulness, especially because of the mention of Lorrie Moore and Aimee Bender. It doesn't hurt that this author has been published in some well-known literary journals and went to one of the top-ranked writing programs. These things don't guarantee a request or offer of representation, but they don't hurt. What's not here, however, is the word count. If it is something like 35,000 words, it's not long enough for the genre. If it's more like 235,000 words, it's way, way too long. If it was one of those word counts and I didn't love the writing in the sample, I'd probably pass on this one without requesting more.

Dear Agent,

Bacon cookies, bacon cakes, bacon tarts, bacon scones! Yes, you can bake with bacon!

BAKIN' WITH BACON is a cookbook based on my popular blog of the same name: bakinwithbacon.com. It features 86 recipes for sweet and savory baked goods that all contain—you guessed it—bacon! Who doesn't like bacon? (Except Muslim and Jewish people, and that's OK.) You may think that bacon oatmeal raisin cookies don't sound delicious, but you'd be wrong. They are AMAZING.

My blog enjoys a readership of 100,000 unique visitors a month and earns over 300,000 page views a month. I have 24,000 followers on Twitter, 78,000 on TikTok, and 16,000 followers on Instagram. I have been featured in the ***Detroit Free Press*** several times in the last year for my unique bacon recipes, as well as on our local ABC affiliate's morning show: ***Good Morning Detroit***, for cooking demonstrations. Please find an introduction, table of contents and 4 sample recipes attached.

All best,
S. Tucker
100 Main Street
Detroit, MI
Susan@fake.com

This one is very promising! The author's platform is robust, especially on specific social media platforms that do well with cooking content. Even better, the author has a strong following on her own website, which isn't subject to the vagaries of megalomaniac billionaires or changing algorithms! If I were an agent who did a lot of cookbooks, I would likely have an opinion on whether I thought the concept worked or not, or had been done before, or I would formulate that after reading the full proposal. If I were an agent just getting started with cookbooks, I would likely read this full proposal and maybe ask around to my colleagues if they thought this had a fighting chance. I'd do a little research to see what else is out there in the bacon space. Cookbooks are hard! But this author's platform is good.

Dear Agent,

I have been an athlete all my life. From soccer starting at age 4, through gymnastics, ballet, more soccer, track and now yoga and weight lifting, I have clocked millions of hours on the field, on the mat, and in the gym. I am a personal trainer, both on and offline, and I have developed a foolproof way to stay active and fit at any age.

YES YOU CAN BE AN ATHLETE is my diet and fitness book guaranteed to deliver results and transform your couch potato self into a fit and healthy person—whatever your goals. Maybe you just want to be able to run a mile. Maybe you want to do complicated yoga poses. Maybe you want to look great in that bathing suit next summer. Whatever your goal, I can help you achieve it with clear diet, fitness, and mindfulness practices.

This isn't a lose-weight-quick plan. It's a total mind-body makeover. For anyone and everyone.

I am a personal trainer in Atlanta, GA with a roster of 500 clients, past and present. I am active on fitness websites and forums as a commenter and moderator and maintain my own blog at youareanathlete.blogspot.com. It receives 1,000 hits a month. My YouTube fitness videos receive at least 5,000 views each.

Please find my complete book proposal attached. I look forward to hearing from you.

Best,
U. Vee
100 Main Street
Atlanta. GA
IMAATHLETE@fake.com

The author's concept sounds good and thoughtful. It's nice to see a project in this space that isn't trying to sell quick fixes or make unrealistic promises. They don't, however, have a big enough platform. They should put more time into building a bigger following on YouTube (or Instagram or TikTok) and leverage their existing clients to help spread the word. Now is not the right time for them to sell a book.

Dear Agent,

LOVE AT THE END OF THE LINE is my 65,000-word young adult novel, perfect for fans of John Green and Rainbow Rowell. It is a story of acceptance, maturity, love, and heartbreak.

Tanya is stoked her incredibly overprotective parents are letting her ride the subway by herself to her new high school. She's always been able to walk to school in her Brooklyn neighborhood, but since she got into Bronx Science (because she's a genius, obvs) it'll take her over an hour to get to school and back on the train. Her parents have no choice but to let her go by herself—and it's not like it's dangerous anyway. She's not a baby anymore—she's 14!

On her third day, she meets Kevin. He's always on the subway when she is, and she notices he's reading the same book she is: THE CATCHER IN THE RYE. They start talking about it, and Tanya can't help but notice his cute smile and twinkling eyes. Day after day, they talk about books, movies, friends, parents, everything. He's always there, every school day.

But soon, Angie gets suspicious. She notices he sometimes wears the same clothes. He is vague about school and family. And then there's his black eye and busted lip. When Kevin won't let her in and let her help, she follows him off the train and discovers the truth about Kevin's life. But can she handle it?

LOVE AT THE END OF THE LINE is my second YA novel. I self-published A BROOKLYN LOVE TALE on Kindle last year and received many 5-star reviews. I'm looking for a literary agent to help me take my career to the next level. Please find the complete manuscript attached.

Best,
I. Jamieson
100 Main Street
Quincy, MA 02169
writerchick@fake.com

This one shows a lot of promise. The author's voice is strong, and I bet that shows in the manuscript too. If I liked the sample chapters, I'd request a full manuscript here. But a few things give me pause (and it's not what you think it is). First, the author describes the book in abstractions, right up front: "acceptance, maturity, love, and heartbreak." This isn't a reason to reject the book outright, but not as helpful in pitching the book. Those don't tell me anything concrete about it. Next, I worry this is the kind of novel where the *real* story is happening to the secondary character (Kevin) and not to the narrator (Angie). It's Kevin in the same clothes, with a busted lip. Angie may be able to help Kevin, but that is a savior archetype, and those stories can be less effective than ones from the point of view of the character experiencing adversity. Because what does Angie ultimately have to lose? The author's self-publishing history is not a red flag, however. It's fine and probably gave the author some great experience. It's heartening to me, though, that this author isn't requesting the agent try to market or resell the self-published book. An agent can't likely take that "to the next level" but might be able to boost the author's career with a new, unpublished book.

APPENDIX 2

One Complete Nonfiction Book Proposal Example

ONE COMPLETE NONFICTION BOOK PROPOSAL EXAMPLE

(For this book! Minus sample pages)

FORGET THE CAT, SAVE YOURSELF

HOW TO SURVIVE WRITING AND PUBLISHING BOOKS

KATE MCKEAN

Represented by Michael Bourret
Dystel, Goderich & Bourret

OVERVIEW

Writing is horrible. Most writers hate the act of doing it, and yet, so many will tell you that their dream is to publish a book. The problem is that you have to write the book to actually get published. Dammit.

Writers want the secret to getting published. They want the magic formula for the query letter and the list of agents who will instantly say yes and the perfect marketing campaign to hit the List. They think that knowing these specific things (and of course there is only one way to get all those things) will make everything fall into place, and they will be bestselling authors. But they don't even know what questions to ask to get those results, and worse, those are the wrong questions.

It's much easier to focus on the nuts and bolts of writing books—the story beats and word counts and query letters and author platforms—than the messy feelings that accompany that writing, like doubt and fear and hope. But the two things are inextricably linked. Writers are not robots at a keyboard. They—we—are feeling humans who have unfortunately chosen to write. But FORGET THE CAT, SAVE YOURSELF: How to Survive Writing and Publishing Books will shine a light on both of those things. It explores the how-tos of writing and publishing alongside the feelings writers experience throughout the process. It will show writers how to weather the ups and downs of writing, the ones that happen in our heads and the ones that happen on the path to publication. The most common question I get as an agent, from clients and elsewhere, is "Is this normal?" I will give writers a handle on the process as well as reassurance that they are not alone, that their feelings are normal too.

I have built a reputation as a literary agent who knows what she's talking about. Writers' conferences, publishing groups, and universities come to me for my presentations and classes on how to get a book published and writers leave not only with that information, but with tools to get through the mental side of writing. Part of my work as an agent is to coach my clients through the whole process, reassuring them when they are insecure, cheering them on when they are triumphant, and helping them untangle how they're getting in their own way. I bring this to my teaching and writing as well.

I am good at this because I have done it myself. I have been bolstered by my writing group. I have been cheered on by my own agent. I have had my own dark nights of the soul with my own books and my own failures. I have my own trunked novels. I can tell clients, and readers, how it feels to write a query letter and wait for editors to read your book and face the hard facts because I have done it all myself. I have been on both sides of this equation. You'd think that would have saved me some heartache, but you'd be wrong.

I've also been dispensing advice and support to writers in my popular newsletter *Agents & Books* since 2019 with the goal of demystifying publishing and putting hard-to-find information all in one place. In the first year, it was easy to write the query letter how-tos and talk about what contract terms meant, but after a while, I have found my more popular posts are ones that deal with the emotional side of writing, like *How to Get Over Professional Disappointment* and *Hating What You Write Is Totally Normal*. People write and say *I really needed to hear that* and *This made me feel so much better* and they enthusiastically share those posts with other writers. There are tons of *how to get your book published* blogs and books out there. But few guide writers through the emotional turmoil of writing and publishing, especially by someone with experience in both. I know all about that emotional turmoil because I've been an agent for over 17 years and a writer myself for even longer. I've seen books published a hundred different ways and written five of my own. Readers trust me for that reason alone.

FORGET THE CAT, SAVE YOURSELF: How to Survive Writing and Publishing Books is a publishing how-to manual meets *Bird by Bird*. It's the book you can give your sister-in-law when she says she's got a great idea for a memoir. It can be used in MFA programs and writers' groups and community writing programs for writers of all types. (Editors, you can just give your authors this book when they are freaking out about their cover or whatever. See? I saved you some time.) It's widely applicable because writers are all the same. We just want to be told we're doing a good job. And frankly, if you're writing at all, then you *are* doing a good job. This book will give authors the information they need to accomplish their goals, and the support to actually see it through.

AUTHOR-LED MARKETING AND PROMOTION

With almost 17,000 total subscribers (+1,100 paying $5/mo or $50/year), *Agents & Books* enjoys consistently high open rates per email—averaging 50% for public posts, over 75% for paywalled posts—and has seen positive subscriber acquisition growth its entire run. According to Substack, 5-10% of my subscribers overlap with other popular newsletters by George Saunders, Anne Helen Petersen, Jami Attenberg, Austin Kleon, and Roxane Gay. *Agents & Books* sees a consistent growth rate week to week, at roughly 750 new subscribers a month, which means readership could double by the time this book comes out, conservatively speaking. As you can see below, the graph keeps going up.

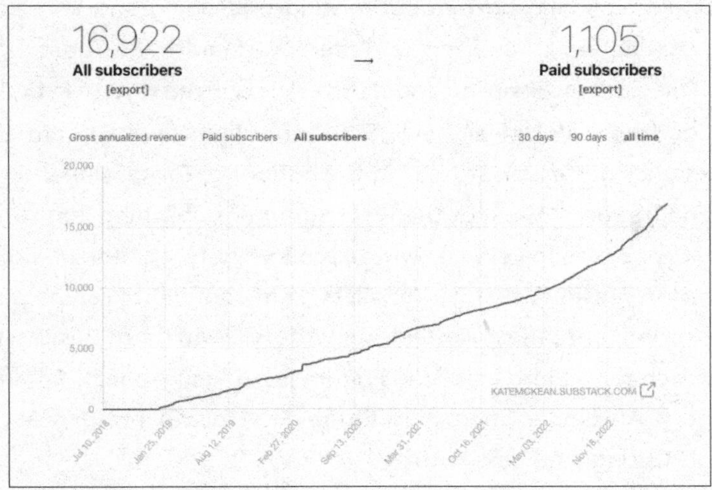

Agents & Books was cited as one of the "20+ of the Best Book Newsletters for Readers" by *Book Riot*, "7 Newsletters That Will Help Get Your Book Published" by *Electric Lit*, "12 Newsletters Worth Subscribing to for Writers" by *The Good Trade*. It has also been featured or mentioned on other popular media newsletters and blogs run by Jane Friedman, Rusty Foster (*Today in Tabs*), Nick Quah (formerly *Hot Pod*), Delia Cai (*Deez Links*) and Anne Helen Peterson (*Culture Study*), as well as the *Slate Culture* podcast. My work in *Catapult* on book contracts was linked in Roxane Gay's *The Audacity* newsletter.

In even more exciting news, I've just secured a monthly column in *Poets & Writers* magazine, slated to start in September 2023. In it I will be debunking publishing myths like "If you don't have a big-name agent, you're sunk" and "The Publisher won't market your book." (You're welcome.) I will be sure to mention FORGET THE CAT, SAVE YOURSELF in my author bio as soon as it's available for preorder.

My other work, both about writing/publishing and some fiction, has appeared in *Poets & Writers*, *Catapult*, *The Toast*, *Popula*, *The Outline*, *Electric Lit*, and others. I received my MA in fiction writing from the University of Southern Mississippi and am also an adjunct professor at NYU in the School of Professional Studies and frequent guest at the NYU Summer Publishing Institute. I have over 33k followers on Twitter, predominately writers, editors, media professionals, and journalists. I am confident I can help secure prominent press. Among the writers I would not hesitate to approach for a blurb are: Jane Friedman, Megan Abbott, Jami Attenberg, Alexander Chee, Matt Ortile, Jen Doll, Glynnis MacNicol, Nicole Chung, and Leigh Stein.

As we all have read, over and over, follower counts do not predict sales. What does, or at least helps the most? Engagement. With such an engaged newsletter following and active social media, my readers will happily and authentically share how my content has helped them on their writing journey. I can also create many other additive ways for new readers and writers to engage with the book.

Teaching

I have twenty years of teaching experience in writing and publishing. I am happy to host classes via Zoom or partner with institutions to create classes, workshops, or webinars around this content, and require book-with-registration where possible. I would also create MFA-program specific content to target those institutions, where there is little to no practical publishing information taught. (And who could also really use the *feelings* part of this book too.) I have taught or spoken at the following institutions/organizations:

- NYU School of Professional Studies
- NYU Summer Publishing Institute
- Stanford University
- Sarah Lawrence Writer's Conference, Publish and Promote
- University of Southern Mississippi Center for Writers
- University of Florida MFA program
- LWC}NYC (Community of Literary Magazines and Presses Conference)
- Pacific Northwest Writers Conference
- Pikes Peak Writers Conference
- San Diego State University Writer's Conference
- Atlanta Writers Conference
- Writer's Digest (extensive online webinars and in-person events)
- Done By Lunch
- Erma Bombeck Writers' Workshop
- Craftcation
- Paragraph Workspace for Writers
- Catapult Don't Write Alone Conference
- Odyssey Writing Workshops
- Lighthouse Writers Workshop
- Writing Day Workshops
- American Society of Journalists and Authors
- Book Doctors
- Independent Editors Group

The book's content can be adapted to meet the needs of writers in any genre: fiction, nonfiction, memoir, even more specifically for science fiction/fantasy, craft/how-to, illustrated/gift, and those writing for adults or kids. Because these speaking engagements and teaching opportunities are part of my day job, and organizations seek me out for these events, book promotion can be ongoing and perennial, leading this to become a strong backlist title. (And the conference usually covers my travel.)

It's easy to incorporate the book's messaging in my routine social media communications. My Twitter (@kate_mckean) following of over 33,000 is used to seeing me promote books and my newsletter, and I will not be shy to promote my own book.

Having spent the last thirteen years on the platform, I am familiar with the different strategies used to promote books, and not just BUY MY BOOK tweets. I can host AMAs or #askagent threads, screenshot short excerpts to start a conversation, and enlist mutuals to retweet messaging.

My personal Instagram (roughly 900 followers, @kate_mckean) is just pictures of my kid, but while writing the book, I can reinvigorate the @agents_and_books Instagram (~500 followers) that accompanies my newsletter, seeding that following for book-related content.

I can create a landing/buy page for the book on my dedicated website: katemckean.com and include information about the book in my bio on all platforms, in the footer messaging on the newsletter, and in any bio in future online publications so that news of the book is never far from wherever I am online.

I will gladly participate in publisher-led marketing efforts including in-person events where/when advisable, "in conversation with" talks, Goodreads promotions, etc.

The manuscript will be approximately 80,000 words and can be completed in about 10 months.

COMPARABLE TITLES

- *Bird by Bird* by Anne Lamott (Pantheon, 1994)
  Oh, *Bird by Bird*. Where would us writers be without it? It is the hug we need while writing. It is the permission we need to write our shitty first drafts. But it was written before Twitter existed and the world of being an author has fundamentally changed. FORGET THE CAT, SAVE YOURSELF will bridge the gap between how Lamott tells us how to feel about writing and how to actually get published.

- *Before and After the Book Deal: A Writer's Guide to Finishing, Publishing, Promoting, and Surviving Your First Book* by Courtney Maum (Catapult, 2020)
  I am so glad this book exists. At first, I worried my book would be stepping on its toes, but I realized it was talking to a very specific audience and is only doing half the job my book will do. It gives good, kind publishing advice but lacks the "feelings" side of FORGET THE CAT, SAVE YOURSELF. Maum's book is aimed at the MFA–literary novel–teaching gig–freelance writer pipeline. My book is aimed at the writer of almost any genre who wants to build a career out of traditional publishing. Readers will trust my perspective as a literary agent and be even more curious about the secrets I can reveal to them. (Spoiler: the secret is it's hard for everyone, lol.)

- *Craft in the Real World: Rethinking Fiction Writing and Workshopping* by Matthew Salesses (Catapult, 2021)
  Salesses' goal is to turn the MFA/workshop culture on its head, and he succeeds. My book's goal is to provide transparency

and compassion to those trying to find their way through the traditional publishing morass. I would love to partner with Salesses to talk to writers and MFA programs to completely blow their minds. Our two books together would be a mini-MFA themselves.

- *Refuse to Be Done* by Matt Bell (Soho Press, 2022)
  The reader who likes Bell's book will love mine as we share a compassionate-but-here's-a-formula-to-get-things-done mindset. Type A, but with a heart. As with Salesses' book, writers will look to complement their craft focused books with my craft and publishing focused book.

- *Save the Cat! Writes a Novel: The Last Book on Novel Writing You'll Ever Need* by Jessica Brody (Ten Speed Press, 2018)
  I love a book with a method, a plan. Writers will find some of the same information in my book, in an additive instead of repetitive way. We often need to be told the same things a few times over. Brody's book is all form and function, but that's only half the job. Addressing a writer's need for both practical and emotional advice in one place is what writers really need.

CHAPTER OUTLINE

Introduction

It's much easier to focus on the nuts and bolts of writing books—word counts and query letters and author platforms—than the messy feelings that accompany writing—like doubt and fear and hope. But the two things are inextricably linked. Writers are not robots at keyboards. Writers are feeling humans who have unfortunately chosen to write. This book explores the how-tos of writing and publishing alongside the feelings writers experience throughout the process, and how writers can survive both. There is little transparency in the writing and publishing process, mostly because there are so many ways to write and publish a book. The most common question I get as an agent, from clients and elsewhere, is "Is this normal?" I hope to give writers a handle on the process as well as reassurance that they are not alone, that their feelings are normal too.

1. Before "The End"
   In many cases, you have to write the whole book, or at the very least a book proposal, before you can start the process of finding an agent or editor. But getting there is a journey of its own. In this first chapter, we'll talk about word counts, plotting vs pantsing drafting strategies, editing tips, manuscript formatting, and how to know if you're really, really done. We'll also talk about how to trust your gut when it comes to editing, how to let go of your work and stop fiddling with it, and steeling yourself for what's to come.

2. What's a Book Proposal and Do I Need One?
   If you're not writing the whole book (sorry fiction writers, this is not you), you need to write a book proposal. There are infinite variations on this, but we'll talk about the baseline components you need, and how to determine if your particular book needs something more. We'll also discuss when/if you need a book proposal if you're writing a memoir. Along the way, we'll deal with how awkward it is to talk about yourself and your accomplishments in a book proposal, and how no one thinks you're bragging. Readers will enjoy this very book proposal as an appendix!

3. What's a Literary Agent?
   This chapter explains what literary agents do, why you need one (of course I'm biased), and how to get one. From where to research them to the dreaded query letter to submission best practices, readers will come back to this chapter again and again. It will also address how *stressful* it is to gather this information, how it feels like sending your work into the void, and how to cope with the inevitable rejections. Not every writer needs an agent, but every writer should know what a good agent does and doesn't do, and how many rejections are about the agent, not the writer.

4. What Happens When an Editor Reads Your Book?
   You got an agent! Yay! Now your book is ready to go out to editors. This chapter explains how a book submission works and what to expect (and not expect). We'll talk

about how a book is acquired by a publisher. On the *feelings* side, we'll focus on how to distract yourself while editors are reading, how not to stalk them online, and what to do in the meantime.

5. Holy Shit You Got a Book Deal
   You got a book deal! Amazing! This chapter will cover what's in a book deal, how it's negotiated, and why it will not evaporate into thin air if you wait a day to think about it. We'll briefly touch on the higher points of contracts and money, as well as when to expect any of it. Authors experience *so* many emotions at this stage: elation, fear, jealousy, uncertainty. And it's all normal.

6. Editing and Publication
   Every book is different (which I will try not to say 100 times in this book), but the production process is roughly the same. We'll go over the process from line edits to 2nd pass pages, as well as marketing, promotion, and the post-publication comedown. Readers will learn how to channel their rage at an editor who kills their darlings and prepare themselves for the emotional whirlwind of the publicity cycle.

7. Self-Promotion Is Terrible for Everyone
   You want to tell the world you wrote a book! But what if no one is listening to you? And shouldn't the publisher be doing most of this whole book promotion thing? This chapter will give readers some best practices for book promotion, as well as reassure them that *everyone* feels

like a huckster saying BUY MY BOOK and why we all have to get over it.

8. What If It All Goes Wrong?
   Not every book is going to find an agent or an editor. Not every book is going to find its audience with readers. So many writers do not sell their first, or second, or third book. That's NORMAL, and writers really need to hear that. This chapter will delve into how to assess what did or didn't work about a book or submission and how not to spiral into a vortex of self-loathing.

9. How to Write the Next Book
   You want to write another book, don't you? This chapter deals with how to recognize what you learned from writing your previous book and how to apply it to your next, as well as how to shake off the Sophomore Scaries and tackle your next book on its own terms.

Appendixes (proposed):

- Brief Explanation About Why This Book Does Not Discuss Self-Publishing
- Query Letter Examples
- One Complete Nonfiction Book Proposal Example (For this book, minus sample pages)
- Mantras to Recite at Every Stage of Writing
- Further Reading

INDEX

N

S

Y

ABOUT THE AUTHOR

Kate McKean is a literary agent at the Howard Morhaim Literary Agency in Brooklyn, New York. She has also worked as an adjunct professor at New York University and earned her MA in Fiction Writing at the University of Southern Mississippi. Her work has appeared in *Poets & Writers*, *Electric Literature*, and elsewhere. She writes the *Agents & Books* newsletter at www.agentsandbooks.com.